The Authentic Organization is an empowering guide, offering an approachable framework for organizations to go beyond diversity and inclusion. Its innovative approach to psychological safety and self-reflection is a standout feature, providing practical strategies for fostering a culture of authenticity and inclusivity. The emphasis on individual expression and authentic self-representation is both refreshing and necessary. This book is an invaluable resource for any leader hoping to gain and maintain a competitive edge in today's talent market!

– Sergio Rodriguez, Senior Manager, Global Workforce DEI Solutions

The Authentic Organization deals with a hugely important topic – how to create psychological safety in the workplace. Through developing an intuitively appealing framework centered on the 5 Pillars, along with a number of practical hands-on tools on how to implement them, the book presents a highly valuable resource for practitioners who seek to create psychologically safe environments in their organizations. The book is insightful, practical, fun, and easy to read!

– Andreas Richter, Professor of Organisational Behaviour, University of Cambridge

This is a timely book, written with heart. There is an increasing focus on psychological safety and Gina brings the concept to life, explaining how to make it a reality for everyone in our organizations.

– Simon Blake, Chief Executive Officer, Mental Health First Aid England

THE AUTHENTIC ORGANIZATION

THE AUTHENTIC ORGANIZATION

HOW TO CREATE A PSYCHOLOGICALLY SAFE WORKPLACE

GINA BATTYE

WILEY

This edition first published 2024

Registered Office(s)
John Wiley & Sons, Inc., 111 River Street, Hoboken, NJ 07030, USA
John Wiley & Sons Ltd, The Atrium, Southern Gate, Chichester, West Sussex, PO19 8SQ, UK

Editorial Office
9600 Garsington Road, Oxford, OX4 2DQ, UK
The Atrium, Southern Gate, Chichester, West Sussex, PO19 8SQ, UK

For details of our global editorial offices, customer services, and more information about Wiley products visit us at www.wiley.com.

Wiley also publishes its books in a variety of electronic formats and by print-on-demand. Some content that appears in standard print versions of this book may not be available in other formats.

Library of Congress Cataloging-in-Publication Data is Available:

ISBN 9781394232277 (Cloth)
ISBN 9781394232307 (epdf)
ISBN 9781394232291 (epub)

Cover Design: Wiley
Cover Image: © pascalkphoto/Adobe Stock

SKY10077573_061324

For the courageous trailblazers paving the way toward safer, more inclusive workplaces and inspiring others to follow in their bold footsteps.

Contents

Preface: Psychological Safety in Action

It was 6 p.m. on a winter's night. The sun had set long ago. It was cold and the rain was bouncing off the floor. I stepped out of the office, pulled my collar up around my ears and headed back to my car after a busy day at work. I was 22 years old. 4 ft 11 inches tall. Tired. Vulnerable. My laptop was slung over my shoulder as I made my way back to the car park on the edge of town, alone.

I had a 15-minute walk ahead of me from the probation office. Around 6 minutes into the walk, I felt a presence appear behind me. A man was now keeping pace with me. He was close. Uncomfortably close. I stopped, hoping he would continue to walk ahead of me. But he didn't. He stopped walking and lingered behind.

Not knowing what to do, I picked up the pace. We had more distance between us now but I could still hear his heavy breath when he exhaled and his footsteps as his boots made contact with the wet floor. I knew I was in danger. I tried to remember protocol. Ah yes, call the office. Step one. I grabbed my phone and called Cath in the office. She was always there at this time of night, waiting for our phone call to let her know we had arrived home safely.

This call was different. I asked her to talk to me until I got into my car. She did, my tone telling her everything she needed to activate Code Red. Within a second, I was on speaker phone with everyone at head office listening in. They had a second line ready to call the police and a third line ready to call the probation office emergency number. Typically, my panic alarm was in the bottom of my bag. Groan.

After what felt like an eternity, my car was in sight. I got in, slammed the door shut (nearly taking my leg off), locked it and drove away in less than 10 seconds. But not before I saw my mysterious stalker. He was a very tall man in his forties. I knew who it was. I had been teaching him for the last three months.

The next day my senior leaders called an emergency meeting with all five of the probation offices I worked in. Security was stepped up for me. My stalker's probation officer was alerted to his behavior and they began the process of dealing with it from their end. The teaching contract I had with him ended immediately.

My stalker continued for three weeks. Every time I was in Dewsbury Office, there he was. Following me. Watching me. I was given bodyguards. I couldn't leave the office without a probation officer escorting me. From the moment I pulled up in the car park to begin my working day, during lunch and tea breaks, through to walking to my car at the end of the day, there was always a male probation officer next to me to protect me.

For those three weeks, I had a phone call at the end of every day with my manager, to check in on how I was feeling, to talk about any concerns I had and to highlight any potential issues that were arising. We talked about my work, my students, my home life and everything in between. I was out as a gay woman at work. Everyone I came into contact with during my working week knew about my sexuality, including my colleagues, students, probation officers and administration staff. Nothing was off limits to discuss with my manager or team if I chose to.

Navigating a High Stakes Classroom

From my first day in the role, my protection, safety and well-being were taken very seriously by my employer. They had to be. It could have been a matter of life or death.

I realize this might sound scary for a first job fresh out of university, so let me help you visualize my work environment and the safety precautions that were put in place to keep me safe.

Rotating around five probation offices across the region during the week, I worked in little consultation rooms, where every hour one ex-offender would leave and another would take their chair – a student for the next 60 minutes. I was there to teach adult ex-offenders English and math. Or so I was led to believe.

The consultation room always contained four things. There were two chairs with a large, heavy desk separating them and a filing cabinet that locked if you kicked it. Hard. The floor was cold, the walls were bare and the windows barely opened. The radiator was broken; permanently fixed to ON at full blast. It was hot, oppressive and smelt funny. Not in a good way.

There was a big, red panic button under the desk (a secret one) and one visible on the wall by the "probation blue" door. Everything in these places was painted royal blue, which was a source of much amusement amongst my colleagues. The panic buttons were placed strategically so we could easily access one from wherever we were in the room, in the eventuality that something kicked off. Which it did. Frequently.

If you pressed one, either on purpose or by accident (for example, when crossing your legs under the table), urgent assistance burst through the doors in the form of large, muscly, shaved-headed probation officers. Imagine sitting there teaching the intricacies of adding and subtracting fractions to a 47-year-old, or how to read ABC style to a 69-year-old, when three muscly men come crashing through the door. Awkward. Yes, it really happened.

My first day in my shiny first proper job went like this. At 9 a.m. I walked up to reception and took my place in the queue, behind a myriad of people that were high, drunk or looked like they hadn't slept in a week. That is what I was dealing with. When it was my turn, I was asked to sign in and directed to wait in the waiting room with everyone else. I looked very out of place in my new trousers, funky animal-patterned shirt, waistcoat, polished shoes and snazzy laptop bag. After what felt like an eternity, someone came to collect me and took me through to the offices.

After initial introductions to the probation officers on duty that day and the office managers I was shown to what they called my "teaching room" and was handed a security fob that would open all the doors in the Probation Office.

As we have already established, the "teaching room" left a lot to be desired. I was hoping it would be behind the safety of all the security doors. It wasn't. I was allocated a room that the probation officers used to meet with their cases, some of which were high risk and would later become my students. I got acquainted with my "new" office for the day. It didn't take long. There wasn't much of it.

I was there to teach people who had committed offenses related to drugs, alcohol, violence, theft, criminal damage, road traffic offenses and sexual offenses. These crimes, the people committing them, and their stories were part of my daily reality. It is safe to say that my workplace was a hostile, aggressive and nerve-wracking environment.

Before I met any student for the first time, I had to read a report telling me everything I needed to know about the person. This included information about their childhood, their education, work history and information about their key relationships and family members. And most importantly, their offenses. In minute detail. Oh, and what I needed to be aware of when I was with this person on my own for the next 60 minutes, including potential risk of harm they may cause me. It was riveting reading.

I had a stack of these reports on my desk and a full diary of students to work with one-on-one. Now remember, this is day one. Talk about initiation by immersion!

I started to read the reports. Within minutes I was overwhelmed by the intensity of what I was digesting. I can honestly say, my mind could not comprehend some of the offenses, especially the animal cruelty cases. I still feel sick to this day about a handful of cases I was involved with.

In 10 minutes my first student was due to walk through the door. And I was beyond terrified. I had never been in trouble with the law and had yet to sit eye-to-eye with someone that had. Terrified doesn't come close to how I was feeling on that first day.

I had read every single morsel of information about this person. I knew who they were, what they thought, what they had said and how they responded under pressure. I knew too much. Any time now I would receive a phone call from reception to collect this person from the waiting room for their first lesson.

For seven months, I met student after student one-on-one, teaching them English and math, just the two of us in a pokey little room. After seven months I was promoted to a senior role within the teaching department. I was exposed to more and more serious offenders and, for the first time, groups.

I got to know these people. And I realized something quickly. The report that I had read. It wasn't them.

What I learnt is that every single person I taught and spoke to had veered away from their true selves to meet external expectations; they had lost touch with their Authentic Self and this is the reason they had committed an offense. They had molded themselves into someone they thought might be more accepted or loved. Some people had put up barriers to protect themselves from being hurt any further, whilst the others had lived up to the expectations that their peers and/or family had of them. If you constantly hear as a kid "you are a bad boy," that becomes ingrained into your subconsciousness. You are more likely to "act" that way. My students told me time and time again that they heard these messages about themselves as kids, so that is what they became.

After a few sessions working together, the desk became a real barrier to their learning, and to our emerging trust and respect for each other. Controversial, I know; we sat side by side. The panic button a million miles away from me. Not one of my students wanted to be there to learn English and math. They had to attend as part of their conditions of probation. Some were dedicated and attended every session with me. Others I only saw once before they were recalled to prison, or they didn't show up at all, leaving me picturing them based on their damning reports.

In that room, nothing was out of bounds for us to talk about. They all knew I was gay. No one had an issue with it, even the people that were in my room due to assault-related offenses. They trusted me and told me their stories, their challenges, their background and I told them mine.

We engaged in intense discussions about their life, the circumstances of their offenses and how they could break the cycle. What emerged through these conversations were the beliefs they had formed about themselves and how they were showing up in the world because of that, beliefs ingrained from early childhood.

This made me think about Psychological Safety and how to cultivate environments where people can thrive. Pillar 1 and the Authentic Self Process was born! But more about that later.

The deep, nurturing conversations we engaged in allowed them to process their old conditioning, past hurts and experiences and to learn new strategies to be their Authentic Self, even when under pressure and influence from others.

Despite the fact I was working with people who had done some very nasty things, I felt safe at work. My employer put safety mechanisms in place: the panic buttons in the offices, my personal panic alarm and the detailed report about the person I was teaching. The teaching room was behind a security door needing a fob to access. I had to phone the head office to sign in and out, every morning when I arrived at work and every evening when I arrived inside my home. We had a Code Red plan which was discussed regularly (and activated in my case). If we felt any sort of unease, we had to phone the office straight away. We all had a weekly check-in with my manager where we discussed health and well-being and were offered support. We could talk about anything – personal or professional. When I was stalked, this became a daily phone call, and I was allocated probation officers to protect me outside the office.

The team working to keep me safe were cross-organizational and included the Probation Service, the company I worked for and the leadership teams within probation offices. Everyone had clear roles, knew what we had to do and when, knew how to initiate the protocol and escalate, if needed. We had established ground rules and were all working to the same goal – "to keep Gina safe." And in my pokey little teaching room (that exceeded 24°C/75.2°F most days), I created and maintained a safe space for myself and my students to learn and to be their Authentic Self.

I learnt a very early lesson in my career: communication is key. This is what kept me safe during those scary three weeks and it is a lesson I have carried with me every day since, ensuring that all expectations are clarified and understood and that messages are communicated and received accurately.

Even though I was stalked by a dangerous man, I felt safe and supported in the workplace. Most importantly, I felt comfortable bringing all of who I was to work and respected by everyone I worked with.

A Toxic Workplace Unveiled

Roll on two years. From the very first day in my new job, I felt uncomfortable with my manager. She was a dictator. Controlling. Manipulative. She made fun of my colleagues in the office, in front of them. She lied. She abused her power. She made people feel unworthy. I watched her bully members of the team out of their roles. When complaints were made about her, she always came out on top and was very smug about that.

A stark contrast from my previous workplace, I was shocked and unnerved to find that homophobia and biphobia were prevalent in the further education college I now worked. Although mostly underlying and subtle, it was particularly noticeable amongst the older members of staff that had worked at the college for years. They had not received any LGBTQ+ awareness training through their annual Continuing Professional Development (CPD) program, and as a result, they were ignorant of their current behavior and evolving standards for conduct and language in the workplace.

From the moment I started my new job, I knew I had to keep my sexuality to myself. I didn't feel safe to be an "out" gay woman in that environment. My colleagues gossiped about gay staff members and students, and frankly, I was disgusted by what I heard.

In one of my early lesson observations, a senior manager gave me the feedback that I have very "gay mannerisms" and needed to tone it down. Not wanting to "out" myself to my colleagues or students, I took their advice. I started to suppress my natural gestures and mannerisms and was noticeably more muted in my teaching style. Over time, this started to affect my creativity with lesson planning and delivery. I questioned every lesson I put together. I ran it through my "heterosexual filter" to make sure that if someone else was watching me deliver that lesson, they would not suspect I was gay.

I had a fear of being outed publicly. I was scared that someone would "find me out" and within minutes everyone in the college would know I was gay. I had a fear of being treated differently and gossiped about behind my back. Not only would it open me up to abuse, harassment and criticism, but it would also impact on my ability to get the promotion I was aiming for. I had aspirations and knew that if I came out, I would be saying goodbye to those dreams for my future, because people like me don't get into leadership positions.

My colleagues could tell I wasn't being my Authentic Self with them and they sensed that I had put up a shield all around me. I was disconnected from them and wasn't going to let them in. They saw the barriered version of me that I chose to show them. I wore a "mask" and pretended I was a straight woman in a heterosexual relationship. They knew nothing about me or my life.

Always on edge and worried about what my colleagues may ask me when we were alone together, I had stories made up in my head, in case they quizzed me about my private life. I ran away from having any personal conversations with my colleagues in the staff room. As soon as they started talking about their partners, kids or what they were doing at the weekend, I would leave the room. And I wouldn't come back until they had finished talking about their plans with their families or other gossip they had fallen into.

They mirrored my behavior back to me. They were equally as distant with me and I was given the cold shoulder. As a result, I didn't feel accepted. I felt excluded from their world and like an outsider. I felt unsafe and vulnerable at work. Isolated and lonely. It made me not want to socialize with them outside of work, and I dreaded the compulsory team Christmas Dinner small talk. I specifically remember sitting around a table with six of my colleagues, with our Christmas Cracker party hats on. You can imagine it, right? I felt super uncomfortable and kept the conversation focused on work the whole time, so I didn't need to talk about my personal life. The company wasn't great and the food was terrible. I couldn't wait to get out of there. The things you remember.

Being in the closet, I couldn't bring my whole self to work. From the moment I arrived at work in the morning I was living in fear. On tenterhooks. Always watching my back. Showing up as a fraction of who I really was. I felt restricted and caged. And I was suppressing my knowledge, skills and creativity in the classroom. I became exhausted. From running. From hiding. From trying to remember what I had told people. From pretending I was someone else.

Around six months into the job, my manager found out about my sexuality and began a torrent of abuse. I experienced daily harassment, in the form of bullying, intimidation and online abuse.

This impacted dramatically on my physical health, which in turn affected my performance at work. The stress that I felt because of the daily hate incidents resulted in me having IBS – irritable bowel syndrome. I became unable to teach classes in the mornings. Whoever heard of a teacher that can't teach in the morning? Well, it happened. I was only able to teach afternoon and evening classes because my IBS symptoms were so severe in the morning; the time my manager was in "full swing."

I hated going to work. I woke with a sense of dread and a heavy feeling in my whole body. From the moment

I stepped into the office and saw her face, to the moment I left work at night, I had the worst feelings in my body. Tight, tense, niggly and running to the toilet every 10 minutes (in the morning). In the afternoon, I was exhausted from feeling so poorly and from internalizing all the nastiness she directed at me. I dreaded her putting her head round the door to talk to me and wished for those phone calls where I could go out to visit a learning provider or when someone called for my support to deliver something.

I didn't report the bullying at first. I was too afraid to "out" myself to the leadership team. I knew I would have to explain the context of the harassment and as soon as I did that, they would know I was gay. I didn't want anyone else at work to know. I had so much evidence, having documented all the incidents, emails, and communications, and I had witnesses willing to speak on my behalf. But I also had so much to lose by going through with it.

It reached a point where I couldn't take it any longer. I reported the harassment and her behavior. HR told me not to progress the case any further because it would highlight my sexual orientation to my colleagues and peers. I felt I had no choice but to drop the claim. In hindsight, I wonder if I had progressed with the claim, if it would have set the wheels in motion for the college to be a more accepting, safe and inspiring place for others to work. What happened to the woman involved? She was promoted.

Two very different experiences. What is the difference between these two workplaces? One cultivated a psychologically safe environment. The other did not.

Life often presents us with unexpected challenges; moments that push us to our limits and redefine our understanding of ourselves. I believe this experience was one of those life-changing moments. They say that the greatest change often emerges from the deepest struggles. These two contrasting experiences led me to dive headfirst into the profound concept of psychological safety and champion the cause of psychological safety for everyone in the workplace.

Creating Work Environments Where People Thrive

I am the founder and CEO of the Psychological Safety Institute. As an organization we predominantly work with multinational corporations and their people. We hear the same conversations over and over again, regardless of the company we are working with.

1. "We know we have an issue with psychological safety (sometimes referred to as a fire) but we don't know where it is, what caused it or what to do about it."
2. "We can't accurately measure psychological safety. We ask a few questions tagged on to other surveys, but we are not getting any useful information back that we can act upon."
3. "Our staff don't feel safe bringing their whole self to work. And that is impacting on communication, teamwork, productivity, creativity – literally everything!"

I believe in one fundamental truth. We all have the right to feel safe at work. Yet, we know that many employees (including leaders and managers) don't feel safe at work and are struggling to be their Authentic Self with their colleagues.

When I first started my work with organizations, there wasn't much data on psychological safety in the public sphere to draw upon. The data that I stumbled across, was delving deep into the catacombs of the archives, was largely unrelated and was being collated along with other employee or organizational data. There was a comment or two in the conclusion of these reports that alluded to issues with psychological safety – but without any real substantial evidence. Mostly the data referred to physical safety, physical and mental health, or issues surrounding team dynamics or effective collaboration.

Over the years, I have worked extensively with multinationals, public sector organizations and the third sector. I have listened to and collated many stories and anecdotes from employees that shared their lived experiences with me. From those stories, I can confirm that individuals at all levels in the business do not feel psychologically safe at work. This often results in them not being their Authentic Self, instead presenting a censored version of themselves. As a result, communication, relationships and team dynamics are negatively impacted. All this insight from organizations, on top of my lived experiences, put a fire in my belly.

I am fiercely dedicated to my mission: to create work environments where people thrive. Initiating a worldwide conversation on the transformative impact of psychological safety within organizations, I aim to challenge and transform workplace attitudes and outdated workplace cultures.

My vision reaches beyond organizational transformation – it touches the very fabric of society and the daily lives of people. I'm determined to drive legislative change by urging governments to embed psychological safety within workplace legislation, which would lead to substantial changes and enhanced protection for employees.

It is these two pivotal workplace experiences that led me to create the world-renowned 5 Pillars of Psychological Safety. These transformative processes and methodologies have been meticulously crafted and refined through years of collaboration with multinational corporations. They come together to form a robust framework for cultivating work environments where people (and organizations) thrive, thereby creating fully inclusive workplaces. I would like to share those learnings with you.

In this book you will find invaluable insights and practical guidance to empower you to be your Authentic Self at work and take an active role in creating a psychologically safe environment for yourself and others.

THE AUTHENTIC
ORGANIZATION

Part I

Background

In this section, we embark on a journey to set the stage for our exploration of psychological safety. We will delve into various aspects of this crucial concept, understanding its nuances and significance.

In Chapter 1, we navigate the fundamental elements that define psychological safety. We unravel the essence of psychological safety, exploring its intricate components, understanding what affects your sense of safety and distinguishing between ineffective and effective implementation strategies. We also delve into the relationship between psychological safety and inclusive culture, debunk common misconceptions and navigate the roles and responsibilities crucial in cultivating a psychologically safe environment.

As we progress to Chapter 2, our focus shifts to the core of the individual: The Authentic Self. Here, we embark on a profound exploration of what constitutes your Authentic Self, understanding the nuanced differences between identity and authenticity. We navigate the challenges of bringing your Authentic Self to work, exploring the obstacles and the transformative power that lies in embracing your true essence. The chapter concludes with a deep dive into the personal decision individuals face regarding whether to reveal their authentic selves in the workplace.

In Chapter 3, we explore the extent of the psychological safety issue. Here, we confront the absence of comprehensive statistics, providing insights on how to identify if your organization has a psychological safety issue. We introduce you to Lux, a powerful diagnostic tool to measure psychological safety. We then shift our focus to understanding the landscape of active industries and countries addressing psychological safety concerns. We draw distinctions between psychological safety and psychosocial hazards, explore success factors and confront the key challenges organizations encounter in cultivating a psychologically safe workplace.

Let us begin our journey, setting the stage for a deeper understanding of psychological safety and its far-reaching implications in the contemporary workplace.

1

Setting the Scene

Psychological safety impacts every single person on the planet and influences every part of your daily life, such as your family interactions, your social life, work, health, relationships, finances, education, your creativity, your engagement with your local community, your spirituality/religion and your digital life.

What Is Psychological Safety?

Psychological Safety is multi-dimensional in nature, making it a complex aspect of workplace culture. Psychological safety is primarily focused on an individual's subjective experience of safety, comfort and confidence within a specific context, whether it is a physical space, an environment, a situation or when interacting with people. It incorporates many cognitive-emotional-behavioral aspects, such as your emotional and mental well-being, your mental processes, your emotional responses, thoughts and the way you behave.

You might be wondering how that translates into the workplace. Psychological safety in the workplace is rooted at the individual level, where cultivating intrapersonal awareness lays the groundwork for bringing your Authentic Self to work. This intrapersonal foundation acts as a catalyst, playing a pivotal role in cultivating positive team dynamics and collaboration.

In other words, psychological safety in the workplace starts with you understanding your thoughts, emotions and behaviors. This self-awareness is crucial because intrapersonal aspects directly influence your performance and behavior in the workplace. This intrapersonal awareness not only serves as a catalyst for bringing your Authentic Self to work, but also acts as a driving force in enhancing and refining communication, team dynamics and collaboration.

In psychologically safe workplaces, communication with crystal-clear clarity is a top priority and the work environment is intentionally designed to facilitate exceptional collaboration and teamwork, promoting a deep sense of belonging where everyone in the team can thrive. Regular opportunities for reflection and creative exploration empower individuals to fully utilize their unique talents and perspectives, resulting in increased innovation and enhanced problem-solving capabilities.

Ultimately, a psychologically safe workplace is one where both individuals and teams can thrive and achieve their full potential.

What Affects Your Sense of Safety?

Sense of safety is an individualized experience. This means that a situation or a conversation with a colleague that feels safe to you may not feel safe to another member of your team.

Let me give you an example. In team meetings, you feel safe bringing your whole self to work, you discuss your projects and openly reflect on your progress with the rest of the team. You feel confident discussing obstacles that you are facing, resolving conflicts and dealing with misunderstandings and miscommunications – because you feel safe. But is that true for every individual within the team? Does everyone in your team feel safe doing these things?

Your sense of psychological safety can be influenced by a wide range of factors. Here are a few to get you thinking about what affects your sense of safety in the workplace.

Conditioning begins the moment you are born. What you believe to be true today as an adult is a result of the social conditioning and messages you heard as a young child. By the age of around six to seven years old, your belief system had been formed from what you experienced around you. Your beliefs are formed through your experiences, inferences, deductions and through accepting what others tell you to be true.

Most of your thoughts and beliefs are not your own. This conditioning comes from a variety of different sources. Close to home the messages come from your parents, family, school, friends, peers, people in your community and religious institutions. External influences are the political system, the government, mass media (TV, magazines, newspapers, radio stations), the books you read, the websites you browse, music and marketing advertisements.

When you were young you didn't question the messages and perspectives that you heard, saw and felt. You accepted the messages were all true and real and you didn't question the assumptions or conclusions you made.

Learning by example, you modeled the behavior and attitudes of those around you. You were taught a certain way of being that is right and "appropriate." You were rewarded with love and praise when you acted in a certain way and punished when you didn't act a certain way. You internalized the critical messages and voices you heard. Some of these beliefs and thoughts about yourself and the world around you were assimilated through osmosis.

In essence, you are trained to have a certain response, whether that is a positive, negative, rational or irrational response to the situation.

The person you are today and your interactions with family, friends and work colleagues are influenced by the social conditioning and messages you internalized during your formative years and, as a result, you are highly likely to have certain biases and perspectives.

You are a product of your environment and upbringing. The messages and beliefs you internalized during childhood play a significant role in shaping your personal and professional identity, impacting the way you present yourself in various contexts, including the workplace. They shape your self-perception, how you interact with others and even how you approach your work.

For example, if you were constantly told as a child that you need to work hard and get a good job to be successful, you may feel pressured to work long hours and sacrifice other aspects of your life for your career.

Additionally, if you were told that success looks a certain way, you may feel like you need to conform to these societal norms and pursue a particular career or lifestyle, even if it does not align with your true passions and desires.

Ultimately, these repetitive thoughts and beliefs can limit your potential and prevent you from fully realizing your true potential at work and in life. And they affect how safe you feel in different scenarios.

Let me give you some practical examples of conditioning from an LGBTQ+ perspective. We live in a world where we are taught (conditioned) that to be heterosexual and cisgender is normal and anything outside of that is wrong or not accepted. Think about it. The mainstream media typically portrays heterosexual and cisgender relationships, right? When there is a program with a steamy LGBTQ+

love scene it hits the news and gets everyone talking. I have been on many radio programs over the years discussing TV shows where there was a "controversial" LGBTQ+ element. Usually that controversial element is an intimate love scene with same-sex couples. Tell me, how often do you hear debates on the radio about heterosexual intimate scenes? I recall . . . never.

In the UK, many LGBTQ+ individuals grew up not having any LGBTQ+ references or a safe space to explore their sexuality, because of Section 28 (from 1988–2003 in England and Wales). On the flip side, non-LGBTQ+ individuals were not educated or given the safe space to ask questions about LGBTQ+ life. The political landscape at the time and social attitudes toward LGBTQ+ people were hostile. Section 28 conditioned us to think LGBTQ+ life is wrong and immoral.

And let's not forget the AIDS crisis. In the mid-1980s there was an intense media focus on AIDS, a new disease that was terrifying and had no cure. It was known as the "gay disease." The AIDS crisis dominated the 1980s for the LGBTQ+ community. I remember it being talked about on the TV when I was a kid and remember when it hit the headlines of newspapers. People were frightened. Terrified. Public health campaigns were rolled out across the UK. A leaflet was sent to every household in the country. There was a week of educational programming on TV at peak time, and family TV presenters were demonstrating condoms on prime-time television.

The AIDS epidemic (and media coverage of this) and Section 28 created misunderstandings and a terrified nation. The information provided by the government and the media about AIDS and HIV was inaccurate, and as a result, homophobia escalated dramatically at this time, with many LGBTQ+ people hiding away in fear.

The impact of all this can be seen today, in the workplace and in society. Misunderstandings. Stereotyping. Judgments. Criticism. Hatred. Aggression. Frustration. Shame. Guilt. Abuse, bullying and harassment. So, you see, as a result of all of this, LGBTQ+ people have more layers of social conditioning to unpick than non-LGBTQ+ people.

Filters. We all have filters. They influence what you see, hear and think, and can cause you to mishear and internalize what has been said in a different way than what was intended. Everything you see and experience in the world is processed through these filters. We are conditioned to have white, heterosexual and cisgender filters. Unconsciously, everyone in your organization is making decisions, having conversations and performing their roles while influenced by these white, cisgender and heterosexual filters. This can have profoundly damaging effects on LGBTQ+ individuals and other marginalized communities.

Privilege. Having privilege means having an advantage that is out of your control and that you didn't ask for. Privilege describes benefits that belong to people because they fit into a specific social group or have certain dimensions to their identity.

Here is an example of heterosexual/straight privilege. "I can express affection in most social situations and do not expect hostile or violent reactions from others." If you don't have to think about your safety when out in public with your partner, you are privileged.

To use your own privilege for good and be an ally, you must be aware, listen and speak up. The first step is self-awareness. Understand and acknowledge your own privilege. The second step is to educate yourself; learn about other people's experiences. Actively listen to the lived experiences of individuals who encounter different oppression from your own. The third step is to support others who are facing oppression. Learn how you can stand in solidarity with them. Break down barriers (or systems, or accepted practices) that perpetuate their oppression.

Ok, so let's bring all that together: conditioning, filters and privilege. How do they impact on an individual's sense of safety in the workplace? They undermine your confidence to express yourself, influence your sense of belonging and directly affect your ability to make meaningful contributions to the collective success of your team.

Let me give you an LGBTQ+ scenario to help you picture how conditioning, filters and privilege manifest in real-life situations. When you walk down the street, you may glance at a heterosexual couple expressing their love for each other in public and not really think about it. But what if this was a same-sex couple? Would you have the same reaction?

In public, many same-sex couples are hyper-vigilant and constantly on high alert. Why? Because the general population are influenced by their conditioning, filters and privilege to regard that behavior as wrong or immoral.

Same-sex couples in this hyper-vigilant state can never be fully in the moment and able to appreciate the love and affection between them and their partner. Subconscious thoughts of "don't let your guard down" and "don't assume everything will be ok" are always with them. Holding hands, a touch to the leg or the arm, a stroke of the face, a glance that says you care – these are always considered. Same-sex couples are always assessing and on guard.

Over the years, I have experienced physical and verbal abuse when in public with my partner. As a result, we are vigilant and always on high alert and never express affection when out in public. We are not alone in this.

In a pharmaceutical company I worked with, I recall having a conversation with an individual who identified as a gay man. He had been with his partner for a few years and was asking for my advice. He was experiencing real issues with public displays of affection (holding hands) due to the negative and aggressive reactions from the general public as well as his colleagues whilst engaging in work social events. This resulted in him and his partner not engaging in public displays of affection at work events or when outside the house. He went on to say that this was starting to impact on their levels of intimacy at home.

Let me tell you. The abuse, the judgments, the disconnection and constantly looking over your shoulder. All that stuff that goes on outside the home, it is not possible to be unaffected by it. It is challenging to take off the masks you wear, quickly and effortlessly when you get home, and it can be difficult to turn the switch from "mask on/distant" to "intimate" with your partner.

So yes, suppressing your natural urges to be affectionate and intimate in public over the years can impact on intimacy back in the home. It isn't like suddenly you stop being affectionate or intimate together. It is more subtle than that. Because you are closing off a part of yourself when you are outside of the home, naturally that begins to seep into your relationship back in the home too. Subconsciously, back in the home you continue to wear that mask and to hold those barriers up.

I hear time and time again my clients say things like "I have noticed I am not tactile with my partner in front of my family or friends anymore. We used to be." Another thing I hear often is "I noticed the other day that we were sitting at opposite ends of the living room. This is our 'new normal.' In the past we would be sat up close, snuggling and sharing a bar of chocolate." Lastly, I hear all too frequently (and a feeling I share) "I still won't walk down the street holding hands with my partner or kiss on public transport, for fear of being attacked. Simple things that heterosexual people take for granted."

Experiencing the subtle homophobia, biphobia and (not so subtle) transphobia that is underlying our society, you learn to hide certain elements, gestures or mannerisms, socially, with your family/friends and in the workplace. You learn to adapt to keep yourself (and your loved ones) safe.

Assumptions and **stereotypes** affect your sense of safety. Let's explore both of these. An *assumption* is something that is accepted as true or as certain to happen, without proof.

Let me take you on the Assumptions Journey. This is how they form:

1. You have an experience. There is an input of raw data and observations from your experience. These are the facts.
2. You filter in information and details from that experience: the environment around you, the sounds and smells.
3. You analyze the situation based on your own life experiences. This may lead you to categorize people and situations incorrectly.
4. You assign meaning to the situation using all the information you have filtered through. This is where you interpret what the information is telling you.

5. You develop assumptions based on the meaning you created in 3 and 4. This blurs the distinction between what is fact and what is story.
6. You develop conclusions based on your assumptions about the person/situation. Here is where emotional reactions are created.
7. You adjust your beliefs about the world around you, including the people involved in your experience of the moment.
8. You take action based on your adjusted beliefs.

Your mind is a powerful tool. It wants to categorize everything. You automatically and intuitively categorize everything around you based on your conditioning, your upbringing, your education, your life experiences and your exposure to groups of people via the media. When you engage in "quick thinking" it leads you to pre-judge others, based on a set of predefined social categories or norms. People in your "in-group" you judge positively, whereas for others you make negative judgments.

You may make assumptions based on one experience or a piece of information without checking whether this is the case for everyone. This can result in people being treated less favorably and not being provided with the same opportunities or choices enjoyed by others. Making assumptions about people may reveal a lack of insight or knowledge.

Now for a practical example to illustrate how an experience can result in assumptions. Walking through an alley way, a homeless man attacks and robs you. This experience results in you associating all homeless people with violence. You now treat all homeless people with disdain.

Daniel Kahneman, author of *Thinking, Fast and Slow*, suggests that your brain has two operating systems. System 1 is the brain's fast, automatic, intuitive approach. System 2 is the mind's slower, analytical mode, where reason dominates. Assumptions come from quick thinking, which is automatic, intuitive and impulsive and demands very little effort. Quick thinking leads you to form impressions and make decisions that often result in errors of judgment. You make assumptions based on stereotypes.

A *stereotype* is a fixed and oversimplified belief about a particular group or class of people. Stereotypes are mistaken ideas or beliefs many people have about a thing or group. These are usually based upon how the person looks on the outside and their behaviors.

Let me give you an example. Imagine a person riding a Harley-Davidson motorbike. You might assume they are rebellious. You picture them dressed in leather, with studs and patches. You think they are older and visualize their hair blowing in the wind out of their open face helmet. A set of wraparound shades usually completes the look. You assume this is a male. In reality, they love the freedom of the open road but defy the stereotype. Their rebellious appearance conceals a warm-hearted personality. Contrary to expectations, they are not necessarily older; age is irrelevant to their passion for riding. The wraparound shades protect their eyes from the sun, not worn as a symbol of defiance. This rider could just as easily be female, challenging the assumption that the Harley-Davidson experience is exclusive to a particular gender. Many stereotypes are rooted in prejudice so you should be wary of them.

Worrying about other people's assumptions of you and if they are stereotyping you can lead to individuals curating their image, hiding elements of their identity and choosing not to bring their Authentic Self to certain situations in the workplace. It can also alter an individual's behavior, where they censor their mannerisms, gestures and communication styles. Ultimately, it impacts on their feelings of safety in the workplace.

Let us move on to **bias**. In simple terms, bias is a tendency to favor certain people or ideas over others, often leading to unfair treatment based on preconceived judgments. *Individual biases* affect someone else's sense of safety. These are where attitudes or stereotypes affect your views, actions and decision-making ability. Individual bias spikes when you are less aware of what you are doing. For example, when you are on "autopilot" or quick thinking.

Systemic biases, also known as structural or institutional biases, refer to ingrained and widespread patterns of prejudice, discrimination or favoritism embedded within the structures, policies and practices of a society or organization. These biases are often woven into the fabric of institutions, influencing interactions, decisions and outcomes on a larger scale. Unlike individual biases that originate from personal beliefs, systemic biases emerge from historical, cultural and societal factors, leading to unequal treatment and opportunities for different groups.

Individual and systemic biases cultivate an environment where individuals are subjected to unfair treatment and unequal opportunities, and as a result they may feel a sense of exclusion, which can destroy their confidence, affecting their physical and mental well-being and overall sense of safety at work.

Empower yourself to address biases by taking proactive steps. Start by acknowledging that everyone has biases and then take time for self-reflection. Question your assumptions, examine your thoughts and consider different perspectives to gain a clearer understanding of your own biases. Be aware of your physiology, recognizing how hydration, hunger and tiredness affect your thinking. After you have corrected any physiological issues that might interfere with your ability to identify your own biases, you can look for opportunities to address bias in the following areas. Challenge your biases by checking the facts behind your opinions and perspectives. Smash stereotypes by recognizing what assumptions you make and the stereotypes you assign to people. Then look for different sources of information. Educate yourself, slow down your thought processes and be mindful to distinguish between "fast brain" and "slow brain" responses. Avoid multi-tasking, reduce stress and actively invite others to challenge your perspectives. Practice allyship by responding to biased comments or behaviors from others.

Personalities can affect your sense of safety – in a few different ways. *Personality* is one component of your identity. Personality consists of predictable behavior patterns. A personality trait is a habitual pattern of behavior, thought and emotion. It is consistent and lasts over time; you carry it from one situation to the next, for a long period of time. You can't change or transform your personality. It is hardwired in the brain.

Personality affects safety in several ways. One, when you experience different personalities to yours; imagine this dynamic. You are in a meeting with someone who is strong, assertive, fast paced and driven. You, on the other hand, are calm, laid back and compassionate in your approach. Or maybe you have someone who is very outspoken and social working alongside someone who is an introvert and reflector.

They have two very different personalities. When you have such strong contrasts, it can lead to clashes, unspoken tension or frustration, and such interactions can make individuals feel unsafe. Navigating these dynamics can be tricky.

A second way personality can affect safety is as a cause of conflict. Some personalities hate conflict and do everything they can to shy away from it. Others prefer to address issues head on, to resolve the situation quickly. In a global study we conducted,[1] we found that many employees were shying away from conflict situations or conversations that could result in conflict situations, instead choosing to not address it with their colleagues. They would internalize the conversation that triggered them, wait until they got home and then start chewing it over and over. This then impacted on their home life, relationships and physical and mental health. The next day, they take all that chewed over emotion and unfinished communication back into the workplace. As you can imagine, this causes long-term impact on relationships, creativity, communication and performance.

Another side of conflict is this. Imagine you have two parties involved – one a supplier, the other the buyer. The buyer raises a concern about the work produced by the supplier. The supplier tries to rectify the situation by increasing the time spent on the project or by addressing the issue with the output. They do not acknowledge the complaint or issue that was raised, either in live conversations or digitally. It is left unaddressed. In this scenario, the buyer, after raising a concern about the work, feels frustrated as the supplier focuses solely on fixing the output without acknowledging the issue.

Three, aspects of your personality can affect how safe you feel at work. Applying Eysenck's Personality Theory,[2] team members who score high in extroversion and low in neuroticism (emotionally stable) are more likely to feel psychologically safe in the workplace. Team members who score low in extroversion (introverts) and high in neuroticism (emotionally unstable) are less likely to feel psychologically safe in the workplace. It makes complete sense. I'll dig into this more in Chapter 6, "Pillar 3."

Another element that affects sense of safety is **power**. I'm referring to the power dynamics between individuals. Interactions and relationships between individuals often revolve around hierarchy, authority and influence, which can significantly impact how safe someone feels in expressing themselves.

Individuals that belong to **marginalized groups** or individuals with protected characteristics may not feel psychologically safe at work due to a history of discrimination, microaggressions and exclusion, which can create an environment where their identities and contributions are undervalued or ignored. Whilst belonging to a marginalized group can influence how safe someone may feel at work, it's essential to note that safety concerns in the workplace are multifaceted and not solely attributed to one factor.

Neurodivergent individuals may feel unsafe when an organization fails to acknowledge and accommodate their abilities and needs. Individuals may struggle to navigate a work environment that doesn't cater to their strengths and challenges. This can lead to individuals feeling misunderstood or even marginalized. The lack of awareness or resources to support individuals with autism, Asperger's syndrome, attention-deficit/hyperactivity disorder (ADHD), bipolar disorder, sensory processing disorder or dyslexia, for example, can lead to misinterpretations, difficulties in communication, unintentional exclusion or feeling overlooked.

Mental health profoundly influences an individual's sense of safety in workplace situations. Struggles with mental well-being can amplify feelings of vulnerability, hinder open communication and create barriers to fully engaging and thriving within the professional environment. Mental health is a big issue in the LGBTQ+ community. I believe this is because LGBTQ+ people experience bullying, rejection, stigma and discrimination and have layers of conditioning to unpick. Those who identify as LGBTQ+ are more likely to develop problems like low self-esteem, depression, anxiety (including social anxiety), and eating problems, and misuse drugs and alcohol, self-harm and experience suicidal feelings and other mental health problems.

Discrimination, harassment, bullying and stigma make people feel unsafe in the workplace. They usually occur due to a lack of understanding or education. There is the added challenge of reporting harassment and abuse, which impacts on how safe individuals feel in the workplace.

Feeling **excluded** at work might manifest in the following situations, such as during conversations about parenting, discussions about family life/relationships and conversations delving into personal details with colleagues. Exclusion may also occur when discussing activities external to work, managing leave entitlement, expressing your gender identity, navigating gender expectations, addressing race-related issues, dealing with cultural and background differences, managing (dis)abilities, confronting age-related biases, and handling discussions related to sexuality, educational background or political views.

Negative behaviors contribute to an unsafe workplace environment. These can manifest through spoken or written words, abuse, insulting behavior, personal insults, offensive emails or comments on social networking sites, as well as images, graffiti, physical gestures, facial expressions and jokes targeting an individual's sexual orientation, gender identity, disability, religion, belief or age. Unwanted physical contact, ranging from touching to serious assault, and intrusion through pestering, spying and stalking are also forms of negative behaviors that individuals may encounter in the workplace.

There are also specific work-related aspects that influence an individual's sense of safety within the workplace. These include the leadership and management style, the effectiveness of communication and trust-building, expectations, roles and responsibilities. The way conflicts are addressed when reported, the feeling of being valued, respected and appreciated, maintaining a balanced workload, job security and organizational policies that promote fairness, equality and ethical behavior also contribute to an individual's overall perception of safety in the workplace. The handling of bullying and harassment within the organizational context further shapes the work environment's safety dynamics.

As you can see, there are many different aspects that influence an individual's sense of psychological safety in the workplace. Which ones of these affect your sense of safety in the workplace?

And let's not forget that these aspects rarely exist in isolation. There might be a whole host of these aspects, intersecting and mixing around together in various combinations at any given moment. Individuals may be unaware that many of these aspects are coming into play.

Ineffective and Effective Implementation

Ineffective implementation of psychological safety can manifest in various ways. Here are a few examples. Training is conducted on an ad hoc basis merely to "check a box." In meetings, individuals remain quiet unless explicitly prompted. Errors are made and not seen as learning opportunities. Micro-management stifles autonomy. High staff turnover and disengagement are prevalent. There is a lack of trust and collaboration. Individuals and teams shy away from risk-taking, leading to limited innovation. Individuals meet the minimum requirements and clock off precisely on time. A culture of blame, miscommunications and conflict is widespread. Measurement of psychological safety is either non-existent or includes only a few employee questions, tagged onto another survey unrelated to this topic.

The consequences of not having a psychologically safe workplace are far-reaching for individuals. Here are a few. Physical, mental and emotional health of individuals are impacted. Poor performance and decision-making are evident. Communication is strained and ineffective. Conflict resolution is minimal. Blame culture emerges, resulting in grievances, conflicts and liability risks. You observe increased absenteeism and withdrawal behaviors in your team. Individuals shut down, feeling insecure and putting up barriers for protection. They compare their performance and abilities to their peers. Stress levels are raised, causing frustration and resentment, which exacerbates existing health issues. Engagement is lowered, with individuals withholding their skills, knowledge and experience. This has a knock-on effect on their levels of satisfaction and sense of purpose at work, affecting relationships, curiosity, creativity and innovation – directly impacting your business.

The impact on the organization is substantial. Turnover, revenue and profit are negatively impacted. Human resources (HR) teams witness increased attrition, with a worrying level of retention amongst the newest recruits. With the employees that remain, engagement is low and absenteeism is high. Productivity takes a hit, and you have missed opportunities for innovation. Ineffective collaboration occurs between individuals and teams. Silo working takes hold. Toxic cultures develop and escalate. There is a greater risk of accidents, incidents and injuries. Problems go unreported and corners are cut. Any wrong-doing, unethical or illegal behavior goes unchallenged. These situations lead to tragic failures, which in certain industries can be catastrophic. All of this could have been prevented if individuals felt safe to bring their Authentic Self to the workplace.

Effective implementation of psychological safety can manifest in various ways. Ongoing discussions about psychological safety occur in various contexts: one-on-one meetings, team meetings and organizational-wide interactions. Individuals are empowered to initiate conflict resolution strategies, promptly addressing issues. You experience open and inclusive communication and a non-judgmental and respectful atmosphere across the business. Trust and effective collaboration are evident, all underpinned by supportive, authentic leadership. You have cultivated a learning culture, and a workplace that exudes empowerment, autonomy, authenticity, alignment (accompanied by supportive policies and practices), as well as accountability and fairness. Psychological safety is measured annually, with the questions focused solely on psychological safety. The results are transparently shared and interventions are openly discussed and agreed upon.

Organizations that proactively cultivate a psychologically safe environment experience a range of benefits, including improved employee well-being (less staff sickness), heightened levels of employee engagement (people giving their all to their work), enhanced creativity and innovation (new ideas for products and services, as well as creative solutions to challenges faced), stronger teamwork and collaboration (high-performing teams and collaborative working), increased opportunities for learning and development, reduced turnover of staff and enhanced talent retention (loyal and happy employees), refined decision-making and problem-solving capabilities and the cultivation of a positive organizational culture and reputation.

Psychological Safety versus Inclusive Culture

Many individuals believe that psychological safety and inclusion are intrinsically linked, that you can't have one without the other. I challenge this view. You can feel psychologically safe in a situation without feeling included or integral to the group. But can you truly feel included if you don't feel safe? Inclusion encompasses a broader sense of belonging and acceptance within a community or group. If you don't feel safe, it is likely to hinder your sense of belonging and your perception of feeling included. In other words, if you don't feel safe it is likely to create obstacles or difficulties, making it challenging for you to experience a genuine sense of belonging and inclusion in a community or group.

Psychological safety is a precursor to feeling included and lays the groundwork for genuine inclusion. Without psychological safety, you can't have a truly inclusive culture. Therefore, cultivating a psychologically safe environment is the catalyst for genuine inclusion. Despite this, organizations often tend to prioritize inclusion initiatives over creating a psychologically safe workplace.

Let me illustrate this through the Hierarchy of Psychological Safety, as shown in Figure 1.1. The Hierarchy maps out organizational responsibilities, embracing both internal and global dimensions.

There are eight levels of responsibility. The first five levels delve into internal dimensions, while the final three levels transcend organizational boundaries.

Level 1 is Individual Safety. This level focuses on establishing a foundational level of psychological safety at the individual level, promoting authenticity, resilience and personal responsibility.

Advancing to Level 2, we experience Interpersonal Safety. This level concentrates on nurturing psychological safety in one-on-one interactions, placing a strong emphasis on effective communication and interpersonal skills.

Figure 1.1 Hierarchy of Psychological Safety

Level 3 introduces us to Team Dynamics Safety. Here, the primary focus is on cultivating a psychologically safe team environment, where everyone in the team can thrive.

Moving on to Level 4, we arrive at Collaboration Safety. At this level, the spotlight is on creating an environment conducive to innovation and collaboration.

Level 5 is dedicated to Organizational Safety. This level broadens the scope of psychological safety to the organizational level, underscoring an unwavering commitment to cultivate a safe and inclusive workplace culture for all employees.

Transitioning into the external dimensions, Level 6 is External Relations Safety. Here, the focus shifts to extending and influencing psychological safety standards in external collaborations. This involves cultivating robust and thriving relationships with clients, stakeholders and partner organizations.

Level 7, Community Safety, shifts the focus toward elevating psychological safety to positively impact the wider community. This level places a significant emphasis on proactively collaborating with the community through various initiatives, extending organizational commitment beyond boundaries.

Finally, at Level 8, Industry and Global Safety, the perspective expands to a global scale. Here, the emphasis is on elevating psychological safety to exert a positive influence on industry dynamics and global contexts. This level is dedicated to challenging and transforming industry and global workplace attitudes, actively working to dismantle outdated practices. The ultimate objective is to establish a global landscape of workplaces and industries that prioritize and cultivate psychological safety.

In the Hierarchy, genuine inclusion is located at Level 5, Organizational Safety, where psychological safety permeates the entire organization. This is often seen as a pivotal stage where an inclusive culture may be more fully realized. Unfortunately, many organizations tend to concentrate solely on Level 5 with their inclusion initiatives, disregarding the foundational Levels 1–4. This neglect results in significant challenges for individuals and teams, ultimately hindering the progress and success of equity, diversity and inclusion (EDI) initiatives.

Feeling safe at work is a fundamental right for everyone. When this sense of safety enables you to express your Authentic Self, you thrive – which leads to increased happiness, well-being, inspiration, connection, engagement and empowerment. These factors contribute to the development of high-performing teams and a genuine sense of belonging. A psychologically safe workplace empowers individuals to perform at their best, driving EDI initiatives forward.

Psychological safety underpins both an inclusive culture and an environment where employees genuinely belong, playing a pivotal role in the success of EDI efforts.

Therefore, focus your attention on cultivating a psychologically safe workplace. It will inherently nurture inclusivity, enrich diversity and positively impact well-being, team effectiveness and overall organizational success.

Misconceptions

Through my extensive work with corporations, it is clear there are misconceptions about psychological safety. Here are a few of the common misconceptions I hear regularly.

"Inclusion takes priority over psychological safety in our EDI initiatives since it doesn't affect everyone." Psychological safety is seen as a "nice to have," once inclusion and belonging have been addressed. Remember, psychological safety underpins inclusion. Without psychological safety, you will not have an inclusive culture. If you want to create an inclusive culture, you need to start with the foundations. Create an environment where people feel safe. Once they feel safe, valued and able to express their Authentic Self, the groundwork for genuine inclusion has been established. Psychological safety serves as the bedrock upon which the pillars of diversity, equity and inclusion stand. Neglecting psychological safety in favor of other initiatives can undermine the very essence of a truly inclusive culture. Prioritize psychological safety from the outset. It will lead to a significant shift in your overall organizational culture. This shift goes beyond just a surface-level approach to diversity and inclusion, as it addresses the core factors that enable individuals to thrive.

"Psychological safety and inclusion are intrinsically linked." This has been discussed in detail in the section above.

"Leaders are responsible for psychological safety." With most corporations operating within a traditional organizational paradigm, characterized by hierarchical structures, power and decision-making are concentrated at the top. Rest assured, the responsibility doesn't lie with leaders.

"Psychological safety only affects a few people, specifically the ones that are susceptible to stress and anxiety." Whilst these factors do play a role, businesses are failing to recognize the impact it has on everyone in the organization, from leaders to employees. This includes employees that work full-time, part-time, temporary, freelance/contract, on job share, shift-workers, volunteers, interns and project-based staff. Everyone. It influences employee health, overall well-being, levels of engagement and ultimately, performance.

"Psychological safety revolves around the fear of speaking up or making mistakes." Psychological safety is a much bigger concept than interpersonal risk taking, with a wider scope that often goes unnoticed or is downplayed. As you progress through the pages of this book and reflect on the Hierarchy of Psychological Safety, I am sure you will see and appreciate the breadth of psychological safety.

"A single training session for everyone in the organization will create a psychologically safe workplace and provide all the tools that we need." Many businesses focus on key performance indicators (KPIs) and short-term goals and fail to measure impact. There is so much pressure to deliver immediate results and meet these KPIs that the bigger picture is often overlooked. Many organizations prioritize productivity and efficiency over creating a psychologically safe environment. A single training event or a one-off conversation will not create a safe workplace. True transformation takes time, effort and a collaborative approach, and sustained attention on it. And you must measure impact. Otherwise, why did you waste all that time, money and resources?

"HR teams, well-being teams and Employee Resource Groups are the ones that should lead the discussions about psychological safety." Whilst these groups of people are often the ones that engage in conversations about psychological safety, it is thought that these groups bear the responsibility and are the ones that tend to initiate interventions for the organization. The discussion about psychological safety must extend to the leadership team and have buy-in from everyone to ensure a comprehensive and organization-wide commitment.

"It is impossible to measure how psychologically safe employees feel at work." It is possible to measure psychological safety. I have developed a tool to accurately do so. More on that in Chapter 3.

Navigating Roles and Responsibilities

Creating a psychologically safe environment is a collaborative effort. Every single individual within the organization plays a crucial role in creating a workplace where everyone can not just survive but thrive. It requires commitment and effort from everyone, regardless of their role or level of seniority. Throughout this book, you will be presented with the methodologies and tools designed to support you on your journey.

You must remember that the responsibility for cultivating psychological safety doesn't sit on one individual's shoulders. It is a shared commitment that involves every single person in the organization. However, there are additional responsibilities that can be divided into three distinct spheres: leadership, managers and HR.

The leadership team has three primary areas of responsibility. The first is the task of developing and communicating a clear mission and set of values that prioritize psychological safety. Second is championing psychological safety as loudly as possible. This includes ensuring the narrative of psychological safety is disseminated throughout the organization and integrated into every aspect of working life, from discussions in leadership meetings, team meetings and one-on-one meetings, to ensuring maximum attendance at training events and organization-wide completion of psychological safety annual assessments. Last, it is important that they lead the way in cultivating a culture characterized by effective communication, mutual respect and collaboration, where diverse perspectives are valued and all employees are treated with dignity and respect. It is essential to recognize that this last responsibility isn't confined solely to the leadership team. It is a collective responsibility shared by all within the organization.

Managers have five primary areas of responsibility. Firstly, they are expected to lead by example and model the behavior they expect from their team members. This involves embracing vulnerability and sharing their own experiences, thereby creating a culture of openness and trust. Secondly, they should encourage open communication and active listening within their teams, to create a safe space for individuals and build trust. Thirdly, a key element of their role involves providing feedback and support to their team members, to help them grow and thrive in the organization. Fourthly, managers play a pivotal role in championing diversity and inclusion. This is manifested through their hiring and promotion practices, recognizing the value and importance of individuals with different backgrounds, skill sets and experiences. Lastly, managers are responsible for addressing any incidents of conflict or harassment promptly and taking a strong stance against these behaviors.

The HR team has several additional responsibilities. These include establishing policies and procedures that support psychological safety, inclusion and equity. They must provide adequate resources and training to support individuals and teams. They are responsible for ensuring all employees have access to confidential resources for support, such as an employee assistance program or counseling services. Monitoring and addressing any issues related to discrimination, harassment or bullying in the workplace need to be prompt and effective. They are tasked with measuring and monitoring psychological safety and taking action to address any concerns or issues, as well as continuously evaluating and improving upon the workplace culture to ensure that it is safe, inclusive and supportive for all employees. Again, it is vital to note that some of these responsibilities are not exclusive to HR. The learning and development team, well-being team, managers and employees each hold specific roles and responsibilities within this collaborative effort.

In this chapter we have begun to explore psychological safety in the workplace. We began by defining the concept of psychological safety and delving into the factors that influence our sense of safety, gaining a deeper understanding of its impact in the workplace. From there, we examined the contrasts between ineffective and effective implementation, as well as the relationship between inclusion and psychological safety. We addressed the most common misconceptions head-on, dispelling myths that often hinder the implementation of psychological safety methodology. Lastly, we navigated the landscape of roles and responsibilities, underlining the collective effort required to cultivate psychological safety throughout the organization.

In the next chapter, we are going to explore the concept of bringing your Authentic Self to work. Buckle up, this is the exciting bit. It might blow your mind a little, but trust me, it is exciting.

Notes

1. Gina Battye (2022). Psychological Safety Global Study. www.thepsi.global.
2. For more information about Eysenck's Personality Theory: https://hanseysenck.com.

2

The Authentic Self

"Being your Authentic Self at work means being vulnerable" is often the first statement leaders and managers make when delving into the concept of the Authentic Self. I want to address this head-on because the Authentic Self is an important concept to understand.

Right now, you are presenting a carefully curated and censored version of yourself. It is a version honed over years to fit in and be accepted. You censor your appearance, your behaviors, body language, mannerisms, what you say, do and how you communicate. Think of it like configuring privacy settings on your laptop. For one user, you'll let them see X. For a different user, you'll let them see X and Y. You show up wearing different "masks" for different scenarios, extending beyond your personal and social life to the version you present at work.

Let me take you back to where it all began. Picture yourself at birth, the authentic real you, as shown in Figure 2.1. This is your Authentic Self.

When you came into this world, you were a blank slate. Innocent, unburdened, unfiltered. Imagine yourself as a brand-new device with factory settings.

As you grew up, you reached a point in your development where you became more conscious and started to question the world around you. Internal dialogues formed, where you started asking questions such as: Why does my brother get more of my parents' attention than I do? Am

Figure 2.1 Your Authentic Self

I not loved? Am I not good enough? Why am I not as slim/tall/clever as everyone else in my class? Why does my family not have much money and all my friends have the latest iPhone, games console and laptop?

These internal dialogues started the process of internalizing the answers, marking the transition from a pristine device to a system laden with bugs and glitches.

Each thought, experience, belief, interaction and each piece of feedback you received contributed to the accumulation of a "layer" that distanced you a little from your Authentic Self. In Figure 2.2 you can see one layer surrounding your Authentic Self, creating a barrier and distancing you from your Authentic Self.

Imagine this process like a layer of an onion building up and up over time, moving you further and further away from that connection to your true essence, your Authentic Self. Figure 2.3 demonstrates this with the addition of a further two layers.

Layers are like intricate threads woven into a complex tapestry. They bear the impressions of the things that shaped you. Woven into each layer are the social conditioning and phrases you absorbed as a child, the beliefs you formed and internalized in your early years (whether they aligned with your Authentic Self or not), the stories you created about specific moments in time, the labels you

Figure 2.2 From Authentic Self to Identity

Figure 2.3 Progression to Identity

"collected" over the years to describe yourself, family expectations, societal norms and personal insecurities. The comments you heard as a child, both encouraging and critical, left their mark. The experiences that left you joyful, hurt, angry or puzzled – you carry those with you.

Over time, these accumulating layers reshape your Authentic Self into a complex, multifaceted identity. In Figure 2.4 you can see that the Authentic Self is buried beneath these layers. The heart at the center symbolizes your Authentic Self, but what your colleagues perceive and experience of you is primarily influenced by the outer layer, which represents your visible identity.

As the layers built up, a subtle shift occurred. You were no longer operating from your Authentic Self. Instead, you began to navigate life through the lens of these accumulated layers. The fear of judgment, the pursuit of validation and the desire to fit in added weight to these layers, reinforcing the façade that concealed your Authentic Self.

You started crafting "masks," different ones for different situations, to safeguard you from vulnerability, rejection and judgment. These masks gradually evolved into a defense

Figure 2.4 Identity Unveiled

mechanism. We tend to wear masks out of fear. In my case, the fear centered on being exposed in certain areas at work: not being good enough at my role, of being an "impostor" and being gay in a heterosexual environment. I was forever dodging the humiliation of being "outed" at work. I didn't want to have that whole "I am gay" conversation over tea and biscuits in the staff room.

Now, you wear these masks to fit into the expectations that society or the workplace has of you, to gain acceptance and avoid conflict.

What happened to your Authentic Self? The layers that have been protecting you inadvertently distanced you from your Authentic Self. What began as a coping strategy evolved into a habitual pattern, a performance you put on each day. Currently, you are living your life on the surface of all these layers, operating from your identity, and not from your Authentic Self, as shown in Figure 2.4.

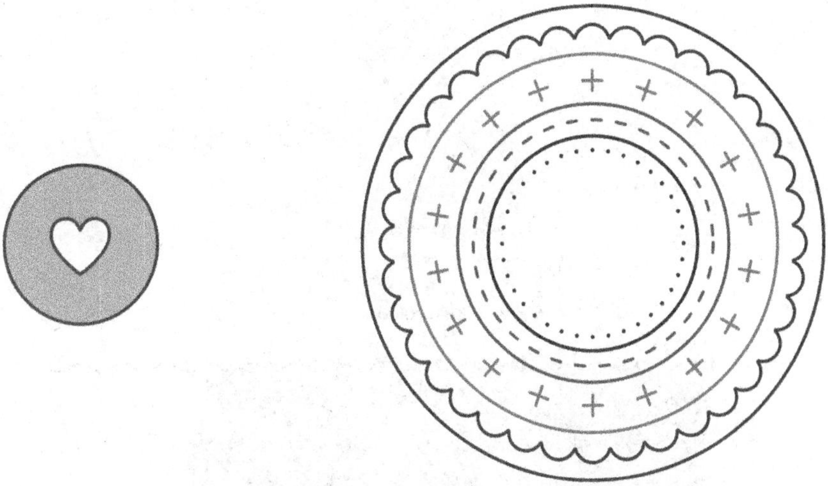

Figure 2.5 Authentic Self and Identity

In Figure 2.5 your Authentic Self is on the left, while your acquired identity and the layers that have accumulated are on the right. This visual highlights the contrast between your Authentic Self and your constructed identity shaped by all these layers, illustrating the transformative potential of reconnecting with your Authentic Self.

Your Identity: How People Perceive You at Work

Imagine the iceberg in Figure 2.6 represents the different aspects of your identity. Identity is how other people perceive you and the way you define yourself, based on your life experiences. Your identity evolves over time through experiences and interactions with others. Identity is essentially a **perception** of who you are.

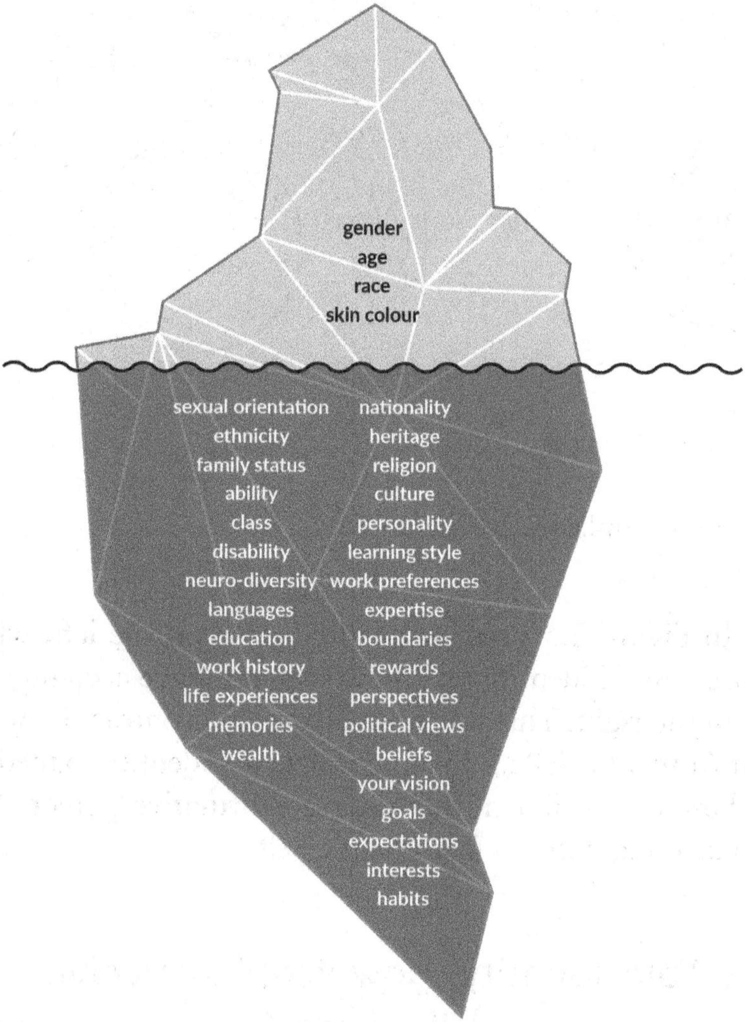

Figure 2.6 Identity Iceberg

The visible portion of the iceberg represents the aspects of your identity that people can see and often use to make judgments, such as your age, gender, skin color and race.

Beneath the surface are things that others wouldn't know about you unless you told them, such as your life experiences, work preferences, perspectives, vision and goals, interests, personality profile, family status, beliefs and all those things that contributed to forming your layers.

Sharing these details of your identity can alter how others perceive you. People often hide parts of their identity because they fear being vulnerable, exposed or hurt. They present a curated version of themselves; they wear a "mask" as a defense mechanism to protect themselves.

At work, many individuals wear a "professional mask." The desire to belong often leads people to present a version of themselves that they believe will be accepted and fit in with the workplace culture.

As a result, your colleagues are exposed to your identity, not your Authentic Self. (Refer to Figure 2.5.)

Understanding the impact of labels and their role is crucial here. From an early age, you begin to accumulate labels for yourself: daughter, son, mother, father, gay, straight, trans, boy, girl, non-binary, creative, unlucky, student, shy – you get the idea. When someone asks what you do, you respond with "I am a . . . health worker, teacher, data analyst, scientist."

When meeting someone new, you instinctively seek a label for them too. You want to make sense of who they are and their experiences in life. In some scenarios, these labels can be useful. In others they can be stifling and debilitating.

Try to describe who you are right now. What words come to mind? Labels often emerge as the initial response. If I ask you "but who are you really?" How would you answer? It is a far more challenging question now that the labels have all been used up, isn't it?

It is easy to become defined by your labels, as they introduce yet another layer to hide behind. Another facet to the mask you wear for the "performance you are delivering" in your life.

Your Authentic Self: The Real You

Your Authentic Self is your truest, most genuine nature and essence. Nestled at the core of your being, it remains unadulterated by external influences, reflecting the purest form of your existence. This untouched core essence is your Authentic Self and is essentially who you **really** are.

Imagine a set of Nesting Dolls – wooden dolls of decreasing size placed one inside another. The little doll nestled at the center of the set is your Authentic Self. But this is not what your colleagues see in the workplace. What they are exposed to is a version of you that you have meticulously crafted over time to navigate the world and your work environment safely. They see the largest nesting doll that sits on the outside. They see your identity.

Your Authentic Self lies beneath these layers. Peel back the layers of the onion, reset your factory settings, strip back all the nesting dolls – you will find your Authentic Self right there, underneath it all. When you strip back those layers and conditioning you begin to reveal and step into your full potential.

The process of reconnecting with your Authentic Self involves a journey of self-discovery. This journey begins by increasing your self-awareness; exploring and understanding your thoughts, emotions, conditioning, motivations and other aspects of yourself. Throughout this process, you will gradually begin to accept yourself for who you really are, instead of conforming to external pressures or societal norms. As a result, you will begin to reveal more of your Authentic Self than just your identity.

When you reconnect to your Authentic Self, you unlock your full potential and become the best version of yourself. Living in alignment with your Authentic Self not only brings a sense of wholeness, fulfilment and meaning to your life but also empowers you to forge authentic, meaningful connections and cultivate thriving relationships that enable you to authentically express your true self.

Bringing Your Authentic Self to Work

Bringing your whole self to work means presenting your **Authentic Self**, rather than your **identity**. In the presence of a psychologically safe environment, your Authentic Self naturally flourishes.

Your identity masks your Authentic Self. Identity is a culmination of your beliefs, experiences and acquired traits and influences how you present yourself in various settings, including your relationships, work, family and social circles. Most individuals are not even aware that they wear "masks" because they are so deeply woven into the fabric of their lives.

As you journey into understanding the significance of bringing your Authentic Self to work, consider the nesting dolls as a metaphor for the layers that you have. By embracing your Authentic Self, you're revealing the smallest nesting doll (the core of who you truly are) to the world and inviting authenticity into your workplace interactions.

The Obstacles

Many individuals don't bring their Authentic Self to work, sharing only their identity or their Authentic Self to a select few individuals. Not everyone feels comfortable sharing every aspect of who they are in the workplace and will present their identity or carefully curated "professional mask." You must remember that everyone has a unique personality, preferences, working style and past workplace experiences. You need to be mindful of this and meet people where they are. Let us explore the common reasons why people don't bring their Authentic Self to work.

Past experiences significantly influence present behavior. Some individuals may have had negative experiences in the workplace when they brought their Authentic Self to work (usually earlier in their career), which they want to avoid happening again.

Professional boundaries vary. While some team members may be open and willing to share everything about themselves, others may prefer to maintain professional boundaries and keep their personal and professional lives separate. In environments with a strong hierarchical culture, employees may feel the need or have been conditioned to maintain a level of formality and distance between themselves and their colleagues to maintain professional boundaries. They may have been accustomed to performing a specific role without discussing anything about their personal life. Their reasons could be varied, such as a result of this conditioning or a carryover from previous workplace cultures.

Your workplace culture might not inherently encourage bringing your Authentic Self to work, possibly stemming from outdated norms. However, if you find a comfortable space to express your Authentic Self with specific individuals within the organization, it is worth exploring. Begin by identifying situations and people where you do feel safe to be your Authentic Self. Define your boundaries, both personal and work. Once these are defined, assess situations where you already feel safe, and think "what do I feel safe sharing with this person and in this situation that I don't currently?" Gradually contribute more while staying within your boundaries. This process creates a ripple effect, much like a pebble in water. As you open up, those around you will notice and realize it is a safe space for them too. By signaling your comfort, a sense of safety will naturally spread, enhancing authenticity throughout the workplace. To reiterate, when you have a psychologically safe environment, your Authentic Self naturally flourishes.

I touched on **power dynamics** in Chapter 1. Power dynamics within a workplace can create an environment and interactions where individuals don't feel safe to bring their authentic selves.

Cultural differences significantly influence how individuals express their Authentic Self in the workplace. Cultures that prioritize collective harmony may lead individuals to conform to established norms, while those valuing individualism might encourage open self-expression. Communication styles also vary; some cultures favor indirect communication whilst others may adopt more direct and assertive approaches, impacting how people express their Authentic Self.

Your **personality** shapes how you interact with others, how you show up in the workplace and how you express your Authentic Self. You are an individual with a unique pattern of thoughts, feelings and behaviors that sets you apart from others. Be aware of how your personality affects you in the workplace and be mindful of different personalities within your team and the impact these have on psychological safety when they intersect. If you are not sure what those different personalities are, take the time to do the work to find out more about your team. You'll read more about this in Chapter 6, "Pillar 3."

Just like you have a unique pattern that makes up your personality, you also have a unique set of **preferences**, which can manifest as a working style. This can impact on when and how you bring your Authentic Self to situations. Take the time to notice and discuss individual preferences within your team.

Positioning is another consideration. While it is important to bring your Authentic Self to work, it is crucial to acknowledge that there are situations where it may not be appropriate to share certain aspects of yourself, and in such cases, different levels of self-disclosure may be required. These situations may call for different behaviors and communication styles. By adapting your approach to fit the environment and audience, you can avoid misunderstandings, maintain respect and create a positive work atmosphere.

Striking the right balance between authenticity, appropriateness and proper positioning requires an awareness of the situation and context and a willingness to be flexible in your approach, while staying true to your core values. It means understanding the perceptions, expectations and preferences of those around you and being respectful of their boundaries. Ultimately, by finding the appropriate level of self-disclosure, you can build stronger relationships and contribute to a more cohesive and productive team. An extreme example, as an LGBTQ+ individual visiting colleagues in an office overseas, where there are strong anti-LGBTQ+ laws in place, you are highly likely to withhold certain information about yourself to ènsure you are safe. You are less likely to discuss your personal life with colleagues there than if you were visiting an office where there are pro-LGBTQ+ laws in place.

Many leaders and managers fear **vulnerability** when expressing their Authentic Self to colleagues, associating it with exposing weakness. Let me address that. Embracing your Authentic Self is a display of strength, authentic leadership and emotional intelligence. When you align with your Authentic Self, you are not just resilient, you are more present and confident in your decisions, knowing you are aligned with who you truly are. You lead by example, embracing your strengths and celebrating your individuality without worrying about other people's opinions or fearing rejection.

Within the workplace, a pervasive concern often takes center stage: the **fear of judgment.** Many individuals worry about how their colleagues, managers and leaders will perceive them if they reveal certain aspects of their identity. They fear being judged, misunderstood or even marginalized for their beliefs, values or personal characteristics.

The pressure to fit in and the **desire to conform** to workplace culture can lead people to suppress aspects of their identity that might make them stand out. They believe that conforming to the norms of the organization is essential for their success and relationships within the workplace.

Individuals might feel a **misalignment** between their Authentic Self and the expectations of their role or industry. They may believe that certain traits or aspects of their identity could hinder their career advancement, so they hide them.

The strain of **performance pressure** can lead individuals to burnout. This is usually because of three things: wanting to meet expectations, fear of falling behind and worrying about other people's perception.

A lack of visible **role models** who are their Authentic Self at work can make it difficult for others to visualize themselves doing and being the same.

Individuals struggling with **personal insecurities,** such as self-doubt or low self-esteem, might believe that their

Authentic Self is not good enough or that they are not good enough.

Conflict with personal and company values. A question I am often asked is "What do you do when your personal values conflict with the company values?" For some individuals, this misalignment can create a challenging work environment.

Let's look at a practical example. Imagine your friend works in a pharmaceutical company. They are passionate advocates for environmental sustainability and animal rights, strongly committed to reducing the environmental impact of the pharmaceutical industry and supporting cruelty-free testing methods. However, the company they work for primarily relies on animal testing for drug development and its environmental practices don't align with their values.

You can see the conflict, right? Their personal values centered on environmental sustainability and animal rights directly conflict with the company's values, which prioritize traditional pharmaceutical testing methods and profit margins.

There are several steps they could consider to resolve this conflict. First, they might take some time to reflect on the extent of the conflict between their personal values and the company's values. It's crucial to assess whether this misalignment is a fundamental issue for them and how it affects their job satisfaction and overall well-being. Next, they can initiate conversations with their colleagues to gauge if there are others who share their concerns. Building a network of like-minded individuals can provide emotional support and help them understand the broader perspective within the company. They should also thoroughly review the company's policies and values statements to gain a comprehensive understanding of the company's position. This can help identify areas where compromise might be possible or where their concerns align with the company's long-term goals. If their personal values continue to significantly clash with the company's values, causing distress or discomfort, they should schedule a meeting with their immediate line manager or the HR department. During this conversation, they can express their concerns, explain the reasons for their discomfort and explore potential solutions. Depending on the outcome of the conversation with their line manager or HR, they may explore the possibility of seeking accommodations, such as working on projects that better align with their values or exploring alternative roles within the company that are more in line with their personal interests. If a resolution cannot be reached within the company, they may need to consider a career move where they seek employment opportunities with organizations whose values closely align with their own. It's essential to prioritize their own well-being and values alignment in the long term.

One last point about bringing your Authentic Self to work. In some cases, not sharing personal information may be a preference rather than a safety mechanism. However, for others, it could be a safety mechanism, and assuming that it is not could potentially put them at risk. As such, it is crucial to respect everyone's boundaries and not pressure them into sharing more than they feel comfortable with. Whether it is asking about their weekend or their views and opinions, some team members may not want to disclose every little detail, and that is okay.

Now, which ones of those resonate with you?

The Power of Embracing Your Authentic Self

When organizations create a culture that empowers individuals to bring their Authentic Self to work, a truly transformative shift occurs. At the core of this culture lies psychological safety. As we have already discussed, psychological safety is the foundation upon which inclusivity, belonging and peak performance thrive. Your Authentic Self flourishes in psychologically safe environments.

We all have the right to feel safe at work. This sense of safety, enabling you to bring your Authentic Self to work, is invaluable. In workplaces where psychological safety thrives, individuals tap into an incredible power. They don't just show up for their job, they show up as their Authentic Self, bringing with them all their unique knowledge, skills and ideas. They feel happy, healthy, inspired, engaged and empowered. They truly thrive. When everyone in your team thrives, guess what happens? These elements all come together giving rise to high-performing teams.

Creating an environment where every individual can confidently be their Authentic Self is absolutely crucial. It's not just the responsibility of one person; it's the collective effort that cultivates the environment. What happens if you don't create this environment? Let's delve into the consequences of operating solely from your identity, examining both the individual and organizational perspectives.

Let's start with the individual. Censoring elements of your Authentic Self is truly exhausting. If you have ever done this, you know. When you are not able to be authentic at work, this creates a sense of detachment and disengagement – from others and yourself. Colleagues pick up on your guardedness and they feel those emotional barriers that are standing in the way of genuine authenticity and communication. Sadly, this can lead to feelings of alienation and loneliness. This inauthenticity also seeps into your connections with family and friends, resulting in a wider sense of exclusion.

It doesn't stop there. These effects have a lasting impact, affecting your physical, mental and emotional well-being. You are more likely to experience heightened levels of stress and emotional exhaustion. This stifles personal growth, creativity and innovation. The workplace transforms into a breeding ground for inauthenticity, frustration, miscommunications and dissatisfaction, leading individuals to feel a diminished sense of fulfilment and purpose in their professional life.

Considering a significant chunk of your life is spent at work, it's only natural to want more: to feel happy, healthy and to be able to thrive at work. To feel valued and respected, have great relationships with those around you and enjoy coming to work. To be able to be creative and innovative in your work. To learn and develop your skills and knowledge and be able to deal with internal and external challenges with ease.

When you bring your Authentic Self to work, it's like a whole new world opens up for you. You are happier and more fulfilled at work and this carries into other areas of your life too. You become a beacon of authenticity, radiating an inner strength that's unmistakable. Others can't help but be drawn to your magnetic presence. Even in the face of challenges, you exude calm and confidence, a trait that extends to all corners of your life. Who do you know that is like that?

Life takes on a different rhythm – one of ease and flow. You manifest easily and quickly, with no effort or striving. Joy, enthusiasm, freedom and appreciation become your natural state. The unique qualities that define your Authentic Self become the driving force behind your happiness, not just at work, but in every area of your life.

Let's look at the impact on the organization. In essence, when you create the culture where everyone can bring their Authentic Self to work, you unleash the full potential of everyone that works in the organization.

When you hire people, you do that based on their unique skills, knowledge and experience. However, when they start their new role, the desire to fit in and be accepted by their colleagues and peers overshadows them. To make sure they fit in, they hide and censor the very aspects that made them stand out during the hiring process.

This has a profound impact on their work, relationships and their levels of curiosity, creativity and innovation. Not bringing your Authentic Self to work results in a domino effect of consequences that reverberate throughout the entire organization.

The impacts of not bringing your Authentic Self to work are far-reaching and deeply interconnected. It can lead to decreased employee morale, a limited diversity of perspectives, reduced innovation, heightened stress levels, lower job satisfaction and a palpable lack of psychological safety, ultimately hindering team dynamics. Such consequences collectively influence the overall success of your business.

At its core, the choice to hide your Authentic Self reaches far beyond your personal experience; it starts a chain reaction that shapes the organizational environment and workplace culture. When individuals feel safe to peel back the layers of their identity and bring their Authentic Self to work, not just with a select few but with everyone in the business, you will feel the transformational ripples across the organization.

A Personal Decision

Not everyone will want to bring their Authentic Self to work. For various reasons, individuals may want to protect their personal life, maintaining a level of privacy amongst colleagues. Some might choose to hide certain parts of their identity with everyone or selectively share with specific colleagues.

While you may not know the reason for this, it is essential to respect their choice and preferences. They are choosing to present themselves in a certain way for a reason, and pressuring them to reveal more can be counterproductive. By respecting everyone's choice and boundaries, you can help to create a workplace that values diversity and inclusivity, one where everyone feels valued and respected.

Encouraging individuals to bring their Authentic Self to work is important, but it is equally important to respect boundaries and not pressure them to share more than they are comfortable with. Creating a supportive workplace environment means recognizing and valuing these differences and working together to create a workplace culture that values authenticity, diversity and inclusivity.

Being your Authentic Self at work can be challenging and may not be the right choice for everyone. Ultimately, the decision to be your Authentic Self at work is deeply personal. Respect everyone's choice and make a commitment to providing support in whatever way you can. Your goal is to create a culture that values authenticity, inclusivity and diversity, where everyone feels comfortable and supported in being their Authentic Self at work.

Remember, no one is insisting that you bring your Authentic Self to work. Instead, the aim is to create an environment where it can naturally flourish.

In this chapter we have delved deeply into the concept of being your Authentic Self within the workplace. We examined the essence of identity, the perception of who you are. From there, we explored the Authentic Self, the core of who you really are. To help understand the interaction between identity and Authentic Self, we used the analogy of the layers of an onion and Nesting Dolls. We discussed what it means to bring your Authentic Self to work and explored the myriad of obstacles that often stop employees from doing just that. From the pressures of fitting into workplace cultural norms to the fear of showing vulnerability, we uncovered the factors that lead you to present your identity and stop you from bringing your Authentic Self to work.

From there we explored the power of embracing your Authentic Self at work and the impact on individuals and the repercussions on the organization when you don't. Lastly, we addressed a question I am asked frequently, what if I don't want to bring my Authentic Self to work.

Exploring the Authentic Self in detail is vital because it plays such a fundamental part in creating psychologically safe spaces. Sadly, this element is often overlooked when companies attempt to create a psychologically safe environment. They focus on conversations and actions that are more comfortable and can demonstrate the achievement of KPIs. They shy away from the elements that are more subjective and can't be easily measured. But think about it. If you are constantly censoring yourself, how safe do you actually feel?

If individuals don't feel safe to bring their Authentic Self to work (if they choose to do so), you are never going to create a safe space or workplace.

In the next chapter, get ready to explore just how extensive this issue really is. We are going to peel back the layers of workplaces and take a closer look at what is going on.

3

The Extent of the Issue

"Do I feel safe and at ease in my surroundings and with the people I am with?" While we may have only recently coined the term "psychological safety," the underlying concept has been a timeless consideration for centuries. So, you would expect we have a million and one pieces of data that have been collected about it, right? Wrong. I mentioned earlier that when I first started out on my psychological safety journey, I couldn't find much data at all. The information I did find was often tied into other data sets, other surveys or focused predominantly on unrelated subjects.

Absence of Statistics

When I first started my business, the concept of psychological safety wasn't talked about in workplaces. I was primarily having conversations about LGBTQ+ inclusion, diversity and equity, with each of these three aspects being separate, distinct and isolated conversations. Over the years, these conversations evolved, with the narrative shifting from equity and diversity, to diversity and equality, then to diversity and inclusion, followed by inclusion and intersectionality, culminating in discussions around belonging and bringing your Authentic Self to work. More recently, there has been a notable shift toward psychological safety and inclusion. However, individuals often misunderstand psychological safety, mistakingly thinking it is intrinsically linked to inclusion.

Psychological safety appears to be a trendy term in organizations – the latest hot topic. My worry is that even though it is currently in the spotlight, the focus on it might fade and organizations could revert to an outdated culture, pushing individuals to retreat back behind their "masks."

Psychological safety is not just a buzzword or a fleeting concept that is here and will be gone tomorrow. If you want a thriving business where individuals genuinely enjoy their work, you need to invest and commit to creating and nurturing a psychologically safe workplace. Inclusion, diversity, equity and belonging all originate from a foundation of psychological safety.

With the recent surge in interest surrounding psychological safety, research on this topic has gained traction. There are different tools, checklists and overarching guidelines available to give you a snapshot of where you are in terms of your organization's psychological safety landscape. Private organizations, academic institutions and individuals are conducting research tailored to specific industries, to understand more about psychological safety and the implications of it in the workplace.

This data collection is great and very welcome but organizations need to be able to see this data and they need to understand what they can do to improve psychological safety in their organization. The overarching guidelines that are in the public domain are not providing practical, actionable steps that organizations can take to significantly improve psychological safety in the workplace.

Working with multinational companies, I frequently hear "We can't accurately measure psychological safety." Exploring the existing methods they use and their experiences with these, it is clear that many organizations are using ineffective methods to measure psychological safety. While some adopt a qualitative approach through observations and interviews, most measurements come from a quantitative approach. This includes employee engagement surveys, well-being surveys, exit data, retention figures, performance management data, performance evaluations, 360-degree feedback and turnover/profit metrics. Yet, these approaches fail to provide a comprehensive understanding of the true level of psychological safety within their organization.

Frustrated, they decide to try something different. They ask a few questions about psychological safety to attempt to gain some insight. Sounds like a solid plan, doesn't it? In theory, yes. However, the challenge arises from the fact that these questions are often sourced through generic searches online, and what comes up may have been originally developed for application in an unrelated industry or they are being used for an entirely different purpose to how they were originally intended to be used.

There are two big mistakes organizations are making here. First, the questions are not tailored to their business/industry. They lack alignment. This means the data they collect is not much use to them. Second, they tag these questions onto something else, another survey that is collecting data on an unrelated topic. This practice sends the signal to employees that their safety is not a high priority to the organization. These tagged-on questions tend to focus on whether employees feel safe making mistakes or feel safe to speak up. They don't ask questions around whether they feel they can bring their Authentic Self to work, about whether their thoughts and emotions impact on their communication dynamics or interactions with colleagues, the nuances of team dynamics, or any of the other aspects that contribute to an individual's level of safety in the workplace. These tagged-on questions tend to focus on the symptoms of an unhealthy work culture, rather than addressing and analyzing the root causes. It is no wonder that organizations are failing to get the insights they crave and urgently need.

The third biggest mistake organizations often make is developing interventions without clear direction or focus, based on the data they have managed to collect. While the data (and anecdotes) highlights there is an issue, it often lacks the necessary depth to be actionable. The precise nature of the problem, its underlying causes and the appropriate actions to take remain unclear. Flailing around in the dark without any other insight available to them, organizations decide to do something, anything, to attempt to address the issue. However, this approach rarely effectively addresses the actual problem. How could it?

Do You Have an Issue?

There are a wealth of signs that may indicate a psychological safety issue within your organization. We delved into some of these when exploring effective and ineffective implementation in Chapter 1. We explored this further in Chapter 2 in terms of embracing your Authentic Self and the consequences when you don't, both at individual and organizational levels.

What about other observable behaviors in the workplace? Here are several red flags to look out for. Individuals stay quiet and don't actively participate in meetings or discussions. Individuals don't actively contribute to team goals, objectives or projects. Ideas, opinions, concerns, knowledge, experience or expertise are not shared, unless asked directly. There is a reluctance to collaborate with others or share their progress on projects. You ask a question and experience awkward silences. You hear discussions about or experience strained team relationships. There is consistent misunderstanding or misinterpretation of messages, resulting in confusion or conflict. There is a reluctance to seek clarification or feedback. Individuals appear unhappy or dissatisfied with their work or team environment, maybe verbalizing this. Personal information is not shared. Vulnerability is not expressed with anyone in the organization. (Bear in mind that the last two points could also be a safety mechanism, so don't use these as standalone criteria.) There is an unwillingness to switch cameras and/or microphones on, unless asked to. There is a steady or large flow of people leaving your organization or team, without expressing the reasons why. These indicators suggest the presence of a psychological safety issue.

Do you recognize any of these behaviors? Do you notice these in your colleagues, managers or leaders?

If you want to delve further into whether you have a psychological safety issue in your organization, consider implementing the Pledges (you will be introduced to these later) and/or the self-assessment questions associated with these. Using these two tools will enable you to identify which of the 5 Pillars of Psychological Safety might require immediate focus and prioritization.

Introducing Lux: Measuring Psychological Safety

As detailed earlier in this chapter, there are many ways, mainly quantitative approaches, through which organizations are trying to gauge if they have an issue with psychological safety. If you are new to the concept of psychological safety and want to do something small to get started, using one or more of these methods may be a good starting point for you. And yes, you can ask questions that you have stumbled upon during online searches. However, it is important to note that these questions might not be tailored for your specific industry or sector. They could have been intended for an entirely different audience or purpose. The results from all these methods must be viewed with caution as they are unlikely to offer you much detail or reveal the root cause of issues. Without precise insight into the nature and origins of your issues, the development of a tailored intervention plan is a challenge.

If you are considering measuring psychological safety in your organization independently, here are some essential guidelines for you to consider.

You need to focus exclusively on psychological safety when you are asking for feedback from your employees. Avoid attaching these questions to other surveys. Instead, pose specific, targeted psychological safety questions, ensuring their relevance to your industry, sector, location and company structure.

It is crucial that you guarantee anonymity for all respondents, both in the data collection and result presentation phases. Particularly in smaller teams, individual identities may become apparent through their responses. In these cases, take it up a level, to the department or directorate above, for example, to safeguard everyone's anonymity.

Results of the survey should be analyzed and provided at appropriate levels within your organizational hierarchy, whether that is on a team, department, directorate or organizational level. Never divulge results on an individual level.

Lastly, ensure that every individual in the organization has the opportunity to participate in the survey, not just a sample or targeted group of people.

If you are genuinely committed to creating a psychologically safe workplace for everyone, not just specific teams or marginalized individuals, and you want to really understand what is going on in your organization, you need to take a different approach.

Many organizations acknowledge the existence of psychological safety issues. However, the data they possess falls short of providing the insights they desperately seek. Additionally, they rely on anecdotal pieces of evidence. It's within this context that the concept of *Lux* was born. My aim was to develop a robust diagnostic tool that would provide accurate data to highlight the root causes of the issues organizations are facing.

Let me introduce you to Lux – a powerful psychological safety diagnostic tool. Lux effectively measures psychological safety across the 5 Pillars of Psychological Safety. It serves as your ally in assessing, identifying and addressing areas for improvement, offering profound insights and invaluable guidance to create psychologically safer workplaces where individuals and teams can truly thrive.

Implemented across organizations globally, Lux is a catalyst for bringing about transformative change, regardless of whether you are a small business or a multinational corporation. The diagnostic tool is designed to be rolled out to your entire workforce, whether you operate from a single office or have global locations. Once all your employees have completed the survey, Lux provides you with the results and bespoke recommendations, enabling you to establish and nurture a psychologically safe workplace.

Lux came into existence for two compelling reasons. The first reason is my mission: to create work environments where people not only survive but thrive. I wanted to create a tool that accurately measures psychological safety within organizations. This tool needed to be designed specifically for organizations, applicable across all industries and sectors and versatile enough to be used by both small businesses and multinational corporations with a global presence. I wanted to create the solution that organizations have been asking me about for years, leveraging the insights I had gained from conversations. I wanted to create the tool for them that didn't exist.

Lux focuses on the 5 Pillars of Psychological Safety, targeting specific elements within the pillars with its 65 questions. Lux provides insights into the functioning of each aspect within your organizational structure, covering intrapersonal, interpersonal, team dynamics, collaboration, curiosity and creativity.

Your Lux interface is customized specifically for your organization. We break down your organizational structure, allowing you to access results for the entire organization, individual or collective directorates, departments, teams and even sub-teams. This granular breakdown empowers you to examine data at each level of your organization and compare it. This enables you to pinpoint the source of issues, as well as identify trends and opportunities for growth.

Within each part of your organizational structure, you will find results categorized by Pillar and country (if applicable) and the ability to filter by year.

When reviewing the Pillars and Questions in detail, you'll see a ranking, from best to worst performing. You can drill down to individual Pillars and questions, so you can identify where to target your efforts as well as facilitate internal benchmarking. Additional filters allow you to narrow down results by year and specific work modes (in-person, online, hybrid). Furthermore, you can track progress over the years, comparing top-level results and analyzing trends across your entire organizational structure over multiple years.

Implementing Lux across your entire workforce will provide you with the data you need to pinpoint the precise issues, their locations in the business, the root causes and most importantly, the means to improve those areas. You will receive tailored recommendations enabling you to target specific areas and implement appropriate interventions to create a safer workplace.

The second reason for Lux's creation is my aspiration to advocate for the inclusion of psychological safety in workplace legislation. To achieve this, data is crucial, but there isn't any relevant data in the public sphere about psychological safety in the workplace. I decided to create a tool to gather global data to support and give weight to my lobbying efforts.

Lux not only equips organizations with essential data and tailored recommendations but also aggregates data on a global scale. This data allows us to identify trends across various sectors, industries, locations, work modes (in-person, remote, or hybrid) and business sizes. From this, we generate an annual Top 100 Psychologically Safe Workplaces List, ranking organizations that have adopted Lux within a year, from best to worst performers.

Our industry, sector and location dashboards provide insights into how each sector, industry and country performs worldwide. They offer rankings, pillar breakdowns and filters for company size and work mode (in-person, online or hybrid). The progression dashboards track year-on-year progress for locations, industries and sectors. Finally, you can benchmark your performance against other companies in your sector or industry. Rest assured, all data is anonymized.

Lux serves as a vital tool for collecting the necessary data to champion the cause of psychologically safer workplaces.

When I was developing Lux, my primary aim was to ensure it was purpose-built and rigorously tested for multinational corporations. Working closely with University of Cambridge experts, we meticulously reviewed and refined the 65 questions integrated into Lux. This process was followed by validation from the Professor of Organizational Behavior at the University of Cambridge. The result is a tool that excels in addressing the specific challenges faced by multinational organizations.

The validation process also extended to the 5 Pillars of Psychological Safety and Lux's methodology, overseen by an expert in Human Behavior Modeling. Their validation process encompassed a comprehensive review, including the validation of the 5 Pillars of Psychological Safety methodology and Lux's methodology, as well as rigorously testing the accuracy and integrity of data within Lux and the coherence and meaningfulness of all charts and data representations.

Through collaboration with researchers and professors from the University of Cambridge, Lux's reliability has been substantiated, while the validation of both the 5 Pillars of Psychological Safety and the diagnostic tool methodology solidifies its credibility.

Let's explore the advantages your organization can gain from implementing Lux. With Lux, you will acquire comprehensive insights that delve into the root causes, rather than just addressing the symptoms. You'll pinpoint areas for improvement, ultimately enhancing the work environment and culture and boosting employee well-being. Tracking progress over time provides valuable data to measure impact, enabling you to evaluate past and present interventions effectively and optimize the outcomes of future interventions.

By leveraging Lux, you'll also gather valuable insights to inform your decision-making processes. By creating a psychologically safe work environment, you will retain and attract top talent, increase productivity, improve communication and enhance customer satisfaction, ultimately creating a high-performance culture. Employees will feel empowered to bring their Authentic Self to work, nurturing creativity, innovation and engagement, which will positively impact both physical and mental health outcomes.

Lux empowers your organization to lead the way in cultivating psychological safety, inclusion and a sense of belonging, establishing you as a trailblazer and industry leader. If you're seeking a robust tool that can accurately measure psychological safety within your organization and will provide clear, tailored recommendations for improvement, Lux is the solution you've been looking for. It is taking the business world by storm and gathering recognition in top industry awards.

Active Industries and Countries

Psychological safety conversations are taking place on a global scale, and they often share common language when describing issues, even though they may use different labels. Some organizations are aware of their psychological safety issues, while others might perceive them as problems related to belonging, inclusion or employees not bringing their Authentic Self to work. While the terminology may vary, the underlying issue remains the same.

It's intriguing to observe the patterns of interest and engagement from organizations over the years. Once a few companies within a specific industry begin discussing psychological safety, we often receive a surge of inquiries from that same industry within the same year. It just goes to show the power of "word of mouth" and industry messaging.

From my experience, the industries that have consistently prioritized their journey toward psychological safety include pharmaceutical, biotechnology, financial services and investment banking.

On the other hand, industries like retail, technology and manufacturing have shown intermittent interest, often characterized by short bursts of training. Some industries, such as transport, education, government organizations, public defense and security (their lack of serious engagement with psychological safety is terrifying), healthcare, marketing, legal, property, engineering, construction and the food industry, have discussed psychological safety but have not engaged deeply in its implementation.

In terms of commitment, the private sector has displayed the highest dedication, followed by the third sector, with the public sector exhibiting the least engagement.

Several countries, including Australia, Sweden, Belgium and Denmark, have taken significant steps to address psychosocial hazards in the workplace by adopting legislation. A *psychosocial hazard* is anything that could cause psychological harm. It refers to unfavorable working conditions in terms of the way work is organized and managed. Common psychosocial hazards at work include job demands, organizational factors, interpersonal relationships and the physical work environment. The associated guidance notes for psychosocial hazards add that psychological harm may include anxiety, depression, post-traumatic stress disorder (PTSD) and sleep disorders; physical harm may include musculoskeletal injuries, chronic disease or fatigue-related injuries.

So yes, while the adoption of legislation addressing psychosocial hazards is a good step forward for employees, providing additional protection in the workplace, it's important to recognize that psychosocial hazards and psychological safety are separate concepts. Let's explore the differences between them.

Psychological safety refers to an individual's perception and feeling of being safe in diverse settings and situations. It encompasses cognitive, emotional and behavioral aspects, which include emotional well-being, mental processes, emotional responses, thoughts and behaviors. Psychological safety is primarily focused on the individual's subjective experience of safety, comfort and confidence within a specific context. Psychological safety extends beyond mental and emotional well-being to incorporate aspects such as intrapersonal awareness, interpersonal dynamics, communication and social interactions, team dynamics, among others. Psychological safety is not the same as mental health. While psychological safety relates to the perception of safety in various situations, mental health encompasses an individual's overall psychological and emotional well-being, including conditions like anxiety, depression and stress.

A **psychosocial hazard** is anything in the workplace environment that has the potential to cause psychological harm to employees. Psychosocial hazards primarily focus on external factors within the workplace that pose a risk to employees' psychological well-being. They are objective conditions or stressors that can affect mental health. Psychosocial hazards highlight workplace conditions, practices and structures that may contribute to stress, anxiety and other psychological issues. Organizations can take proactive steps to recognize and manage psychosocial risks in order to prevent or reduce their negative impact on the mental health and well-being of their employees.

The key differences lie in the fact that psychological safety revolves around an individual's subjective experience of feeling safe and comfortable in various settings, whereas psychosocial hazards consist of objective workplace factors that have the potential to cause psychological harm. Psychological safety is closely tied to an individual's perception, emotions and behaviors, whereas psychosocial hazards relate to the external conditions and stressors present in the workplace that may impact employees' psychological well-being. While addressing psychosocial hazards can help enhance psychological safety in the workplace, it is crucial to recognize that these are distinct concepts.

Success Factors

The businesses that make the most progress in establishing and nurturing psychologically safe workplaces are those that demonstrate a commitment to the cause, embed it in their long-term agenda and secure buy-in across all levels of the organization. Additionally, businesses that operate within a flat or relatively flat organizational structure, favoring a more agile or Teal style of working, tend to thrive rapidly when adopting the 5 Pillars methodology.

The Teal style of working is a holistic organizational approach characterized by self-management, an evolutionary purpose that adapts with the organization's growth and a focus on cultivating an environment where individuals can bring their authentic selves to work, thereby nurturing creativity and collaboration.

On the other hand, businesses with a hierarchical structure characterized by numerous layers may take longer to identify and address issues and to develop and implement interventions. However, when they wholeheartedly commit to this process, they experience significant positive impact on individuals, teams and the organization as a whole.

Additional success factors include the following. Successful organizations view psychological safety as an ongoing journey rather than a destination. They communicate their commitment to psychological safety and the benefits it brings throughout the organization and it is embedded into every conversation and every meeting. Clarity in communicating this commitment helps employees understand the organization's goals and their role in creating a safe environment.

They continuously seek ways to improve and adapt their strategies based on evolving needs and challenges. They implement effective assessment and feedback mechanisms, such as annual surveys and anonymous reporting systems, to continuously monitor and improve psychological safety. Listening to employee feedback and acting on it is crucial. They provide ongoing training and education on psychological safety concepts and practices which significantly contribute to success. This ensures that employees at all levels understand the importance of psychological safety and know how to cultivate it, for them and their colleagues. Recognizing and celebrating achievements related to psychological safety can reinforce its importance too. When organizations acknowledge and reward behaviors that promote psychological safety, it encourages further adoption.

Being flexible and adaptable in implementing psychological safety measures is essential. Different organizations may require tailored approaches, and being open to adjustments is key to success. Lastly, organizations that have leaders actively advocating and modeling psychological safety tend to be more successful.

Key Challenges

Let's explore the key challenges businesses are facing, backed by statistics from my own research. These issues transcend industries, sectors and locations and revolve around four primary aspects: Authentic Self, communication, safe spaces and team dynamics. Let's examine each of them individually.

Authentic Self

This category raises several concerns reported by many organizations. A widespread issue is the reluctance of individuals to bring their Authentic Self to work. Unfortunately, this self-censorship intensifies communication problems and disrupts team dynamics.

In the workplace, employees often encounter difficulties when it comes to managing their emotions, which can be traced back to the lasting impact of negative past experiences. Identifying triggers for negative emotions, thoughts or behaviors in the workplace often presents issues, resulting in delayed issue resolution. As a result, employees carry these negative interactions home with them, impacting both their physical and mental health, as well as straining their relationships outside of work. Lastly, navigating workplace expectations also proves to be a challenge for employees. Some individuals worry about how their colleagues perceive them, which can lead to feelings of inadequacy or impostor syndrome.

Notably, the challenge of employees not feeling safe to bring their Authentic Self to work is particularly pronounced in the Asia-Pacific, Middle East and Africa regions.

Let's delve into the results from the global study we conducted, which sheds light on the extent of these issues.

80 percent of respondents said they wish their organization was a safer place to work.

75 percent reported hiding or censoring elements of their Authentic Self, including their abilities, skills and knowledge when interacting with colleagues, management and customers.

When asked about the factors that affect their performance and behavior in the workplace, 37 percent reported they don't bring their Authentic Self to work due to past negative experiences and a fear of a repeat; 30 percent expressed concerns about how others perceive them, both in their work and personal lives; 20 percent of respondents felt that they fell short of meeting the expectations set by others; and 13 percent reported difficulties in communicating with or forming positive relationships with colleagues.

When asked about the barriers stopping them from bringing their Authentic Self to work, 44 percent answered negative past experiences, 26 percent reported wanting to protect their personal life, 17 percent said specific fears, whether related to something or someone; and 13 percent reported their views and values don't align with those of their colleagues or the organization they work for.

We asked "What do you want and need to be able to bring your whole self into the workplace?" Here are the top six priorities they identified, in order of importance: 21 percent of employees expressed the need to stop worrying about what other people think of them, their work and their personal lives; 18 percent of respondents want to get rid of the feeling of "I'm not good enough"; 17 percent said they valued the ability to define, communicate and assert their personal boundaries in the workplace; 16 percent said impostor syndrome is a concern to them and look for ways to combat these feelings of self-doubt; 14 percent highlighted the importance of personal leadership strategies; and the remaining 14 percent believed that changing the way they think about certain situations and people would help them to bring their Authentic Self to work.

Anecdotally, many employees shared their challenges in bringing their Authentic Self to work. They mentioned that they find it difficult to be their Authentic Self at work and it is easier to hide behind a persona or professional mask. This self-protective behavior was viewed as a safety mechanism rather than a preference.

What about the impact on their personal lives? The consequences of not being able to be their Authentic Self extends beyond the workplace. A significant number of employees (58 percent) worry about what colleagues think of them, the work they produce and their personal life. The impact on emotional well-being is also evident, with 33 percent of employees unable to manage their emotions effectively when faced with negative or unwanted situations at work.

We delved deeper to understand the connection between work and personal life. When asked if they "ruminate and stew over things that happened at work when they are at home," a striking 87 percent responded yes.

Additionally, when asked whether taking negative work situations home had a negative impact on them and the people around them at home, a whopping 92 percent confirmed that their work experiences directly affected their personal lives.

These results highlight the profound impact that the inability to bring your Authentic Self to work can have, affecting not only employees' well-being in the workplace but also spilling over into their personal lives.

Communication

Effective communication poses a challenge in most organizations we work with. There are three areas of concern here. The first challenge is communicating your message so it is received in the way it was intended. The second is receiving a message in the way it was intended by the sender. The third challenge involves the overall exchange of communication and navigating conversations effectively. Organizations commonly encounter several areas of concern with communication. Effective handling of misunderstandings, miscommunications, disagreements, conflicts and microaggressions proves to be a significant hurdle in communication, with many individuals shying away from addressing these issues directly.

Another area of concern is the choice of language, where individuals may unintentionally exclude others, convey unintended messages, overcomplicate their message or fail to deliver it clearly and succinctly. Choosing an appropriate way to transmit a message adds a further problem in communication. Emotional triggers can further complicate matters, leading to inappropriate responses and exacerbating conflicts. Some individuals find it challenging to express their emotions, needs and concerns when communicating with colleagues. Lastly, accurately understanding or decoding messages is another aspect that often goes awry, leading to misunderstandings and tensions in relationships.

In our global study, we discovered the following key findings about communication: 25 percent of employees find it challenging to interpret incoming communications accurately; 30 percent struggle with communicating a message so that it is received in the way it was intended; for 45 percent of employees, the most significant challenge lies in the exchange of communication – this incorporates managing conflicts, expressing disagreement, asserting ideas, addressing microaggressions and navigating difficult conversations.

When it comes to their confidence in ensuring team members receive their messages as intended, 62 percent expressed feeling confident, whilst 38 percent remained unsure that they had received the message as intended.

In terms of successfully handling miscommunications, misunderstandings and conflict with colleagues, 34 percent stated they are unable to do so effectively.

With respect to having the confidence, ability and resilience to express their feelings, needs and concerns to colleagues, 38 percent indicated that they do not possess these qualities.

These results highlight the vital importance of addressing communication challenges to enhance collaboration, innovation and overall workplace well-being.

Safe Spaces

Establishing safe spaces within organizations presents several challenges. The primary concern is creating an environment where everyone feels safe. This incorporates defining ground rules, implementing conflict resolution strategies and effectively communicating expectations, work and personal boundaries. Common challenges in creating safe spaces include encouraging participation, facilitating decision-making processes, addressing conflicts or issues that may arise, promoting collaboration, innovation and creativity, ensuring effective communication and extending the concept of safe spaces to accommodate remote or hybrid workers.

In our global study, we posed a series of questions to employees to gauge their perception of safe spaces within their organizations.

When asked if they feel safe in their team meetings, employees were encouraged to consider various aspects, such as their ability to bring their Authentic Self to work, discuss their work openly and reflect with their team, manage conflicts and address misunderstandings, miscommunications, unacceptable behavior and microaggressions: 67 percent of respondents reported feeling safe in their team meetings, taking into account these factors; 33 percent indicated that they do not feel safe in their team meetings.

In response to the question "Does the organization you work for actively encourage you to reflect on and learn from the work you are doing, individually, in teams and as an organization?," 51 percent responded negatively, indicating that their organization does not actively promote reflection and learning.

This data highlights the need to address challenges in cultivating environments that prioritize employees' feelings of safety and well-being – to ensure everyone can thrive.

Team Dynamics

Organizations often grapple with several key issues in this area. These include establishing clear personal and work boundaries, navigating the diversity of work and communication preferences among team members, recognizing and effectively working with different personality types within the team, adapting to various work modes (including remote working, hybrid arrangements and in person collaboration) and ensuring the expectations within the team are well defined and effectively managed. Failure to address these elements often leads to strained communication, misinterpretations and low morale in teams.

In our global study, we sought to understand how frequently teams discuss and reassess critical aspects of team dynamics. We asked employees "In your team, how often do you discuss (and reassess) your personal and work boundaries, your work preferences, your communication preferences and how you like to celebrate milestones with your colleagues?" The responses were as follows: 60 percent of respondents indicated that such discussions never occur within their teams; 20 percent reported that these discussions happen often, on a weekly or monthly basis; 14 percent said they discuss these topics one to two times a year; 6 percent stated that these discussions occur three to four times a year.

Additionally, we asked "Which of these personality traits best describes you, in the workplace the majority of the time?" Respondents identified themselves as follows: 39 percent stated they are introvert and emotionally stable; 34 percent stated they are extrovert and emotionally stable; 14 percent stated they are introvert and emotionally unstable; 13 percent stated they are extrovert and emotionally unstable. More on the implications of this in Chapter 6 "Pillar 3."

It is intriguing that, when asked about their current priorities, 49 percent of organizations responded with a desire to "create environments where teams thrive"; 18 percent of organizations responded with "effective communication to create a psychologically safe workplace"; 17 percent of organizations responded with "creating environments where everyone can bring their whole self to work and be authentic"; and 16 percent of organizations said "Other" with only a few organizations offering examples, mostly unrelated to psychological safety.

Back to the 49 percent of organizations that responded with a desire to "create environments where teams thrive," the data we have collected this far consistently underscores the crucial need to establish the foundations first, ensuring that everyone feels safe to bring their Authentic Self to work. Bypassing this essential step (Level 1 in the Hierarchy of Psychological Safety) and directly attempting to create an environment where teams can thrive (Level 3 in the Hierarchy) is pointless and a waste of time and resources. If someone doesn't feel safe within your "safe" space, you have failed in creating an environment where they can thrive. Right?

Public Sector

Lastly, the challenges affecting the public sector. They consistently report a lack of resources and funding constraints, a noticeable lack of buy-in and leadership support, siloed working practices, issues with team dynamics and a widespread issue of employees not feeling safe to bring their Authentic Self to work.

The data on team dynamics underscores the significance of understanding and proactively addressing these dynamics, as doing so is vital for improving communication, resolving conflicts and enhancing overall team cohesion and productivity.

In this chapter, we delved into the extent of the issue surrounding psychological safety in the workplace. We began by looking at the data-related challenges organizations face when striving to create psychologically safe environments. We explored key indicators or "red flags" to look out for that will help you to recognize if you have an issue with psychological safety in your organization. We discussed how organizations are measuring psychological safety and the reasons these are proving to be ineffective, before introducing a more robust and accurate method to measure psychological safety effectively. We observed the patterns of interest, commitment and adoption of legislation across industries, sectors and countries, with some consistently prioritizing psychological safety, while others show intermittent engagement. We uncovered the success factors that enable businesses to establish and nurture psychologically safe workplaces. Lastly, we discussed the key challenges businesses are facing, backed up with statistics from the global study we conducted.

Next up, we are moving into the Teachings. We are finished with defining the problem; now we will explore solutions. We will start with an introduction to the 5 Pillars of Psychological Safety and then we will take a deep dive into each Pillar, exploring them in detail.

Part II

The Teachings

The 5 Pillars of Psychological Safety are the comprehensive framework being used around the world to create fully inclusive workplaces. They provide practical support enabling individuals and teams to take an active role in creating a psychologically safe workplace. In essence, they cultivate an environment where organizations and their people thrive.

The 5 Pillars of Psychological Safety are shown in Figure P2.1.

My graphic designer was perplexed when I asked for a graphical representation of the 5 Pillars of Psychological Safety, without traditional pillar imagery. I set them a creative challenge, leaving the parameters wide open for interpretation. The graphic we landed on perfectly captures the essence of the 5 Pillars framework, which are as follows. Pillar 1 is Self. Pillar 2 is Social. Pillar 3 is Collaboration. Pillar 4 is Curiosity and Pillar 5 is Creativity.

The first three Pillars are critical components in cultivating a safe, inclusive and thriving workplace that empowers both individuals and teams to achieve their full potential. By prioritizing intrapersonal awareness, authenticity, effective communication and creating a supportive environment that nurtures a sense of belonging among team members, the workplace becomes a safe and

Figure P2.1 The 5 Pillars of Psychological Safety

welcoming space where individuals can collaborate effectively and feel supported in achieving their goals.

Pillars 4 and 5 build upon this foundation by providing structured opportunities for continuous learning and innovation. Through the dedicated Curiosity Sessions and Creativity Workshops, teams can explore new ideas and discover different perspectives, which encourages and promotes a culture of curiosity and creativity. These scheduled sessions offer a structured time for reflection, exploration and experimentation – inviting individuals to step out of their daily routines, challenge themselves and embrace the possibilities of what could be.

Together, the 5 Pillars form a robust framework that cultivates psychologically safe, inclusive and forward-thinking workplaces, where authenticity, effective communication and collaboration, as well as innovation and creativity are deeply valued. By empowering both individuals and teams to achieve their full potential, the 5 Pillars create a vibrant and supportive workplace culture that inspires employees to thrive and facilitates a strong sense of belonging.

In the pages that follow, you will delve deep into each Pillar. In each Pillar chapter you will find the following information.

An introduction to the Pillar. This sets the scene for the chapter.

Pillar Framework. A systematic framework for understanding and exploring the 5 Pillars of Psychological Safety. This framework includes **First Principles**, followed by the **Dimensions** and **Pillar Highlights**. For clarity, "First Principles" are the fundamental concepts on which the 5 Pillars of Psychological Safety are based. "Dimensions" are how we explore and measure each First Principle. The "Pillar Highlights" are the key areas of focus within each Pillar. At the beginning of each chapter introducing the Pillar, you will be introduced to the respective framework.

Next, you will explore the **Pillar Methodology**, before deconstructing the Dimensions into their individual components and diving deep into the Pillar Highlights, the key focus areas within each Pillar.

At the end of each chapter, you will find the **Pillar Pledges** and the **Pillar Self-Reflections**, giving you the opportunity to assess your current levels of psychological safety associated with each Pillar.

The processes, methodologies and insights I am going to share with you in the following pages have been meticulously crafted and refined through years of collaboration with multinational corporations. They have been tried and tested. They have been validated and they have been interrogated rigorously. They come together to form a robust framework for cultivating work environments where people (and organizations) thrive, thereby creating fully inclusive workplaces. These are the 5 Pillars of Psychological Safety.

4

Pillar 1: Self

Pillar 1 is Self and focuses on empowering individuals to thrive in the workplace by cultivating intrapersonal awareness. This lays the groundwork for individuals to bring their Authentic Self to work. If you don't feel safe to be your Authentic Self at work, your workplace isn't psychologically safe. Unfortunately, the concept of bringing your Authentic Self to work and intrapersonal awareness is often overlooked by organizations in their efforts to create a psychologically safe environment. As discussed earlier, the focus tends to be on having conversations and taking actions that demonstrate the achievement of KPIs. Instead of prioritizing the Authentic Self, they direct their attention toward creating an environment where people can thrive, without laying the necessary groundwork. Pillar 1 is the foundational pillar. Without addressing the Pillar 1 Highlights, individuals won't feel safe to bring their Authentic Self to work (if they choose to do so) and as a result you will never create a truly safe workplace. You can't leave this Pillar out.

Recognizing when you are not being your Authentic Self at work involves being mindful of various red flags. These signs include feelings of low confidence, self-worth issues (extending to money and relationship issues), loneliness and isolation, as well as low self-esteem, a lack of creativity, mental health challenges and the ever-persistent impostor syndrome. Often these indicators manifest as an overarching sense of not feeling good enough.

If you find yourself feeling out of sorts without a clear reason, facing continual uphill battles in your life, work or finances, or sensing that you are disconnected from your carefree, fun-loving inner self, it's essential to pay attention.

Likewise, exhibiting defensive, argumentative, protective, deceptive, hostile or aggressive behaviors can all be an indication of a misalignment with your Authentic Self.

Striving excessively to please others, pushing to achieve something or to avoid trouble, trying to be someone you are not or ignoring your genuine desires and intuition – all these actions can be telling signs of losing touch with your Authentic Self. If you find yourself lying, exaggerating or making things up to create a more favorable image, it's time to take notice. Recognizing these signs is the first step toward reconnecting with your Authentic Self.

Let's explore how you can recognize when you are being your Authentic Self. You'll experience inner peace, maintaining calmness even in challenging or demanding situations. Confidence will naturally radiate from you – it gently oozes out of your pores and is apparent in all areas of your life. When you enter a room, you'll exude an inner power so tangible that others can't help but notice. Others are magnetized to you. Life will flow effortlessly and manifestations will occur easily and swiftly, without the need for excessive effort or striving. Positive emotions such as hope, optimism and self-belief will dominate. You'll also feel happiness, enthusiasm, eagerness and passion for what you do, along with a sense of joy, freedom, love and appreciation. If these qualities resonate with you, it's because you are experiencing being your Authentic Self.

Consider this. You have been working super hard for months on end and you have a family vacation planned. You are counting down the days, the hours, the sleeps. The day before your holiday, you finish up all your work, do the relevant handovers and log off. Vacation autoreply is on.

Day one of your holiday. You have arrived at your destination with your family. You are ready to relax, to soak up the sun and enjoy some much-needed downtime. But what happens? It takes a few days before you can truly switch off. Before you can let go of everything and fully embrace the holiday spirit. Day four or five, you can feel the transformation. You are more relaxed, content, happy, joyful even. You have stopped thinking about work and are fully immersed in the moment.

Now, think of the difference between how you feel on day one and day five. Day one is you living from your identity. Day five is you living from your Authentic Self. No barriers, no censoring, just being yourself, hopefully!

That is the feeling we aim to capture when it comes to being your Authentic Self at work. Relaxed, playful, creative, joyful. Got it?

Remember, no one is insisting that you bring your Authentic Self to work. Instead, the aim is to create an environment where it can naturally flourish.

Now that you have a good idea of what it means to bring your Authentic Self to work, let's look at the Pillar 1 framework.

Pillar 1 Framework

First Principle. This is me: all of me. This is the fundamental concept on which Pillar 1 is based.

Dimensions. Pillar 1 has three Dimensions. These are how we explore and measure the First Principle from different angles and perspectives. In Pillar 1, individuals ask three questions. The three questions provide a practical approach for individuals to understand and apply the First Principle. Question 1 is "What affects my performance and behavior at work?" Question 2 is "How can I take back control of the things that affect my performance and behavior at work?" Question 3 is "What can I do to achieve my personal and professional goals at work?"

Pillar Highlights. Pillar 1 encompasses several Pillar Highlights, or key areas of focus within the Authentic Self Process. The Pillar Highlights provide more specific guidance or subtopics within each Dimension to help individuals delve deeper into understanding and applying the First Principle in various aspects of their work and life. We will explore these in detail in the Pillar Highlights section later.

When you thoroughly engage with Pillar 1 and embrace the Authentic Self Process, you embark on a journey of self-discovery and empowerment. By the end of Pillar 1, having applied the transformative Authentic Self Process, you will have identified and examined the factors that impact your performance and behavior at work. Equipped with a powerful toolkit of insights and strategies, you'll thrive in any workplace situation.

Armed with heightened self-awareness and unwavering confidence, gained through unleashing your Authentic Self, you will not only excel professionally but also become a catalyst for meaningful change. The Authentic Self Process empowers you to create a positive impact in your workplace, inspiring those around you to do the same.

It is powerful stuff.

Pillar 1 is the one that empowers individuals to thrive in the workplace. It transforms people, enabling them to bring their Authentic Self to work. For years I have organized Authentic Self Retreats overseas, bringing together leaders, managers and teams. These retreats create a dedicated space and time for individuals to work through the Authentic Self Process with my team. The process takes every individual on a personalized journey, resulting in profoundly unique experiences for everyone. They return to the workplace with the skills and insights they need to thrive in the workplace.

Pillar 1 Methodology: The Authentic Self Process

The Authentic Self Process underpins Pillar 1. The Authentic Self Process is an extraordinarily powerful three-step system that unlocks your untapped potential, enabling you to thrive in the workplace, assuming the environment is safe.

The Authentic Self Process empowers individuals to bring all of who they are to work, tap into their hidden capabilities and excel in their professional lives. The Authentic Self Process directly addresses the six key obstacles identified in a global study we conducted that prevent employees from bringing their Authentic Self into the workplace.

In addition, this transformative process provides employees with powerful techniques that can facilitate deep and lasting changes, unlocking new levels of personal and professional growth that can positively impact every aspect of their lives (see Figure 4.1).

Step 1 of the Authentic Self Process is known as "Raise" and is associated with the Dimension "What affects my performance and behavior at work?" In the first step, individuals are encouraged to explore and uncover what factors influence their performance and behavior in the workplace. By delving into their emotions, thoughts and triggers, individuals gain a deep understanding of the elements at play. This heightened self-awareness allows them to identify and recognize any limiting beliefs or conditioning that may be

Figure 4.1 The Authentic Self Process

acting as barriers to their growth and realizing their potential. This self-awareness is crucial for initiating positive change and personal development. We will delve into the specific key areas that affect performance and behavior in the workplace a little later, providing a comprehensive understanding of this Dimension.

Step 2 of the Authentic Self Process is known as "Release" and is intricately tied to the Dimension "How can I take back control of the things that affect my performance and behavior at work?" The second step centers on empowering individuals to regain control over the factors that may have a negative impact on their performance and behavior in the workplace. Through the process of self-reflection and the implementation of targeted strategies focused on releasing and reprogramming, individuals actively reclaim control over their responses to triggers, overcome self-imposed limitations and skillfully reprogram unhelpful patterns, cultivating personal growth and enhancing resilience. As a result, a more authentic and empowered approach to work emerges, enabling individuals to thrive and excel in all workplace situations.

To guide you further, you will be provided with a selection of activities or probing questions at the end of each section addressing the aspects influencing your performance and behavior at work. These activities are designed to help you navigate through the "Raise" and "Release" phases of the process. However, it is essential to note that a comprehensive suite of activities and questions are available through dedicated resources such as our live training sessions, the Psychological Safety Toolkit and Authentic Self Journal, e-learning programs and retreats. These comprehensive resources are intentionally omitted here, as they require expert guidance and support to navigate the emotions and thoughts that may arise during the transformative process. These can be sourced through the website detailed in the endnotes.[1]

Step 3 of the Authentic Self Process is known as "Reconnect" and is associated with the Dimension "What can I do to achieve my personal and professional goals at work?" In the final step, individuals are guided to thrive in the workplace by embracing personal leadership strategies. They are encouraged to set and pursue their personal and professional goals with renewed confidence and authenticity. By reconnecting with their authentic selves, individuals skillfully unleash their full potential, leading to increased satisfaction, enhanced productivity and the ability to make meaningful contributions in their professional lives. You will be provided with a flavor of the mindful practices for personal leadership that we endorse, as well as the strategies you need to master personal leadership for professional success. These practices and strategies are instrumental in the "Reconnect" phase.

The Authentic Self Process not only addresses the obstacles that hinder authenticity in the workplace but also equips individuals with powerful techniques for lasting change. As a result, individuals can experience new levels of personal and professional growth that positively influence every aspect of their lives. By actively engaging in this transformative process, individuals contribute to the creation of a workplace environment where they feel safe and empowered to bring their Authentic Self, cultivating a culture defined by authenticity and curiosity.

The Process in Practice

We begin by raising your self-awareness, as we delve into Dimension 1. Here, we uncover the various aspects that impact your performance and behavior in the workplace. Top level. These aspects may surface all at once or emerge one at a time. We prioritize them based on their severity and the impact they have on you. We then take a deep dive into each aspect individually, digging into what the issue is, how it manifests for you, and explore other areas of your life it shows up in. We go to the core of the issue, if we can, to find the underlying stories and triggers associated with it. Our goal is to unearth everything that needs attention. Once we feel everything has been uncovered that needs to be, we transition into the process of releasing. This can take many forms, depending on what the issue is that we are working through. The aim is to reprogram the stories and beliefs attached to it, creating more empowering narratives or beliefs and extracting the valuable lessons from the issue. Releasing usually culminates in a powerful releasing ritual, which we will discuss later.

We repeat this process for every aspect that influences your performance and behavior in the workplace. Once you have raised your self-awareness on all these aspects, and completed the releasing and reprogramming, we move into Dimension 3, "Reconnect." Here, we explore personal leadership strategies to ensure you have the skills and knowledge you need to thrive in any workplace situation.

Pillar 1 Dimensions: Deep Dive

Now, let us delve into the Dimensions in greater detail. The Dimensions enable us to effectively explore and measure the First Principle from different angles and perspectives. What makes these Dimensions particularly impactful is that they are framed as questions, encouraging a practical approach for individuals to apply and understand the First Principle. When we ask a question, we naturally begin to search for answers, leading us toward a greater understanding of ourselves and the world around us.

In this section, we will explore each Dimension in turn, with a brief explanation. We will then uncover the key components or subtopics that are integral to each Dimension, known as "Pillar Highlights." In the next section, you will explore each of the Pillar Highlights in detail, within the context of the Authentic Self Process. This will facilitate the raising of your self-awareness and begin the releasing process.

Dimension 1: Raise

The first Dimension prompts us to ask "What affects my performance and behavior at work?"

Drawing on the insights gathered from our global study, employees identified various factors that impact on their performance and behavior at work. It's important to note that the way these issues are described can vary based on factors such as location, age and culture. However, the underlying essence of these issues can be categorized into several key elements.

These key elements significantly influence an individual's performance and behavior in the workplace and often stop people from bringing their Authentic Self into the workplace. They encompass your thoughts and mindset, the impact of your past conditioning, the stories and narratives you tell yourself, events or individuals that trigger negative emotional responses, managing overwhelming emotions, the influence of limiting beliefs, negative past experiences and the navigation of expectations.

These key elements collectively form the foundation of the Pillar Highlights. As you delve into these areas, along with any others that may arise during the self-awareness stage, you will initiate a powerful shift, leading you on a journey toward authenticity in the workplace, empowering you to thrive as your Authentic Self.

Dimension 2: Release

The second Dimension prompts us to ask "How can I take back control of the things that affect my performance and behavior at work?"

Following the exploration within Dimension 1, where you uncovered and raised your awareness on the factors that influence your performance and behavior at work, the focus now is on processing, releasing and reprogramming these elements. That is our focus here: the art of releasing and reprogramming.

A note here about control. In your life, three key factors play a significant role in shaping your thoughts, emotions and behaviors. You. Other people. Something bigger than both of those. You might refer to this as the Universe, broader cosmos or natural world, among other names. I will use Universe for ease to illustrate my point.

Here are the elements at play: (1) What you think, feel and do – these are within your control; (2) What other people think, feel and do – you can't control these, only they can; (3). What the Universe thinks, feels and does – no one can control these.

Let's delve deeper. Firstly, what you can control. In your life, there are things you aspire to achieve. Some you've taken action on, while others may have been temporarily set aside as you attend to responsibilities such as family, relationships or caregiving. These choices are yours to make.

Secondly, your parents, guardians and friends may have had a significant influence on your life choices. Maybe they are the reason you got into your chosen career, relationship or the leisure activities you enjoy. They may have specific expectations or desires for your path, like marriage or career choices. It's essential to recognize these external influences, but know that you can't influence what others think, feel or do.

Thirdly, there are factors entirely beyond your control, like natural disasters, gravity, aging and the weather. Wishing for different weather conditions won't alter them.

You can control what you think, feel and do. That is the work we are doing here. Attempting to control what lies outside your sphere, such as other people's thoughts or the forces of the Universe, can lead to frustration, suffering and detachment from your Authentic Self.

A key question you can ask yourself here is "Am I focused on me right now, other people or the Universe?"

Remember, there is no judgment on where you are right now. The important thing is you are here, you are showing up to do the work on yourself and you are open to new ideas.

Isn't it fascinating that old stories and thoughts dictate how you live your life, even when they no longer serve you? Many of these hold us back. It is time to uncover those that are negatively impacting you and let them go. Dimension 1 raises your awareness about these influences, while Dimension 2 empowers you to release and reprogram anything that is holding you back.

Don't worry, you will only release the things you are ready to release and at a pace that feels comfortable to you. Think of it like peeling an onion, one layer at a time.

Dimension 3: Reconnect

The third Dimension prompts us to ask "What can I do to achieve my personal and professional goals at work?"

In our global study, employees consistently highlighted the importance of personal leadership strategies as a key element in their journey to being their Authentic Self in the workplace. This Dimension naturally builds upon the groundwork laid in Dimensions 1 and 2.

When you ask the question "What can I do to achieve my personal and professional goals at work" many ideas and strategies may come to mind. These can be broadly categorized into two areas: adopting mindful practices for personal leadership and mastering personal leadership for professional success.

Within Dimension 3, we introduce mindful practices aimed at nurturing personal leadership. These practices incorporate various aspects of self-awareness and growth. The mindful practices we endorse are as follows. Managing and overcoming feelings of overwhelm, strategies for maintaining your physical and mental health, exercises in pausing and reflecting on your actions and decisions, exploration of the balance between ego-driven choices and intuitive decision-making and a comprehensive process we call "charting your life's journey." This involves creating a timeline of your life, reflecting on what you are attracting into your life, extracting life lessons, setting intentions and releasing the attachment to specific outcomes.

In terms of mastering personal leadership, these take on a practical application and encompass a wide range of essential aspects. They include setting personal boundaries to safeguard your well-being, ensuring a healthy separation between your personal and professional life, embracing accountability for your actions and decisions, cultivating curiosity, harnessing the power of language to positively influence your self-image, prioritizing self-development and self-care, decluttering both your physical space and the mind, reflecting on the influence of your inner circle, striving for work-life balance, creating daily routines and rituals that promote efficiency and well-being, utilizing journaling as a tool for reflection and growth, cultivating gratitude to reshape your perspective, addressing and replacing any harmful habits with positive ones, prioritizing physical activity for holistic well-being, nourishing the body with wholesome foods and raising your vibration and energy. These strategies collectively empower individuals to navigate their path toward personal and professional success while staying connected to their Authentic Self.

Pillar 1 Highlights

The Dimensions enable us to effectively explore and measure the First Principle from different angles and perspectives. The Pillar Highlights provide more specific guidance to help you to delve deeper into understanding and applying the First Principle.

Let us delve into the Pillar 1 Highlights in detail. We will take a deep dive into the key elements that significantly influence an individual's performance and behavior in the workplace, often stopping people from bringing their Authentic Self into the workplace. These elements are your thoughts, past conditioning, stories and narratives, triggers, emotions, limiting beliefs, past negative experiences and expectations. We will examine each of these in turn. At the end of each Highlight, you will be presented with an activity or a set of probing questions designed to raise your awareness and initiate the releasing process in that area.

Thoughts

Your thoughts are a powerful force. They create your reality. Your thoughts have a profound impact on your emotions, behavior, what you say, the opportunities you attract and those you miss out on. Every aspect of your life is influenced by them. It's essential to become aware of them and understand how they affect your performance in the workplace.

Let's talk about the "Law of Attraction," an ancient principle with roots possibly tracing back to Greek philosophy prior to Socrates. Throughout history many philosophers, scientists, writers and even filmmakers have explored the law of attraction. In essence, the law of attraction states that "like attracts like" or as I prefer to explain it, "what you think about, you bring about." You have the ability to bring about everything you desire, whether you are conscious of this or not. Everything you have experienced in your life to date is the culmination of all the thoughts you have ever had. While this may seem overwhelming, it highlights the impact your thoughts have over your reality.

Consider these real-life personal and workplace examples individuals have shared with me, illustrating the law of attraction in action.

Picture a scenario where you've been invited to join your new partner and their friends for an evening out. You don't really know your partner's friends, and for some unexplained reason, you don't seem to connect with a few of them. Despite your reservations, your new partner is enthusiastic about you joining them. However, you have doubts, thinking to yourself, "I'm going to have an awful night. I am not going to enjoy it. I am going to be bored and fed up. I really don't like . . . and we'll end up bickering all night." Upon reflection the next day, you find that all these negative expectations materialized into reality. It was indeed an unpleasant night, lacking enjoyment, filled with boredom and frustration and spoiled by bickering.

Now imagine this situation. You receive an invitation to attend a family wedding where you'll have the opportunity to reconnect with people you haven't seen in a long time, family and friends you've been eager to catch up with but somehow never found the opportunity. You are excited and you've already got the perfect outfit in mind. You think to yourself "I'm so excited about this. I'm really looking forward to seeing . . . and catching up with . . . I'm going to have an amazing time, dancing and having fun." Upon reflection the next day, you find yourself lying in bed, overwhelmed with the vivid memory of an incredible time, filled with heartwarming conversations and laughter that resonated throughout the day.

Now, consider this workplace scenario. You found yourself in the middle of a challenging project, doubting whether your team had the necessary skills and resources to successfully complete it within the defined time frame and to the high standards you expect. You openly expressed to your colleagues that you believed it was impossible to accomplish the project successfully due to various constraints. This belief genuinely took hold in you. But what was happening behind the scenes? With the belief that success was impossible, you inadvertently refrained from seeking solutions, lacked the motivation to invest the required effort and gradually disengaged from the project. As a result, it's no surprise that the project missed the deadline, failing to reach completion.

Lastly, imagine a team leader preparing for an important project presentation. The leader enters the meeting room with a confident and positive attitude, envisioning a productive and engaging discussion. They focus on the desired outcome, a well-received presentation that gets the full support from the team. During the meeting, the leader's enthusiasm is contagious. They actively engage with team members and they maintain a positive outlook, believing in the team's capabilities and the success of the project. As a result of this positive energy, team members are motivated and inspired. They actively participate in the discussion, sharing valuable insights and innovative ideas. Everyone is aligned on the project's goals and strategies.

In this last scenario, the leader's positive mindset and approach to the meeting set the stage for a successful and productive discussion. This positive energy attracted collaboration, passion and creative problem-solving among team members, ultimately leading to a successful outcome for the project and the meeting.

If you constantly think negatively, you may start to attract negative situations and people into your professional life. Negative thinking can hinder your interactions, performance, behavior, productivity and creativity in the workplace. However, if you shift your focus to positive thinking, you may start to attract more opportunities, positive experiences and supportive colleagues into your work environment. No doubt you will have heard someone say "it is important to cultivate a positive mindset and visualize success in your career." It is vital to note that if you change your thoughts, you change your outcomes.

In our global study, we identified several common triggers that often lead individuals into specific thought patterns and immerse them in negative narratives. These triggers cover a range of experiences, which I will detail here. Regret over past actions, wishing they had said or done something differently in a past situation. Imagining possible future scenarios, instead of being present in the moment. The self-imposed pressure of meeting personal expectations, as well as concerns about meeting external expectations and the fear of potentially disappointing others. The lasting influence of childhood messages and beliefs, such as the scarcity of resources/money.

Immersing in fears or anxieties. The influence of their self-image and their perspective on their current life situation. The tendency to compare themselves to other people or conform to societal expectations. Can you relate to any of these triggers? When you are triggered, you disconnect from your Authentic Self.

Let us look at the thought process. Imagine your thoughts as if they were moving along a conveyor belt. This conveyor belt carries an endless stream of your thoughts, as depicted in Figure 4.2. Your thoughts continuously come and go and you have little control over their arrival or departure. These thoughts race through your mind at quite some speed.

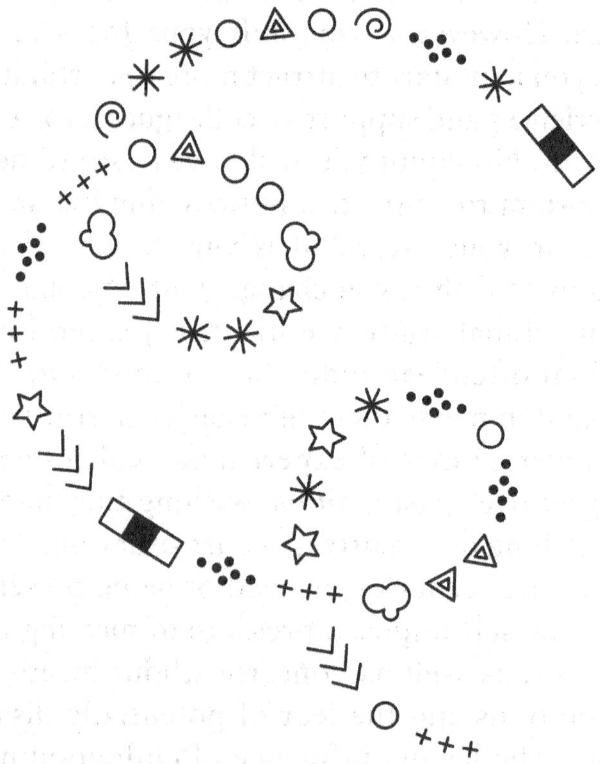

Figure 4.2 Thought Process

On average, you have around 80,000 thoughts per day. Surprisingly, around 98 percent of these thoughts are old and recycled – repetitions of the thoughts you have thought before; yesterday, the day before that, the week before that, the month before that, the year before that. Only 2 percent are original, fresh and innovative thoughts. So, you can see, your thoughts tend to follow automated and repetitive patterns. You need to actively manage and control them to prevent negative or unproductive thinking patterns and to be able to introduce new, empowering thoughts.

By observing and managing your thoughts, you can learn to harness their power and use them to your advantage. You have the power to choose which thoughts you entertain and which ones you let go of.

This is what happens in an untrained mind. You have a thought. As soon as your conscious awareness identifies with the content of that thought, you start actively thinking. Processing. Attaching to that thought and creating stories. Bringing in other thoughts that resonate with it and that are on the same vibration level. Before you know it, half an hour has passed and you emerge from the mental vortex, probably feeling lower in energy and enthusiasm than when you first had the initial thought.

When you start thinking in this way, you activate the ego and disconnect from your Authentic Self. That thinking might be in the form of a judgment about yourself, the pattern of thinking that there is something wrong with you or that you are not good enough.

I am going to be bold here and say to you – you are not your thoughts. How can I be so sure? Because I meditate every day and this is what I have noticed. When I sit in a quiet space with my eyes closed, I rest in the silence, observing what's happening in my mind. A thought arises. If I grab onto that thought and start to wonder about its meaning, it takes me into a mental process where my thoughts spiral and build on top of each other. Later, I may realize that I have followed that initial thought and return to simply noticing my thoughts, sometimes berating myself for getting caught up in it. Alternatively, I can choose to observe the thought. I notice it. I can acknowledge the thought without attaching to it and without following the path it wants to lead my mind down. And then, I let it go.

The simple fact that I can observe a thought tells me something crucial: I am not my thoughts. And neither are you. Think about it. The fact that you can think about your thoughts implies you are separate from your thoughts.

Now, contrary to popular belief, there are no issues with thoughts. You may have heard people say "when you meditate, you need to empty your mind." I don't agree with that and here's why: it is impossible. Your mind doesn't stop while you are awake. It can slow down, and speed up but it never stops. What if those thoughts that come in meditation are a form of release? Perhaps they serve as a de-stressing technique that your body automatically engages in to help process and release trapped emotions.

When you attach to your thoughts, or as I like to call it "lasso a thought," this is what causes you suffering, pain and fear. Let me repeat that. It is not the thought itself that causes you suffering or harm. It is the act of attaching to the thought, believing it and making it your truth in that moment. That is what causes you suffering. The emotions that surface and the corresponding responses you experience when attaching to a thought stem from your dissatisfaction with "what is." You are not happy with your current reality. Figure 4.3 illustrates how you attach to thoughts and hook into them.

You have two choices at any given moment. You can either hook into a thought, becoming an active participant in the story, or you can choose to observe the thought, as in

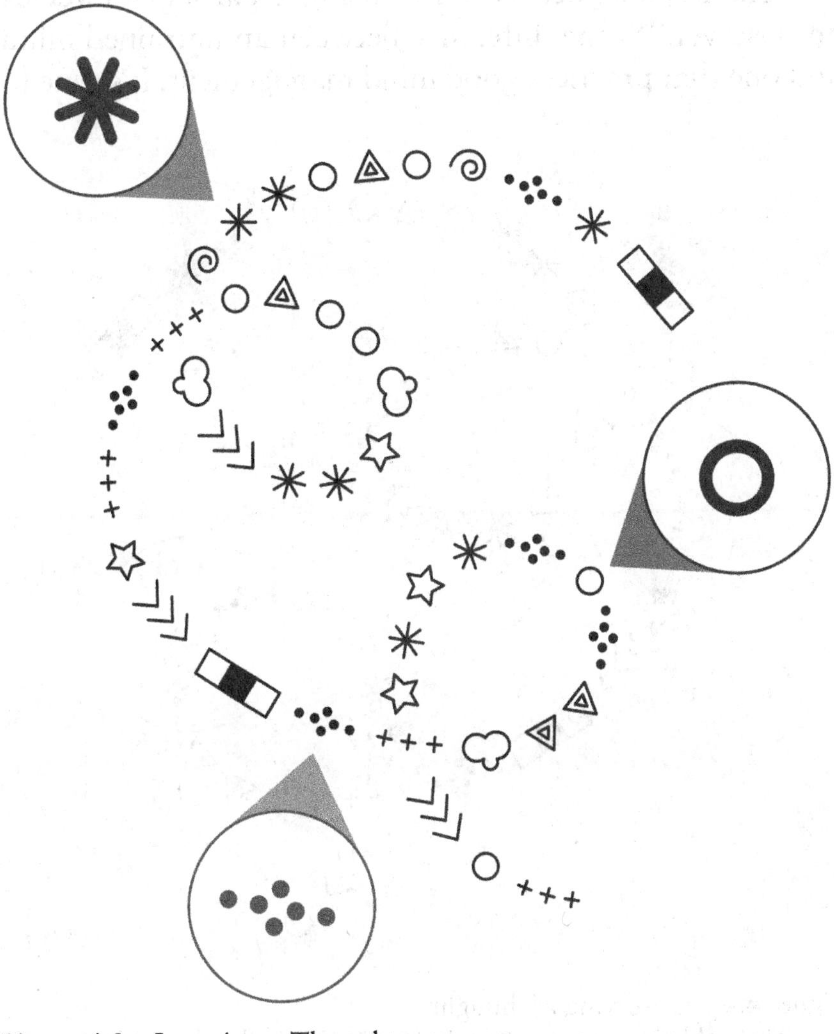

Figure 4.3 Lassoing a Thought
Key: The enclosed circles symbolize the thoughts from your stream of consciousness to which you attach significance and hook into.

Figure 4.4. By participating in your thoughts, you disconnect from your Authentic Self and take on the role of a character in the story. You don't want to be a character. The more empowering choice is to be the observer. It is much more powerful. When you observe, it establishes a profound connection to your Authentic Self.

The key distinction lies in being a participant versus an observer. It's the difference between an untrained mind and one that practices good mind management. It's time to

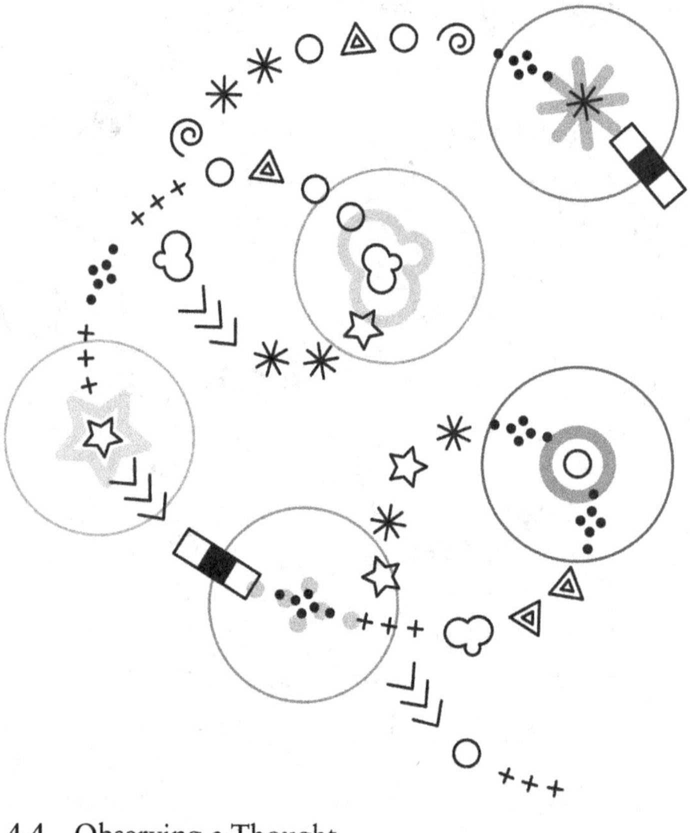

Figure 4.4 Observing a Thought
Key: The highlighted icons within the stream signify the ability to observe thoughts without active engagement, cultivating mindfulness and self-awareness.

cultivate the skill of good mind management. Practice the art of observation rather than participation. Recognize when bad management of your mind is engaged and gently resist the urge to follow those thoughts. Instead, redirect your focus to observing and release the thoughts gently, calmly and peacefully, as illustrated in Figure 4.4.

Another thing to consider is that when you attach to a thought or fixate on one thing, you may inadvertently overlook or prevent other opportunities from coming your way. The thought you have lassoed may be limiting you and your potential, whilst another thought, just over there, might be the key that takes you forward, offering more influence or greater opportunities for you.

Think of it in this way. Imagine a squirrel collecting food for the winter. It has spotted one nut on the forest floor. It has homed in on it and is focused on this one nut in a beautiful wooded valley. If the squirrel turned around, it would discover a huge pile of nuts that fell from the tree during an overnight storm, just a few feet away. The one nut it found had been blown away from the larger pile by the wind. If only the squirrel turned around. It might even see the potential mate observing from a low hanging branch.

When you focus on a particular thing happening at a certain time in a specific way, you risk overlooking other possibilities that may be available to you. This narrow focus can restrict what you receive and potentially shut off a whole spectrum of ideas, resources and interactions.

For instance, let's imagine you are striving for career advancement within your organization. You might often find yourself thinking "I need to secure a promotion to the next level." Let's explore alternative perspectives. What if the career progression you desire isn't solely tied to moving up the hierarchical ladder? What if it involves lateral moves, taking on special projects or acquiring new skills in a different department? By fixating solely on one specific path to advancement (the promotion), you may unintentionally limit your potential for growth. To embrace a broader range of possibilities, consider that career success can come from various avenues, some of which you may not have considered initially. It's crucial to remain open to diverse opportunities that may lead to your desired career progression, even if they deviate from your original expectations. And remember, what you want may not manifest in the exact way you envision and in the timescale you expect.

When you become fixated on what you want and the specifics of how you want it to be, you not only limit what can come to you but also miss the richness of the journey and the nuances along the way. In doing so, you close yourself off from the joy and happiness available to you in this very moment.

Lastly, it's crucial to be aware of common thinking errors that can affect you and your colleagues at work. These thinking errors can impact how you make decisions, communicate and get things done. Here are the most common thinking errors:

- All-or-nothing thinking is where you see things as either really good or really bad, with no middle ground.
- Overgeneralization is where you use one example to make big, sweeping statements such as "it always happens."
- Mental filtering is where you only focus on the negative things and ignore the rest.
- Disqualifying the positives is where you ignore or minimize positive experiences, leading to a skewed perspective.

- Jumping to conclusions is where you make negative assumptions without enough proof. This includes thinking you know what someone else is thinking (mind-reading) or believing something bad will happen even if it's unlikely (fortune-telling).
- Catastrophizing is where you think the worst will always happen, even when it probably won't.
- Magnifying and minimizing is where you make things seem bigger or smaller than they really are, such as your achievements.
- Emotional reasoning is where you believe that if you feel bad, things must be bad.
- "Should" statements are those that include words such as "should," "must," and "ought to." These can lead to unrealistic expectations.
- Labeling is an extreme form of over-generalization where instead of describing your error, you give yourself or others harsh labels.
- Personalization is where you blame yourself for things that aren't your fault.

Being aware of these thinking errors can help you and your colleagues make better decisions and work together more effectively.

Do you recognize any of those within you or your team? Recognizing and addressing these cognitive biases and thinking errors is essential for nurturing effective problem-solving, cultivating healthier interpersonal relationships and promoting overall well-being in the workplace.

Now over to you. Here are two activities designed to raise your awareness of how your mind works, the thoughts you think and how they impact your performance and behavior in the workplace.

Activity 1

Find a comfortable, distraction-free space where you can sit for 10 minutes. Set a timer if you are concerned about time. Close your eyes and sit in silence for 5 minutes, allowing your mind to do what it does. At the end of the 5 minutes, reflect on what happened. What thoughts surfaced? Write down all the thoughts you remember. Did you engage in any of those thoughts and follow them or did you merely observe them as they drifted past? Which of those thoughts did you hook into? What else did you notice? Draw your conclusions. Were there any patterns? Were your thoughts mainly positive, negative or neutral? Did they feel to be empowering thoughts or destructive overall? Did you mainly observe or participate in your thoughts?

Activity 2

Throughout the day, write down any repetitive thoughts you encounter. At the end of the day, reflect on these thoughts to identify any recurring patterns, common themes or emotions that surfaced when you kept thinking those thoughts. Take note of which of these thoughts had a negative impact on you at work. Now that you have identified these repetitive and recycled thoughts, decide which are helpful to you and which are unhelpful. Write a list of all the unhelpful thoughts you keep thinking. You will need this later when we explore releasing and reprogramming thoughts and situations. The reason you are thinking these thoughts will become apparent when we delve into stories and past experiences.

Past Conditioning

Building on our earlier discussion in Chapter 1 about conditioning and how it affects your sense of safety in the workplace, let's delve deeper into how past conditioning affects your behavior and performance within the workplace. We will draw insights from practical examples shared by individuals during our retreats.

To begin to understand the profound impact of our past, particularly our childhood experiences, on our performance and behavior in the workplace, let's begin by revisiting messages many of us encountered during our formative years. Did you, like so many others, hear any of these messages throughout your childhood? "You can't have ice-cream unless you eat your greens." "Put it back; we can't afford that. Money doesn't grow on trees." "You need to go to school, get an education and secure a good job." "It's just a graze. You're okay. Stop crying." "Boys wear blue, girls wear pink." "Don't talk to strangers." "Wait until your mother/father gets home." "You're not good at X (art, math, spelling). Stick to what you're good at." "When you get married to a handsome man, you can . . ." "Don't play with dolls/dress up. You're a boy. Boys don't play with dolls/dress up." "You're so small/tall/fat/skinny."

These messages, however well intentioned, often lay the foundation for your beliefs and shape your perception of success. Did you hear messages that success looks a certain way? For many, success was presented like this: a big house, a good job with benefits, a loving partner of the opposite sex, a fairytale wedding, children, a manicured lawn, a white picket fence and an adorable puppy. This, in the eyes of society, was often recited as one of the definitions of success. And what about the influence of the media? The idea that possessing items such as the latest iPhone, a top-of-the-range car and a shiny new laptop equates to success. But what does this do to you? Your kids? Reflect on that for a moment.

Understanding how these early experiences continue to affect you is essential for personal growth and professional achievement. By examining your conditioning, unraveling your beliefs and recognizing any limiting thought patterns that may have been ingrained, you can break free from the constraints of your past and achieve your full potential in the workplace.

Let us explore practical examples in four key areas: career path, financial decisions, productivity and communication/collaboration. These are all examples shared by individuals during our retreats. They are not isolated comments, they are recurring narratives shared by individuals globally.

Career path. Traditional career paths often come with the belief that "you need to go to school, get an education and secure a good job." Individuals raised with this belief may prioritize stability over career satisfaction. They might be less inclined to take entrepreneurial risks or explore unconventional career paths that align better with their passions.

Childhood conditioning around gender roles can significantly influence workplace behavior. Messages like "boys don't play with dolls/dress up" and "boys wear blue, girls wear pink" can lead to individuals conforming to expected gender norms instead of expressing themselves authentically or pursuing their desired career paths. For example, it may discourage individuals from pursuing creative or caregiving professions if they identify as male. Men may feel pressured to be the primary breadwinners and to excel in their careers, while women may prioritize family over their career due to societal expectations.

Early conditioning about the idealized image of a "loving partner of the opposite sex" and a "fairytale wedding" can impact personal choices and behavior in the workplace. This may inadvertently lead some individuals to prioritize marriage over their career aspirations, making career sacrifices to fulfill traditional family roles.

Lastly, media portrayals of success can also influence career choices. For instance, someone exposed to glamorous depictions of certain professions (doctors, lawyers, dentists) may feel compelled to pursue those careers, even if they're not aligned with their true interests and talents.

Financial. Messages like "money doesn't grow on trees" can instill a deep fear of financial instability. Individuals with this conditioning may become overly cautious with their finances, hesitating to invest in personal or professional development due to the fear of running out of money. In the workplace, this caution can translate to a reluctance to take calculated risks or invest resources in projects, potentially causing missed growth opportunities out of fear of financial loss.

Those conditioned to associate success with material possessions, such as big homes, high-end cars and the latest gadgets, may prioritize accumulating these items over their professional growth. This materialistic focus can lead to excessive work hours and stress as they strive to afford these luxuries.

Lastly, the media's emphasis on consumerism can lead to impulsive spending habits and financial stress. Employees caught in this cycle may experience workplace stress and distraction due to personal financial concerns.

Productivity. Childhood routines and schedules can significantly influence your approach to time management.

Individuals raised in structured environments may excel at meeting deadlines, while those with less-structured upbringings might struggle with punctuality and effective time management.

Growing up in an environment that exclusively praised perfection can lead to perfectionist tendencies in the workplace. These individuals may spend excessive time on tasks, struggle with delegation and feel anxious about making even minor errors.

Media-driven messages promoting the latest gadgets and material possessions can foster a sense of inadequacy and comparison with peers. This can lead to perfectionism at work, as individuals strive to attain a perceived standard of success set by external influences.

Messages like "you can't have ice cream unless you eat your greens" can lead to a belief that tedious or less enjoyable tasks (the greens) must be completed before more rewarding ones (the ice-cream). In the workplace, they might lead to delaying tackling challenging projects until simpler tasks are finished, hindering productivity.

Those conditioned to equate success with external validation may seek approval from colleagues or supervisors in the workplace. This desire for validation can impact decision-making and behavior, potentially compromising authenticity and self-confidence.

Messages like "wait until your mother/father gets home" can foster a reliance on higher authority figures' input or approval in decision-making at work. They are likely to avoid taking initiative or making decisions at work.

Childhood experiences with calculated risk-taking can affect an individual's willingness to take professional risks. Someone accustomed to taking risks in a controlled environment may be more open to entrepreneurial ventures, while those raised to avoid risks might stick with safer, more traditional career choices.

Repeated messages during childhood that mistakes were unacceptable and would lead to punishment can result in a strong fear of failure in the workplace. This fear can make individuals risk-averse, avoiding undertaking challenging projects or pursuing innovation that could lead to professional growth.

Messages like "you're not good at X (art, math, spelling). Stick to what you're good at" can lead to self-doubt and avoidance of tasks they believe they're not naturally skilled at, limiting their willingness to learn and adapt in a changing work environment.

Communication/Collaboration. Messages like "it's just a graze. You're okay. Stop crying" that encourage the suppression of emotional expression can hinder an individual's ability to acknowledge and manage emotions at work, impacting effective communication, teamwork and conflict resolution.

A strict interpretation of "don't talk to strangers" can make networking and relationship-building challenging in the workplace, as individuals may hesitate to initiate conversations or collaborate with colleagues they don't know well.

Comments about physical appearance, such as "you're so small/tall/fat/skinny" can lead to body image issues and reduced self-confidence, affecting an individual's assertiveness, self-esteem and willingness to take on leadership roles in the workplace.

Messages of success conveyed by the media can lead individuals to prioritize social status and image. This can result in workplace behavior aimed at maintaining a certain appearance or status, potentially affecting interpersonal relationships and team dynamics.

An upbringing emphasizing strict respect for authority figures can make it challenging for individuals to voice nonconforming opinions or provide constructive criticism to supervisors or colleagues, potentially hindering team dynamics and innovative thinking.

Depending on their upbringing, individuals may lean toward valuing independence or collaboration in the workplace. Those raised to prioritize self-sufficiency might struggle with teamwork, while those taught to prioritize group harmony may find it difficult to assert themselves independently.

Early exposure to communication patterns at home can influence how individuals express themselves at work. For example, those from households with open and direct communication may excel in negotiations, while those from more reserved backgrounds might avoid confrontation.

Childhood experiences with family conflict can shape an individual's approach to workplace conflicts. Those from families that avoided conflict may struggle with addressing issues head-on, potentially allowing conflicts to fester.

These examples illustrate how childhood conditioning can silently influence an individual's priorities, values and behavior in the workplace, often without them realizing the extent of these influences. Recognizing these conditioning factors can empower individuals to make deliberate choices that better align with their personal and professional goals.

As you reflect on these examples, take a moment to consider whether any resonate with your own experiences.

They might even trigger memories of alternative messages you received during your childhood. Reflect on the messages you heard as a child and consider how they continue to impact your behavior in the workplace. Raising your awareness of your childhood conditioning will provide valuable insights into the origins of your thought patterns, emotional responses and actions in various workplace situations.

Now over to you. Here is an activity designed to raise your awareness of the childhood conditioning that has influenced you.

Activity 3

Ask yourself the following questions. "What do I believe to be true about my childhood, family life, health, fitness, relationships, career, money, love, education, success, failure and self-image?"

If you are struggling to identify your beliefs, try this. Imagine you are talking to a friend and they ask you about those areas mentioned above. What do you say to them? Take note of how you respond and the language you use in your conversation with them. These responses reflect what you genuinely believe to be true about those areas of your life.

Once you have completed this activity, reflect on what it revealed. Are there any areas where your beliefs might have a negative impact on your thoughts, feelings or behaviors in the workplace?

Stories and Triggers

For every single event, situation, experience and conversation in your life, you create a story. You attach an emotion and meaning to that event. It might be a positive, neutral or negative emotion.

You create stories for every aspect of life. You have stories about food, money, relationships, career, success, self-worth, health and friendships. It is a way for you to make sense of who you are, the people around you and your life experiences.

When you look at the story you tell about a certain area of your life, it gives you an insight into what you believe to be true about that. Imagine you are out for dinner with a friend and they ask "How are you feeling? You weren't feeling well the last time we met." Listen to what you say in response. This is what you believe to be true about your health, your body and your well-being. This belief becomes the story you tell.

The stories, or narratives, you created about past events impact on every situation, conversation and experience you have today. These stories are repeated thoughts you think and share with others about the situation, highlighting and shaping what you believe to be true about the event. They are hiding beneath the surface, steering your every move, thought, action and decision. The story you created in a single moment in time has become a reality that affects your present and future experiences.

Let me give you a couple of workplace examples to illustrate this in action.

Imagine this. You have applied for a new job. You pour your heart and soul into the application. You give it everything. You feel empowered, you feel passionate and you really believe you can secure the position. Then, a rejection letter arrives.

The first thought that crosses your mind is "They don't think I am good enough." And now you are hooked into that thought. "I am not good enough at my job."

Those thoughts escalate and now you are creating a story around it. "I am not good at my job. What am I going to tell people at work? Where else am I not good enough? I am a rubbish parent and child. I am not a good partner. I can't get the job I want which means I will never get the money I want to do X. I am not good at . . ." You find every area of your life that this feels true to you and you search out every ounce of evidence to prove it.

How does this make you feel? You feel dejected, frustrated and embarrassed. You start doubting yourself, questioning yourself. Remember that your emotions significantly influence your actions. You walk into work with a slouched posture, giving off lower energy vibes to your colleagues. You are less creative, your confidence has dropped, you start to distance yourself from your colleagues and don't really want to be there. This echoes out into your personal life. You are despondent and withdrawn, you are snappy with your loved ones causing them to keep their distance from you. You feel lonely and isolated.

The initial thought you had in that one moment has triggered something in you and now it is affecting every part of your life.

Next, picture yourself working on a project with a team of colleagues. During a critical presentation to your manager and senior leadership team, one of your team members makes a minor mistake in their part of the presentation. The error doesn't significantly impact the overall outcome, but it is noticeable.

After the presentation, you notice that they appear visibly flustered and self-critical. You and your team reassure them that the mistake was minor and easily correctable. However, over time, you start to notice a pattern.

Every time they are involved in a presentation or a high-stakes meeting, they become anxious and occasionally make small errors.

Over time, you internalize this pattern and assign meaning to it. You might think, "They can't handle pressure well and they are not reliable in high-pressure situations." Once you've settled on this interpretation, you start constructing a story around it. You might start believing "They are a liability on our team. Their performance in critical situations is always below par."

As a result, every time they are assigned to an important project or presentation, you approach it with the preconceived notion that they will underperform. Instead of offering support and constructive feedback, you find yourself expecting them to make mistakes and doubting their abilities.

In this scenario, your initial perception of your colleague's performance has evolved into a story that influences your interactions with them and the overall dynamics of your team. Rather than addressing any specific needs or exploring potential solutions to help them, you default to your preconceived story about their performance under pressure, which can hinder their professional growth and impact the team's dynamics.

The key takeaway. Your interpretations and stories about yourself and your colleagues in the workplace can significantly impact your interactions and decision-making, often without you realizing it. Recognizing and challenging these stories and preconceived narratives is essential for nurturing a more positive and productive work environment.

What influences your interpretations of situations and the story you attach to them? Many factors play a role here, including the conditioning and messaging you heard as a child, your filters in that moment, a difference in perspective, mishearing what the other person said, distractions that prevent you from being fully present in the conversation, unconscious bias, a feeling of power imbalance in the relationship, your physical and mental state in the moment, the people around you and how you feel in their presence, the physical environment you are in – and so much more.

If you attached a negative emotion and story to a past event, when you experience a similar situation now, you may be "**triggered**." This means you have a negative emotional response that is caused by a particular action or situation. It is possible that the trigger could originate in your personal life but manifest in a workplace scenario because something reminds you of the original situation. It could be a word, phrase, sound, smell or feeling that triggers the emotional response.

Common areas that trigger negative emotions include unresolved past experiences, striving to achieve perfection driven by internal expectations, comparing yourself to other people, self-doubt expressed through thoughts like "I'm not good enough" or "I'll never succeed," childhood messages that continue to affect you, limiting beliefs and negative self-talk, worrying about meeting perceived external expectations, feelings of overwhelm and inadequacy around workload expressed through thoughts like "I have too much to do," negative interpretations or misunderstanding situations and a sense of lacking control. These triggers can evoke strong negative emotions and impact your well-being, thoughts and actions.

Do any of those areas trigger negative emotions in you? If so, pay attention and observe what is going on in you when you are triggered. The person or situation that triggered a reaction within you highlights the belief you need to work on within yourself. This is a growth opportunity. More on that in a moment.

What happens when you are triggered? Let us look at this process in more detail. Consider the cycle illustrated in Figure 4.5. Something happens. Unconsciously, your beliefs are activated, which triggers "old" emotions in you. The emotions you attached to the story you created in the past rise up within you and directly influence and impact on the thoughts you think in the present moment about the situation you are in. These thoughts you have in the moment, mixed with your "old" emotions, impact on how you feel in this situation unfolding in front of you. Which then impacts on how you act and behave in this moment.

In essence, the cycle is: Event – beliefs – emotions (trigger) – thoughts – feelings (a mix of old and new) – behavior – response.

The usual approach to break this cycle is to change the feelings that have risen to the surface. You try to change those feelings by looking outside of yourself. You might use food, alcohol, drugs or money to numb those

Figure 4.5 Trigger Cycle

feelings or to give you some temporary release. What would have more impact is to change the belief, which triggered the old emotion, that influenced the thought that caused the new feeling.

Here is a practical example of this in action. You are in the office having a conversation. A is your manager. B is you.

A: "I didn't see you had sent that to me. Where is it?"

B: "I definitely did!"

Your manager said something that you misinterpreted. You think they are insinuating that you have not sent it, that you are lying.

What your manager does not know is that you experienced a situation in a previous workplace where your manager said the same thing which resulted in a conflict situation. You proved you had sent the document to them but it left a negative feeling between you. You internalized that situation as a negative experience and formed the belief that "They think I am a liar."

Now, in this situation, you have heard similar words that were used in the past and your belief has been triggered. In a very short space of time, all the old emotions have risen to the surface and you are feeling uncomfortable. Flustered. All the old thoughts have rushed into your mind – thoughts of "they thought I was lying" which you have made into a present statement "they think I am lying."

The old emotions mix with new emotions and without realizing you have directed your uncomfortable feeling toward your manager, which then leads you into a conflict situation. You get defensive, they are confused and the whole situation has escalated.

The conflict in you arises when something has been triggered in you. The other person may have said something neutral, yet you heard different words, or a negative tone or were reminded of a past experience.

For the untrained mind, it is easy to miss when you have hooked into a story. As we discussed earlier, it all begins when you grab hold of a passing thought that is whizzing along the conveyor belt in your mind. Much like spotting your bag on a conveyor belt in the airport, grabbing hold of it, yanking it off the belt and clutching it tightly as if it were a prized possession you won in a game of "hook-a-duck." Just as your guardians would say "Get that one!" and you would aim your little hook to grab it out of the water. Now you "own" it, it is yours and you can claim the prize. That is what you are doing with your thoughts and stories. You are grabbing hold of them and holding on to them tightly.

Here is the surprising twist. When something triggers you, those intense feelings are flagging up something vital. This is a growth opportunity for you. What triggers you is here to teach you something about yourself. It is flagging up a belief, a fear or the conditioning you have experienced throughout your life that needs working through.

This is an opportunity to question your thinking and your stories. When these feelings surface, they are often accompanied by an unquestioned, unexamined and potentially untrue story that is bubbling up and taking over you. That uncomfortable feeling is telling you "I am here. I am causing you discomfort. Work on me."

If you don't take this opportunity to work through it, the universe tends to keep sending you situations and people that trigger the same response until you recognize it and work through it. Don't just let it go. Don't think "I will deal with it later." Take back control and actively work through it. You can start the process by completing the activity below.

Over to you. Here is an activity designed to raise your awareness of the things that trigger you.

Activity 4

Step 1 is to raise your awareness. Notice what triggers negative emotions, thoughts and behaviors for you at work. You may experience this as tension or friction. This will highlight where you have attached a negative story to certain situations that happened to you. Write a list of the things that trigger you.

Step 2 is to release and reprogram your triggers. Reflect on these situations. Ask yourself what the person said or did that triggered you to feel conflict or to feel uncomfortable. What did they touch upon? For example: is it the belief "I am not good enough"? Is it that they may find out you are a fraud? Is it your fear of lack or losing control or looking silly in some way? Also, consider what expectations you had in that moment (your own and what you think others expected of you). Identify what is going on for you when you are triggered. How do you feel in the moment, what are the thoughts you have, does it remind you of a certain event in your past, how does it impact on how you interact with your colleagues? When you have explored all your triggers in detail, reflect to see if there are any common patterns, trends, people, situations, emotions and language used. This will give you insight into specifics that tend to trigger you.

Step 3 is to reconnect. How can you reduce the impact these triggers have on you?

Emotions

Being aware of your emotions is a vital skill for success in the workplace. Once you are able to identify and understand your emotions, you can manage them in a way that helps you to perform better. Remember, your emotions are linked to your thoughts and beliefs and can be triggered by stories.

Imagine this. During a team meeting, one of your team members made a comment about your recent presentation, suggesting that it lacked the detail they had expected. Instantly, you feel your face flush and embarrassment and defensiveness rise within you. You put a lot of effort into that presentation and this comment really catches you off guard. You have had a negative emotional response triggered by your colleague's criticism.

Consider these two different approaches. Number one, you deal with the trigger promptly and effectively. After the team meeting, you take a moment to collect yourself and reflect on your emotional response. You realize that their comment triggered you because you value your work and strive to make positive contributions to the team. You acknowledge that the comment, although critical, was intended as constructive feedback and treat it as such.

You decide to address the situation proactively. You ask your colleague if you can have a conversation to discuss their feedback. You explain your intentions, emphasizing that you were committed to delivering quality work that adds value to the team and are open to suggestions for improvement.

During the conversation, you both gain a deeper understanding of each other's perspectives. Your colleague clarifies their intention was not to undermine your efforts but to highlight areas for improvement. They give you some really good suggestions, which you take on board and will use to plan your next presentation. You appreciate their feedback and agree to work together more closely on future projects, wherever possible. This positive experience strengthens your working relationship.

By addressing your emotional response promptly and effectively, you not only diffuse any potential tension but also use the trigger as an opportunity for growth and improved collaboration.

If you recognize that you have been triggered and want to address the issue straight away but need some space or time out to think or to compose yourself first, be proactive and ask for it. For example, you could say "I need to take a break, can we reconvene . . .?" (insert time in here – 10 minutes, later today, tomorrow). It might be helpful to get a drink, go somewhere quiet for a few minutes or go for a walk. Use this time to compose yourself and understand what it was that triggered you. Then, when you go back to the conversation, you will have a clearer idea of what you need to clarify or discuss with the person.

Number two, you allow your emotions to fester. Following the team meeting you choose to avoid addressing your emotional response. You feel that confronting the situation might make things awkward between you and your colleague, so you decide to let it go.

You can't stop thinking about it though. You take the situation home with you, chewing over it, considering all the things you could have said or done differently in the moment. Over time, you notice that you become increasingly anxious about interacting with this colleague, even a little resentful. You start second-guessing yourself and your work, constantly worrying about receiving criticism. This affects your self-esteem and you find it challenging to communicate effectively with your colleagues, leading to misunderstandings and miscommunication on various projects.

The unaddressed emotional trigger lingers, affecting not only your self-confidence but also your overall performance, working relationships and team dynamics. The situation continues to deteriorate and you become less satisfied with your work and the environment.

In this scenario, not addressing the emotional trigger allows it to fester, with it gaining more negative energy, leading to ongoing challenges in your workplace relationships and overall well-being.

Considering these two different approaches, you can see that recognizing and managing your emotional response in situations is crucial for maintaining healthy work relationships and preventing your emotions from negatively affecting workplace interactions. When you are aware of your emotions, you can acknowledge your feelings and respond in a way that is appropriate for the situation. You are less likely to react impulsively or let your emotions get the best of you, which can lead to better decision-making, improved communication and stronger relationships with your colleagues.

By learning to manage your emotions effectively, you will be better equipped to handle the challenges and opportunities that arise in the workplace.

Your emotions can make you sick. Remember the last time you were stressed. How did you feel? Did you notice you became sick, irritable or disconnected from those around you? Maybe you experienced stiff shoulders, a bad back or pain in your knee. Maybe you had a sore throat, sniffles or a full-blown cold. Or a headache, nausea and sleepless nights. The physical symptoms you experienced were likely a result of trapped emotions that were not fully experienced or released.

When you trap or suppress emotions (when you don't feel them and experience them fully) you will notice your physical body respond. Many ailments and health conditions are a result of trapped emotions in your body. When you fully experience an emotion it washes through you, usually in less than a minute. And then it is gone.

The common thing most people do when they feel an emotion is to get busy. They do something to take their mind off it or they try to diffuse it. Don't do that. Feel it. Experience it. Take deep breaths and notice it come and go. Treat it like a thought. Observe it and don't participate in it. Don't react or respond in that moment. Simply let it wash through you.

If you don't, you suppress the emotion and it becomes "stuck" in you, until you release it. Negative emotions can fester, resulting in something much worse than a cold. Suppressing or ignoring them can lead to a variety of ailments and health conditions that can hinder your performance and well-being.

Becoming acutely aware of your emotions in the workplace is crucial for your physical and mental health. It is vital that you become aware of your emotions – how you are feeling at any given moment – and fully experience all of that emotion. By fully experiencing and managing your emotions you can maintain your health, improve your performance and create a more productive and fulfilling work environment.

A note here on fear. Fear is a strong emotion that arises when you don't feel safe. It is caused by a perceived danger or anticipation of something negative happening. Fear can have a significant impact in the workplace, affecting both individuals and the overall organizational culture. Fear can create a toxic and unhealthy work environment, leading to high levels of stress and burnout among employees. Constantly living in fear can trigger stress-related health issues, resulting in absenteeism and reduced overall well-being. A culture of fear can lead to high turnover rates, where employees who consistently feel unsafe or unsupported in the workplace may seek opportunities elsewhere. This turnover can be costly for organizations in terms of recruitment, training and lost institutional knowledge.

Common fears that prevent people from bringing their Authentic Self to work include the fear of a past negative experience repeating itself, fear of what other people think, their reactions or behaviors toward you, fear of being judged, fear of discrimination, fear of change, fear of failure or making a mistake, fear of confrontation or conflict, fear of public speaking/presenting and fear of losing your job. Do any of these fears resonate with you?

The power that drives fear is the unknown. Fear grows in the darkness. When you take the time to consider the worst-case scenario and formulate a plan to address it, fear tends to lose its grip. By naming and acknowledging your fear, you turn the light on, bringing it out into the light.

Now, over to you. Here is an activity designed to raise your awareness of your emotions and how they impact on your performance and behavior in the workplace.

Activity 5

Write down the emotions you are feeling/have felt today. Make a brief note of what triggered you to feel that emotion. What happened? Who were you with? What was going on in your mind to trigger that emotion in you? How did you deal with this emotional response? Did you observe it? Did you get hooked into it? Were you aware of it in that moment, or only when you reflected back on the situation? Did you allow yourself to feel the emotion or did you suppress it? Did this have a positive, negative or neutral impact on the situation you were in?

Look back at your notes and reflect on the role your thoughts played in influencing your emotions, the stories that underlie these emotional responses and any recurring patterns you may observe.

Limiting Beliefs

Earlier in this chapter, we talked about recurring or repetitive thoughts and you completed an activity to identify what those thoughts are. You might be wondering, where do your repetitive thoughts originate from? The answer is that a repetitive thought is a belief. In essence, a belief is a thought you keep thinking and accepting as true.

Beliefs are powerful. They can significantly impact your life, including your experiences in the workplace. Your belief system is formed by the age of six to seven from what you experienced and heard around you as a child. These messages seep into your subconscious mind and shape what you believe as a child, and later as an adult.

Your current beliefs are a result of the social conditioning and messages you heard from childhood. Unless you have actively worked to change them, your current life is still being dictated by those early beliefs – the same you had when you were six years old. Think about that. The decisions you make in the workplace are based on the beliefs you formed when you were six to seven years old.

How you view yourself, others and the world around you is heavily influenced by your beliefs. These beliefs can either empower you or limit you, affecting how you feel, how you behave, how you approach challenges, how you interact with colleagues and how you interpret events in your life – leading to the creation of stories. You may be carrying beliefs that no longer serve you and may be holding you back from achieving your full potential.

A limiting belief is a belief that you hold about yourself, others or the world that limits your potential and prevents you from achieving your goals or living the life you desire. It is a belief that you accept as true, even though it may not be based on factual evidence or objective reality. Limiting beliefs can be formed through your upbringing, past experiences or social conditioning, and they can manifest in different areas of your life such as relationships and career.

The most common limiting beliefs are "I'm worthless," "I'm going to be found out," "I'm unlovable," "I don't deserve/am not worthy of . . . (success, love, happiness)," "There is something wrong with me," "I'm different (this results in comparing yourself to others)," "I can't be my real self or I will be judged," "Everything is my fault," "They are going to abandon/reject me" and "I'm a failure." When you dig deeper into these, they all point to the same thing; there is one belief that underlies all of these. "I'm not good enough."

It is crucial to understand how your beliefs impact you in the workplace. Limiting beliefs can hold you back and prevent you from taking risks or pursuing your goals. Let's take the belief "I am not good enough" and look at how that could affect someone in the workplace.

Ali, a talented marketing professional, is assigned to a crucial role in a team project. They believe that they are not good enough to take this role despite their qualifications and experience. This belief affects their behavior and contributions to the project significantly. How?

Ali holds back on taking the lead in project meetings and doesn't propose the innovative ideas they have in their head. They defer to their colleagues, assuming they have better insights, which hinders the team's progress and results in missed opportunities for creativity and problem-solving.

Ali is afraid of being judged by team members and worries about making mistakes. This fear paralyzes their decision-making and problem-solving abilities. They constantly seek validation from their colleagues, which slows down the decision-making process and creates unnecessary dependency on others.

Ali's belief of not being good enough leads to heightened stress and anxiety throughout the project. They constantly feel like they are on the verge of failure, which takes a toll on their mental and emotional well-being. This increased stress also affects their physical health, resulting in sick days, and impacts on their overall job satisfaction.

Ali avoids seeking leadership roles within the project and taking on the more challenging tasks, believing that others are more capable. As a result, they miss valuable opportunities for skill development and career advancement.

Ali's self-doubt affects the team's dynamics. Their colleagues are frustrated with their reluctance to contribute and take ownership of tasks. This leads to a lack of trust and cohesion within the team, compromising the project's success.

In this scenario, the limiting belief "I am not good enough" significantly impacts Ali's career by limiting their confidence, decision-making and willingness to take on challenges or seek advancement. Addressing and overcoming this limiting belief through self-awareness and positive self-talk can help them unlock their true potential and have a more positive impact on the project and their overall career.

By proactively working on your limiting beliefs, you can improve your performance and achieve your goals.

Limiting beliefs can be challenged and overcome through self-awareness, positive self-talk and personal development.

Remember these key points. What you believe to be true is a direct reflection of what you experience in your life. If you don't like what you are experiencing in your life, you have the power to change it. Change your thoughts. Change your beliefs. Change your life.

Now, over to you. Here are three activities that will transform your life. Don't take my word for it. Try them out and see for yourself.

Activity 6

You are going to uncover your beliefs. Step 1 is to raise your awareness. When a friend asks about your career what do you say to them? Write down the "stories," the words and the phrases you typically use to describe it. Now, look at what you just wrote down. What do you notice? What do you tell them is good about your career? What do you tell them about your career that is not working right now? Are there any recurring or wonky thoughts about any aspect of your career, your relationships at work, your current tasks or projects or how you show up in the workplace?

Step 2 is to release and reprogram. Explore your responses to those questions in more detail. Step outside of the "story" you just told about your situation for a moment and analyze it objectively. What is going on behind the words you tell your friend? The stories you share with your friends are reflections of the beliefs you hold about the situation. Identify the beliefs you have about your career. What do you believe to be true about it?

Step 3 is to reconnect. Now, you are going to extract the learning. What are the empowering beliefs you have? What are the limiting beliefs you have? How do these beliefs influence you, your work and your interactions in the workplace? Do you notice any recurring keywords? What other insights do you gain now that you've uncovered these beliefs?

Activity 7

This is a simplified version of the process I take people through to reprogram a limiting belief. Take one limiting belief that you want to work on and change.

Step 1 is to raise your awareness. Begin by identifying the limiting belief you want to work on and change. State it in one sentence – clear and concise. Reflect on where this belief shows up in your life: at work, at home or in social situations.

Step 2 is to release and reprogram. Examine the belief you have identified. Do you genuinely believe it to be true? Explore the impact of this belief. What happens when you think that belief? Contemplate who you would be without that thought. List three pieces of evidence that support the limiting belief. For each piece of evidence, question whether you truly believe it. If yes, list the reasons behind why you believe it. If no, strike them from your list of evidence and think of another.

Step 3 is to reconnect. Consider the opposite of the limiting belief or what you want the new, empowering belief to be. Provide three pieces of evidence that support this new belief. Reflect on the insights gained through this process. What is the emerging reality about this belief?

Activity 8

The Releasing Ritual. Step 1 is to raise your awareness. Refer to your notes from Activities 6 and 7 and identify three things you want to release, let go of or purge. These could be thoughts, patterns, programming, conditioning or physical items.

Step 2 is to release and reprogram. Write down what you want to release on a piece of paper. As darkness falls, stand outside and take a few deep breaths. Read aloud each item individually, pausing in between each one to take a deep breath. As you breathe out, release all the things associated with what you have just read aloud; the beliefs, fears, grief, negative emotions, worries and anxiety. Let go of anything that holds you back, no longer serves you or stops you from being/doing what you want. Aim to release all these emotions and energies. Once you have completed this for all three items, burn the piece of paper. As you watch the flames, imagine the night air and wind carrying away these burdens, stripping them of their power. Observe the flames until they die down; as you do, you'll sense the weight lifting from your mind and body.

Step 3 is to reconnect. Pause to take deep breaths. Visualize the future that lies ahead of you. Envision the exciting experiences, valuable opportunities and meaningful connections that you have created the space for. Recognize that now is the time to take ownership of your journey and pursue it with confidence.

If you find the idea of the Releasing Ritual a little unconventional or "woo-woo," I challenge you to step beyond your initial skepticism and give it a try. On the last evening of every retreat we facilitate, this is how our time together ends. It is a culmination of all the inner work we have undertaken through the Authentic Self Process, which includes the activities I have shared with you here in Pillar 1. During the day, leaders and managers engage in an activity where they summarize the lessons and insights they've gathered from our work together. They are then tasked with crafting an object, using materials sourced from the local environment, which they will offer to the fire during the Releasing Ritual.

When night falls, we gather around the fire. At first, some may be skeptical, unsure of what to expect. We ease into the evening by sharing our week's experiences and insights, setting the stage for the Releasing Ritual. When we begin the Ritual, everyone is invited to share what they are releasing, whether by reading from their paper or speaking from the heart. When they are ready, they place their paper and object into the fire, watching as the flames consume them. In these moments, we hold space for each other. The release of emotion in those moments is palpable. It resonates within all of us.

After the Releasing Ritual, we take the time to reflect on our feelings, experiences and newfound insights. The transformation in people is undeniable. Those who were initially skeptical or hesitant, even those who doubted the process, undergo a profound change.

So, if you are feeling uncertain or questioning the purpose of this activity, I strongly urge you to set aside your reservations and give it a chance. You might just discover its transformative power for yourself.

Negative Past Experiences

A major factor that prevents individuals from bringing their Authentic Self to work is negative past experiences. You know about my two negative past experiences in the workplace. They are a perfect example of this in action. Homophobic bullying significantly impacted on every aspect of my life, which resulted in me hiding and censoring myself in future situations. Let me tell you about Sam's experience. I met Sam when I was delivering training for a Fintech company.

Sam, a highly talented software developer, had been with the company for six years before I met them. Sam is neurodivergent and in our conversations they disclosed that they excel in their work but sometimes encounter challenges related to noise, social interactions and communication.

At their previous workplace, they experienced something that had a significant impact on them, resulting in them leaving the company and hiding parts of their Authentic Self in their new role. During a team meeting, Sam was presenting a project they were leading on to colleagues. They had meticulously prepared the presentation and felt confident walking into the room. During the presentation a colleague new to the team interrupted them, making comments about their unique presentation style and speech patterns in front of the entire team.

They told me the incident was not just embarrassing, it was emotionally distressing for them. They felt humiliated and exposed, as if their neurodivergence had been put on display for ridicule. The comments really threw them off and they struggled to complete the presentation. The stress of the situation heightened these traits, making them more pronounced. Afterwards, they felt as though everyone was talking about them behind their back.

Despite being a highly skilled professional who added immense value to the team, Sam couldn't help but feel like an outsider in their own workplace. This negative experience took a significant toll on Sam's mental well-being, affecting both their performance and behavior at work.

Eventually, Sam made the difficult decision to leave that toxic work environment, seeking a place where they could be appreciated for their talents without fear of discrimination. When they were telling me about their experience, it was evident the scars of that incident still haunt them and they disclosed they now approach certain workplace interactions with caution. They choose to hide or downplay their neurodivergent traits to avoid being vulnerable to similar negative experiences.

This heartbreaking incident demonstrates how past negative experiences can influence an individual's behavior at work and lead them to hide elements of their Authentic Self, even when it involves something as fundamental as their neurodivergent identity.

In the global study we conducted, negative past experiences were identified as the top reason why individuals don't bring their Authentic Self to work. Like Sam, bringing their Authentic Self to work may have triggered negative events or situations. Experiences like this often lead individuals to create a story around the situation. When they experience similar circumstances in their current work environment, they are triggered. Many people choose to hide or censor their Authentic Self to avoid the possibility of reliving a similar negative experience and to make sure they stay safe. For some, these past experiences may remain in their conscious awareness, while others may have suppressed them and remain unaware of their lasting impact.

For some individuals, these negative past experiences may have been in the form of racism, microaggressions, homophobia, neurodiversity challenges or hate crime (for example) and resulted in trauma, PTSD, mental health issues or social anxiety. Situations such as these can deeply impact an individual, causing physical, mental, emotional and psychological issues.

For other individuals, they may have experienced negative situations such as misunderstandings, miscommunications and conflict situations with their colleagues, which resulted in them being more cautious or putting barriers up to protect themselves. These situations, if dealt with in the moment, could have been successfully resolved. In this Highlight, I refer to these situations, not trauma-related situations.

All moments in time are neutral. It is the human brain that attaches negative or positive charge to them. Things happen. You experience things every single day. What one individual may deem as a negative experience, you may deem as a positive experience, and vice versa.

Imagine, you are in a team meeting where there is a heated discussion about a project that you are working on. If you are directly impacted by this discussion, you may internalize this as a negative experience. A colleague who is not impacted by this discussion may internalize this as a positive or neutral experience.

How you internalize experiences is based on how you feel in the moment. If you feel any tension, anxiety or frustration you are more likely to internalize the situation or experience in a negative way. You attach a negative story to it, probably chewing it over and over in your head, until the point where you can't let it go. On the other hand, if you feel upbeat, happy or supported in the situation you are more likely to internalize the experience in a positive way and forget about it.

That is the key here. All the things you have held on to from your past are there because in that moment you attached a negative story to it. You are likely to have continued to build on that story in the days, weeks, months and years following the creation of it, and internalized it as a belief.

Stories and triggers play a pivotal role in understanding and addressing negative past experiences. Pay close attention to the stories you share with your family and friends about these experiences. These are the stories you have associated with those events, and they reflect your current beliefs. It might be helpful to reassess these stories to see if they still align with your present reality. These negative stories could be the underlying source of your triggers in the workplace, whether consciously or subconsciously.

Every negative experience that you have held on to from the past is a result of the story you attached to it in that moment. You have the power to change that story in an instant. Are you ready to challenge those stories and rewrite them to serve you better?

Over to you. Let us explore and reprogram a negative past experience.

Activity 9

Think of a workplace situation where you have associated a negative story with it. What happened? Who was involved? What triggered you at that moment? How did you feel? How did you respond at the time?

Reflect on how your perspective might have differed if you had been in a different mindset, had greater insight or gained more experience. Is it possible that your interpretation of the situation or experience could have been different?

Activity 10

You are going to delve into and reprogram the stories attached to a past experience. Take one thing that triggers you, using your notes from the Stories and Triggers activity. Choose the one that has the most impact on your performance and behavior in the workplace. Ask yourself these questions.

Step 1 is to raise your awareness. Was there a specific moment in the past where this trigger originated from? If so, what story did you attach to that past experience? How is it impacting your life today?

Step 2 is to release and reprogram. Challenge that story. Is it entirely true? Can you state every single part of that story is accurate and true? What was happening for you at the time? Were you fully present or were you distracted? Did something in that moment trigger you? What could have been going on at the time for the other person? Who could have been influencing them? Was there anything else going on in your life that might have influenced how you experienced this situation?

Step 3 is to reconnect. What were you unaware of about the situation at the time? What have you learned about that experience since, whether through hindsight or external perspectives? How else could you view the experience you had? What other perspectives are there? What else could this experience mean to you? What other meaning could you attach to this that is more empowering for you?

Expectations

When expectations haven't been clarified or expressed, tensions occur. I will reiterate this key point many times because it is such a significant aspect in communication, team dynamics and collaboration. Expectations play a significant role in both your personal and professional life. In the workplace, expectations can have a major impact on your performance, relationships, job satisfaction and overall well-being.

You have different types of expectations that you carry with you every day. These expectations can be a source of anxiety and frustration, and can affect how you interact with your colleagues, approach your work and view yourself.

There are three types of expectations: the expectations you have of yourself, other people's expectations of you and the expectations you have of others. Understanding the three types of expectations can help you navigate the workplace more effectively, improve your relationships with colleagues and reduce stress and tension in your professional life. Let's look at each in turn.

Expectations of yourself. The main source of anxiety and frustration for people is the expectations they have of themselves. These are standards you have set for yourself, whether realistic or otherwise. Usually, the bar is high for the expectations you set for yourself.

Let me share an example with you. Quinn, an investment banker, openly acknowledges their strong perfectionist tendencies and extremely high standards when it comes to their work. They disclosed that they struggle with impostor syndrome, so they do everything they can to make sure they are fully prepared for anything that comes their way. This commitment to perfection drives Quinn to produce meticulously detailed financial analyses, aiming to impress both clients and colleagues.

However, Quinn went on to tell me about the challenges this brings. They are their own toughest critic, often resulting in late nights at the office, relentless revisions and a constant state of stress. The fear of making even the slightest mistake can be overwhelming at times. This self-imposed expectation of perfectionism impacts on them bringing their Authentic Self to work.

Quinn shared that during investment meetings or presentations, they often hesitate to share their financial strategies or ideas unless they are absolutely certain and prepared to present flawlessly. They fear that their colleagues will scrutinize any potential imperfections or question their expertise. They are reluctant to seek advice, help, support or collaborate openly, perceiving it as a vulnerability. They often take on an excessive workload, convinced that delegating tasks may result in outcomes that don't meet their expectations.

When I asked Quinn how they believe their colleagues perceive them, they mentioned that they think they are recognized as a highly skilled and detail-oriented investment banker; they are also seen as distant and reserved. They acknowledged that their relentless pursuit of perfection often hides the creative and authentic person behind the mask they present at work. They rarely share their challenges or even their unique personality traits with their team.

Quinn was trapped in a cycle where their own demanding expectations limited their ability to connect, collaborate and authentically express themselves in the workplace. Since my conversation with Quinn, I learned they reached breaking point, experiencing burnout that resulted in them taking a substantial period of time off work. As a result of this, they realized they could not continue to work in this way. Quinn has since been actively working on relaxing their demanding expectations and addressing their struggles with impostor syndrome.

Over to you. You are going to identify the expectations you have of yourself.

Activity 11

Step 1 is to raise your awareness. Think about the expectations you have set for yourself, both in your personal and professional life. Ask yourself, what standards have I set for myself for my work and relationships with colleagues? Write them down.

Step 2 is to release and reprogram. Take each expectation one at a time. Examine each expectation and ask yourself "Is this realistic? Would I expect the same from others?" Then, reflect on the impact these expectations are having on you. Are they influencing your performance and behavior at work? Your interactions with colleagues? Do they stop you from bringing your Authentic Self to work? If any seem unreasonable to you, ask "Why would I expect this from me but not from other people? What would I expect from other people?"

> Step 3 is to reconnect. It is time to relax your expectations. For those expectations you identified as not realistic, ask yourself "How can I relax the conditions I have placed around this to make it more achievable?"
>
> For instance, let's say you have the expectation that you will consistently work overtime to meet tight project deadlines. This means you work late into the evenings every day for months on end, even though you know this can lead to burnout and affect your work-life balance. It is time to relax the conditions you have placed around this. The aim is to meet the deadline, right? You may need to re-evaluate and adjust your approach. Your relaxed condition could be "I will commit to focusing on deadline-related tasks during regular working hours. For anything else that needs my attention, I will communicate with the people involved to manage their expectations effectively."
>
> What about a health-related expectation? If you have set a personal goal to exercise for 60 minutes 5 days a week but are struggling to keep up, relax the conditions you have placed around it. The aim is to regularly exercise, right? Your relaxed condition could be "I will exercise for at least 20 minutes 3–5 times per week."
>
> By re-evaluating and adjusting your expectations, you will experience work and life differently.

Other people's expectations. The next type of expectation that causes significant anxiety for people is what other people expect of you. Do you feel like people have expectations of you to be or perform in a certain way? Have you ever felt the weight of these perceived expectations from colleagues or peers? These expectations are often not voiced by the other person – but instead are assumptions you are making about what they expect of you. Often, these are not real. They are perceived expectations – what you think people expect of you. For example, your manager hasn't explicitly stated it, but you sense that they expect you to always be available for last-minute meetings and urgent tasks.

Over to you. Let's look at the unspoken expectations you think other people have of you.

Activity 12

Take a moment to reflect on what you believe is expected of you by your colleagues. How do these perceived expectations affect you? It's essential to recognize that these expectations may not be grounded in reality.

Now, challenge each one of these. Are they based on facts or assumptions? Have you sought clarification from the relevant people to confirm these expectations? Evaluate if you are comfortable with these perceived expectations. If not, take note of what actions you can take to address them. If any of the expectations are unfounded, let them go, freeing yourself from unnecessary burdens.

If you find yourself feeling anxious or frustrated due to these perceived expectations, ask for clarification from the relevant party. Refrain from making assumptions.

This proactive approach can help establish clear expectations from the start, reducing the potential for miscommunications and misunderstandings.

Expectations you have of others. The last type of expectation we carry is the unspoken set of expectations you hold for those around you: your partner, your kids, your parents and your colleagues. These are usually unspoken expectations you place on the other person to do (or not do something). You may recognize these unexpressed expectations when you catch yourself saying "Why is it always me that has to . . . [insert action here]?" or "I wish you wouldn't do that."

For example, consider this common workplace scenario. You expect your close colleagues to proactively share updates on the project you are collaborating on, without you having to explicitly ask. When they don't meet this unexpressed expectation, it often leads to frustration.

Let's shift the focus to you. Let's look at the expectations you have of other people.

Activity 13

Take a moment to identify situations in your workplace interactions that have caused tension or frustration. Name these situations and reflect on how they impacted you. Next, reflect on the expectations you had in those moments that you didn't express. Then, consider the general expectations you hold for others, which may be unconscious. Think about your colleagues, team members, managers, leaders, stakeholders and clients. Consider the standards to which you are holding them. Then, question if those standards are realistic, if you can relax those standards or release them entirely.

Releasing unrealistic expectations or overly demanding expectations you have set for others can bring more peace to your professional life. Keep in mind that everyone has their strengths and limitations. It is important to communicate clearly and establish realistic expectations to prevent misunderstandings and disappointment.

During moments of workplace tension or conflict, it can be helpful to take a step back and reflect on not only the expectations you have for yourself but also those you believe others have of you. Setting realistic expectations for yourself and engaging in open conversations with colleagues to understand their expectations is essential. Additionally, it is essential to communicate and discuss any expectations you have of others. Proactive and effective communication of expectations contributes to a workplace that is more harmonious and conducive to productivity, enabling individuals to bring their Authentic Self to work.

Pillar Highlight Summary

After delving into the Pillar Highlights, you will have a heightened awareness of the key elements significantly influencing an individual's performance and behavior in the workplace. These elements often stop people from bringing their Authentic Self into the workplace. The activities at the end of each Highlight will further your understanding of how these elements impact you personally in the workplace, providing you with valuable insights and setting in motion the releasing process.

Working through the three Dimensions and Pillar Highlights in-depth initiates a profound and lasting transformation, both in your professional and personal life. When you wholeheartedly commit to the Authentic Self Process, you unlock a range of benefits, including increased self-awareness and unwavering confidence. This heightened emotional intelligence enables you to identify and manage triggers and emotions in real time, resulting in reduced stress levels. You'll gain the ability to apply personal leadership strategies to navigate diverse workplace situations and enhance your adaptability to change, ultimately improving your capacity to overcome challenges. These qualities, combined with increased resilience, empower individuals to bring their Authentic Self to work, enabling them to thrive in any workplace scenario.

Next, you will find the Pillar 1 Pledges and questions for you to self-reflect on, providing you with the opportunity to assess what may hinder you from being your Authentic Self at work.

Pillar 1 Pledges and Self-Reflection Questions

For each Pillar, you will be introduced to Pledges. These are statements that we ask organizations to commit to. We ask you to commit to these pledges and discuss them regularly in team meetings. Here are the Pillar 1 Pledges and questions for self-reflection.

Pillar 1 Pledges

1. I manage my emotions when they arise.
2. I manage the thoughts I have that affect my performance and behavior at work.
3. I am aware of the things that trigger negative emotions, thoughts and behaviors for me at work and strive to manage these effectively.
4. I actively work on changing the way I think about my past experiences.
5. I know and manage how my conditioning and expectations impact on my relationships, teamwork and decisions at work.
6. I take responsibility for my behavior, actions and how they impact on other people at work.
7. I communicate and assert my personal boundaries at work, when necessary.

Pillar 1 Self-Reflection

To what extent do you agree with the following statements? Score yourself for each of the statements.

If you strongly disagree, score yourself 1 point. If you somewhat disagree, score yourself 2 points. If you neither agree nor disagree, score yourself 3 points. If you somewhat agree, score yourself 4 points. If you strongly agree, score yourself 5 points.

1. I am capable of effectively managing my emotions as they arise.
2. I can effectively manage thoughts that negatively affect my performance and behavior at work.
3. I have the ability to manage triggers for negative emotions, thoughts and behavior at work, ensuring they do not impact my work and relationships.
4. My past experiences (in other workplaces, socially or personally) do not significantly influence my performance and behavior at work.
5. I successfully manage how my conditioning and expectations impact my relationships, teamwork and decisions at work.
6. I take full responsibility for my behavior, actions and their impact on other people at work.
7. I effectively communicate and assert my personal boundaries at work when necessary.

Each of the statements refers to a Pillar 1 Pledge. If you score less than a 4 for any of these statements, revisit the relevant section(s) of Pillar 1. Anything under 5 means you have room for improvement. If you score less than a 3, make improvement a priority.

Summary

Pillar 1 is the bedrock of the 5 Pillars of Psychological Safety, forming the essential foundation for a thriving workplace. It's not rocket science. If you can't freely express your Authentic Self at work, your workplace lacks psychological safety. This safety is crucial for effective communication and collaboration with colleagues, cultivating an environment where everyone can thrive.

This pillar requires dedicated time and effort. Take the time, do the groundwork. It involves personal introspection and growth, both on an individual and collective level. Encouraging others to embark on this journey is equally important. With the Authentic Self Process at your fingertips, you have the tools to thrive in any workplace scenario.

Next up is Pillar 2. Let's delve into communication.

Note

1. For more information about the Psychological Safety Institute and our services, training programs and resources: www.thepsi.global

5

Pillar 2: Social

Pillar 2 is Social and focuses on mastering the intricate art of workplace communication. Building upon the transformative foundation laid by Pillar 1, Pillar 2 is exclusively dedicated to honing your communication skills. As you master the art of workplace communication through Pillar 2, you will not only build stronger relationships but also set the scene for seamless collaboration to thrive. Let's take a look at the Pillar 2 framework and methodology.

Pillar 2 Framework

First Principle: This is how I communicate effectively. This is the fundamental concept on which Pillar 2 is based.

Dimensions. Pillar 2 has three Dimensions, each offering a unique perspective. The Dimensions are how we explore and measure the First Principle from different angles and perspectives. In Pillar 2, individuals ask three questions. The three questions provide a practical approach for individuals to understand and apply the First Principle. Question 1 is "How can I make sure I communicate my message clearly and in the way I intend it to be received?" Question 2 is "How can I make sure I receive messages from other people in the way they were intended?" Question 3 is "How can I get the most out of my exchange of communication with colleagues?"

Pillar Highlights. Pillar 2 encompasses several Pillar Highlights, or key areas of focus within the Communication Cycle. The Pillar Highlights offer more detailed guidance within each Dimension to help individuals delve deeper into understanding and applying the First Principle.

We will explore these in detail in the Pillar Highlights section later.

As you engage with Pillar 2, you will acquire the necessary skills to implement all aspects of the Communication Cycle. You will be able to adjust your communication based on feedback and have a toolkit of dynamic and powerful communication strategies at your disposal to tackle any workplace scenario.

By mastering the communication strategies in the Communication Cycle, you will enhance and nurture your relationships in the workplace, enabling you to connect more effectively with colleagues, clients and stakeholders. From delivering a compelling pitch to navigating a difficult negotiation, the tools and techniques you learn in the Communication Cycle will empower you to communicate with unwavering confidence and crystal-clear clarity.

Pillar 2 is the one where individuals master workplace communication. It transforms individual interpersonal skills and relationships and helps build social capital in the workplace. It addresses a fundamental gap in our education system by focusing on the soft skills we often lack in navigating interpersonal dynamics, resolving misunderstandings, managing conflicts and effectively asserting our ideas in professional settings. These skills are not just valuable, they are essential. Just as Pillar 1 empowers individuals to thrive, Pillar 2 equips us to build stronger, more meaningful connections in the workplace and beyond. Through the Communication Cycle and the insights gained within this pillar, you'll possess the tools to bridge the gap between intention and interpretation, cultivating a collaborative and productive environment for everyone.

Pillar 2 Methodology: The Communication Cycle

The Communication Cycle is at the core of Pillar 2, providing a comprehensive framework designed to empower individuals to master effective workplace communication. It provides a structured approach to enhance your ability to connect, collaborate and convey ideas with unwavering confidence and crystal-clear clarity.

Engaging with the Communication Cycle immerses you in a profound understanding of the key elements that drive successful workplace communication. Whether you are striving to deliver impactful messages, actively receiving feedback or facilitating seamless conversations, the Communication Cycle equips you with the essential skills and strategies to navigate any communication scenario.

The Communication Cycle consists of three elements, as shown in Figure 5.1: *communicating* your message, *receiving* a message and the *exchange* itself. These three elements directly influence and impact the success of your communication efforts.

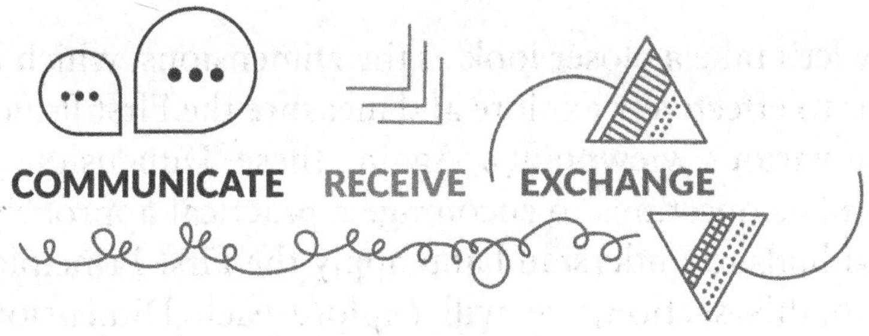

Figure 5.1 The Communication Cycle

The first element of the Communication Cycle is known as "Communicate" and aligns with the Dimension "How can I make sure I communicate my message clearly and in the way I intend it to be received?" In Communicate, individuals focus on the "Sender to Receiver" process to ensure the clarity and intention of their messaging.

The second element of the Communication Cycle is known as "Receive" and is intricately tied to the Dimension "How can I make sure I receive messages from other people in the way they were intended?" In Receive, individuals shift their perspective to "Receiver to Sender" to ensure accurate interpretation of a message.

The third element of the Communication Cycle is known as "Exchange" and is associated with the Dimension "How can I get the most out of my exchange of communication with colleagues?" In Exchange, individuals shift their focus to "Navigating Interactions with Colleagues" exploring the various factors that impact their interactions and conversations with colleagues.

Pillar 2 Dimensions: Deep Dive

Now let's take a closer look at the Dimensions, which enable us to effectively explore and measure the First Principle from various viewpoints. Again, these Dimensions are framed as questions to encourage a practical approach for individuals to understand and apply the First Principle.

In this section, we will explore each Dimension in turn, with a brief explanation. We will then uncover the key components that are integral to each Dimension, known as "Pillar Highlights." In the next section, you will explore each of the Pillar Highlights in detail, within the context of the Communication Cycle.

Dimension 1: Communicate

The first Dimension prompts us to ask "How can I make sure I communicate my message clearly and in the way I intend it to be received?"

Drawing on the insights gathered from our global study, 62 percent of employees stated they felt confident that their messages were received as they were intended, when communicating with their team members and 38 percent of employees stated they were unsure this message had been received in the right way. Think about that. Over a third of your people are not sure they are being understood correctly. What impact do you think that has on individuals, teams and the organization, not to mention productivity, creativity and innovation?

When asked if they have the confidence, ability and resilience to express their feelings, needs and concerns with their colleagues, 38 percent of employees stated they do not. Again, over a third of your people are not confident, and therefore don't express their feelings, needs and concerns. Can you imagine what impact that is having?

Let's think about the elements that you need to be aware of when communicating a message. Key considerations include verbal and non-verbal communication cues, the language you use, the clarity of the message, your method of transmission and making sure the other person received the message in the way you intended. We will explore these in the Pillar Highlights.

Dimension 2: Receive

The second Dimension prompts us to ask "How can I make sure I receive messages from other people in the way they were intended?"

Several elements influence how you receive messages from others and whether you grasp their intended meaning. Reflect on your most recent conversation with a colleague. During this interaction, various factors came into play. These factors affected how you interpretated and decoded the message and impacted on your ability to stay present in the conversation, your inclination to seek clarification, your practice of non-judgmental and active listening and your observation of the other person's verbal and non-verbal communication cues. Together, these factors either support or hinder you in the process of interpreting the message being conveyed to you. We will explore these in more detail in the Pillar Highlights.

Dimension 3: Exchange

The third Dimension prompts us to ask "How can I get the most out of my exchange of communication with colleagues?"

Reflect on a recent conversation you have had and you will notice a sequence of events. It typically starts with an opening (icebreaker and small talk), followed by turn-taking, occasions of overlapping speech, possibly interruptions as you tried to interject a key point, shifts in topics and ultimately ends with the closing of the conversation.

Conversation involves many different skills, including active listening, asking questions, sharing information, asserting your viewpoint, proposing new ideas, summarizing your understanding, building upon ideas, respectfully disagreeing, offering support, introducing new thoughts and perspectives, ensuring everyone is included in the conversation and moving things forward.

In Exchange, individuals are encouraged to consider their communication exchanges and focus on specific aspects, such as responding rather than reacting, code-switching, managing emotional triggers, initiating conversations, regulating turn-taking, effectively closing a conversation, confidently asserting their ideas, navigating interruptions, handling disagreements, addressing conflicts, recognizing microaggressions, challenging someone and reconciling conflicts between personal and company values. You will learn more about navigating exchanges effectively in the Pillar Highlights.

To illustrate the extent of the issue individuals have with communicating effectively in the workplace, here are more results from the global study we conducted. An alarming 34 percent of employees reported that they struggle to successfully navigate miscommunications, misunderstandings and conflict with their colleagues. This represents just over a third of your workforce. They feel they don't have the skills to deal with these situations.

When asked if they ruminate and stew over things that happened at work when they are at home, a staggering 87 percent of employees admitted to doing so, with 92 percent acknowledging that this negatively impacts both them and their loved ones. What happens at work is directly impacting their personal lives. Consider the potential toll on individuals' physical and mental health, their overall well-being, their willingness to bring their Authentic Self to work and the repercussions for workplace relationships, team dynamics and collaboration.

Pillar 2 Highlights

The Dimensions enable us to effectively explore and measure the First Principle from various perspectives. The Pillar Highlights offer more detailed guidance, encouraging a deeper understanding and practical application of the First Principle.

In this overview, we will cover the basics. We have a comprehensive suite of activities and questions related to the Communication Cycle that can be accessed through our live training sessions, the Psychological Safety Toolkit, Authentic Self Journal, e-learning programs and retreats. More information about our resources can be found on our website, details of which can be found in the endnotes.[1]

Let's delve into the Pillar Highlights in detail. We will take a deep dive into the key elements that significantly influence communication in the workplace, using the Communication Cycle as the framework.

Communicate

In this section, we will delve into important considerations to ensure that your message is communicated clearly. One of the most common pitfalls in communication is when individuals deliver their message but don't check in with the other person to make sure it has been received as intended. This is where most misunderstandings occur.

Let's start with a scenario. In a team meeting to review the progress of an ongoing project, four colleagues (A, B, C and D) gather around a conference table. Unfortunately, A is feeling frustrated because of several setbacks in the project. A has a slouched posture, crossed arms, frequently lets out deep sighs, frowns throughout the meeting and is noted doing the occasional eyeroll. A says things like "I can't believe this project is still dragging on. It's taking forever and it seems like no one is on top of things."

B leans forward throughout the meeting, nodding and smiling and frequently offering verbal sounds like "yes" and "ah" signaling active listening. C looks relaxed and has open body language, smiles and makes eye contact with everyone. D sits upright with open body language, nodding frequently and has a friendly expression throughout.

So, what have we got going on here? There are a few verbal cues in the conversation, with A exhibiting negative cues and the other three individuals exhibiting positive cues.

Let's not forget that verbal communication cues encompass more than just the actual words you use. It is important to recognize there are other factors at play here that can influence how your message is received. You may have come across the saying "It's not what you say, it's how you say it." The content of your message is important, but most important is the way in which you convey it, along with the non-verbal cues you exhibit. How you speak can tell the listener many things. In the 1970s, psychologist Albert Mehrabian suggested that communication is formed from 55 percent non-verbal cues, 38 percent vocal cues and only 7 percent the actual words you use.

Let's look at the various **verbal cues** to be mindful of during conversations. Pay close attention to your pace when speaking, as well as your volume, tone and filler sounds which indicate that you are thinking or understand, such as erm, um, uh-huh, ahh, yes, no. Be aware of how you use pauses and silence. Think about the rhythm (speed and flow), pitch and intonation, making sure you vary it to avoid sounding monotone. You might want to put emphasis on specific words to highlight key points and be aware of repetition and rephrasing, which help the other person to understand the key points to your message.

I like to think of verbal cues in a conversation as a musical score. Imagine a sheet of music with all the musical notation on it. It has many elements contained within those sheets, not just the musical notes to play. When you listen to that great piece of music (think classical) you can hear all those aspects mentioned earlier at play: pace, volume, tone, filler sounds, pauses and silence, rhythm, pitch, intonation, emphasis on certain notes or phrases, repetition and rephrasing.

Let's look at each of these in relation to a musical score. The tempo of a piece of music sets the mood. Your speaking **pace** does the same thing. Your pace can express urgency, excitement or calmness. A fast pace is likely to express enthusiasm, while a slower one may indicate thoughtfulness or hesitation.

The **volume** of your voice can mirror the crescendos and diminuendos in music. Speaking loudly can express a strong sense of conviction, whereas a softer tone may indicate a sense of intimacy or vulnerability.

Your **tone** is like the timbre of musical instruments. Think of it like the unique quality and character of the sound of your voice. Tone carries the emotional nuances of your words. A warm, inviting tone can create a harmonious atmosphere, whereas a harsh tone may bring about a sense of disharmony or conflict.

Filler sounds are like pauses and rests in music, indicating moments of reflection or transition. They can express understanding, hesitation or contemplation.

Like rests in the music, strategic **pauses** and **silence** can add depth to your message. They provide the listener with time to absorb and reflect on what you've said.

The **rhythm** of your speech reflects the ebb and flow of a conversation. It can convey a sense of engagement and connection, similar to the rhythmic patterns in music.

Pitch and **intonation** resemble the melodic aspects of music. Varying pitch and intonation can infuse your words with emotion and emphasis, preventing your speech from becoming monotonous.

Just as a musician may accentuate certain notes or phrases, **emphasizing** specific words or phrases can highlight key points or emotions in your message.

Repetition and **rephrasing** are like recurring themes in music. They can reinforce key ideas and help ensure understanding.

All these elements are present in the musical score. For a beginner musician, they may simply play the notes they see, but a more advanced musician will read the other elements, interpret them and make the song their own.

By tuning into these verbal cues, much like a musician interpreting a musical score, you can gain valuable insights into a person's intention, emotions and the nuances of their communication.

What about **non-verbal communication cues**? You were introduced to a few in the scenario with A, B, C and D earlier. Re-read it and see if you can identify all the non-verbal cues.

Understanding non-verbal communication cues, such as body language, facial expressions, gestures, posture, body movement, eye contact, physical contact and personal space, is essential in ensuring you get the message across to someone as you intended. Let's look at each of these briefly.

Body language is the use of expressions, gestures, mannerisms and physical behaviors, often being instinctive rather than conscious. Remember that B, C and D all displayed positive body language – leaning forward, maintaining an open posture and engaging in direct eye contact. A, on the other hand, exhibited closed body language, with crossed arms and a slouched posture. What do you deduce about these individuals and their attitude from their body language?

Facial expressions allow you to convey emotions without uttering a single word. In a performance review, an employee smiles when discussing their accomplishments on a particular project. This indicates they really enjoyed the work they did and have pride in their achievements. In the earlier scenario, A frowned and occasionally rolled their eyes, while B, C and D were smiling and had welcoming expressions. What do these expressions reveal about them? Paying attention to facial expressions can offer valuable insights during conversations.

Gestures. Common gestures include pointing, waving, using your hands when talking, thumbs up/down and beckoning someone to come toward you. Be aware that not all hand gestures mean the same thing around the world. Imagine you are on a multinational video call when one of your colleagues from the United States gives a thumbs-up gesture to signal agreement with a proposal. However, a colleague from a different country (Afghanistan, Iran, parts of Italy and Greece) interprets this thumbs-up as a rude gesture, causing a misunderstanding that requires intervention.

Posture. How people sit, stand, walk or hold their head affects perceptions. In an idea generation session, one team member slouches in their chair, avoiding eye contact. Another team member actively participates with an upright posture, maintaining eye contact and nodding in agreement. These contrasting postures impact how their input is received by the group, influencing the dynamics of the discussion.

Eye contact. This is an especially important type of non-verbal communication. The way you look at someone can communicate a multitude of things. It also helps you to gauge interest and response in the conversation, as well as helping to maintain the flow of conversation. Be aware that not everyone is comfortable with maintaining eye contact, such as some neurodiverse individuals, those with a history of trauma or PTSD or social anxiety, introverted individuals and those with a lack of confidence.

Physical contact. You can communicate so much through physical contact. Consider how you feel when you experience the following situations. A weak handshake versus a confident handshake, a reassuring hand on a shoulder versus a controlling grip on the arm, a warm compassionate hug versus a hug that holds you at a distance. Quick hand-to-hand contact (such as handshaking, fist bumping, high-five) or a light tap on the shoulder to attract attention is generally acceptable in the workplace. Think "quick." Extended or inappropriate contact can lead to discomfort, feelings of unsafety or even harassment concerns.

Personal space. The amount of personal space you feel you need depends on several aspects, such as the situation, the person you are speaking with, how comfortable and safe you feel with the person, the environment you are in and the culture. Be aware of personal space when speaking with your colleagues. Imagine you are in a crowded meeting room and you see a team member instinctively take a step back when engaging in a conversation with a colleague they know is sensitive about personal space. This minor adjustment helps maintain a comfortable interaction despite the limited physical distance.

We have explored verbal and non-verbal cues. Let's delve into the words you use now. **Language** and the use of it is a powerful tool. It reflects and influences attitudes, behaviors and perceptions.

You may have heard the term "inclusive language." In essence, inclusive language is language that strives not to exclude anyone. It avoids expressions that may imply or express sexism, racism, homophobia, transphobia, ageism, ableism or any other form of bias, prejudice or insult toward anyone. Inclusive language recognizes and respects diversity, remains sensitive to differences and encourages everyone to bring their Authentic Self into the workplace, if they choose to do so.

Let me give you some examples of conversations that use exclusive language. See if you can see the issue within these examples.

Example 1. At an event, the host introduces a speaker named Jordan:

Host: "Ladies and gentlemen, it's my pleasure to welcome our next speaker. He has an impressive background in the field, and we're thrilled to have him share his insights with us today."

Did you see the issues? In this introduction, the host mistakenly used "he" and "him" pronouns for Jordan, making an assumption based on their name and unintentionally misgendering the speaker. Jordan actually uses "she/her" pronouns. The phrase "Ladies and gentlemen" is binary, excluding non-binary, genderqueer and gender-nonconforming individuals who may not identify as "ladies" or "gentlemen." Using this phrase can inadvertently make some people feel marginalized or invisible. Also bear in mind that not everyone identifies with the gender traditionally associated with their biological sex. Addressing them as "ladies and gentlemen" may not align with their gender identity and can be considered disrespectful or invalidating. Lastly, in some cultures, the use of gender-specific language is considered either less suitable or not the norm, making "ladies and gentlemen" culturally inappropriate in those settings.

To address these concerns, many modern events and organizations are shifting toward more inclusive language. This means avoiding gendered language and striving to use gender-neutral terms. For example, use "they/them" pronouns when you don't know a person's gender instead of defaulting to "he/him." When referring to a collective group, use terms like "everyone," "colleagues," "team" or "people."

Example 2. A new member of staff has just joined your team. Your manager is introducing them:

"Everyone, I'd like to introduce our new team member. She's a fantastic addition to our team and brings a unique perspective, but I thought you should know that she suffers from a hearing impairment."

Did you spot the issue here? In this example, the phrase "suffers from a hearing impairment" uses exclusive language tied to ableism. It implies that the team member is a victim of her condition rather than highlighting her abilities and skills. A more inclusive introduction would be "Everyone, I'd like to introduce our new team member. She's a fantastic addition to our team and brings a unique perspective. She has a hearing impairment so this is how she prefers to communicate . . ." This focuses on her abilities and contributions rather than focusing on her circumstances.

There are many other common examples of ableist language, which can be identified by words or phrases that devalue individuals with disabilities or use disability as an insult or expression. Phrases like "that idea is crazy" and "it fell on deaf ears" are other examples of ableist language. Strive to focus on people, not circumstances.

In the examples above, you have seen instances of exclusive language related to gender and ableism. Now, let's explore other phrases and words that can be exclusive.

When it comes to race, exclusive language includes terms like "mixed race," "black" (note that the "b" is uncapitalized), "Indians," "Eskimo" and "Aboriginal." Phrases such as "master bedroom," "nitty gritty," "no can do" and "hip hip hooray" can also be exclusive. Have you ever noticed the use of "black" to denote something negative? Think about "black sheep," "blackmail," "black market" and "blacklist." Instead, choose inclusive language such as "biracial," "multiracial," "Black" (note the "b" is capitalized), "BIPOC" (Black, Indigenous and People of Color), "First Nations," "First Nations People" and "Inuit." For phrases, choose inclusive alternatives such as "leader/follower" or "primary/replica," "the basics" or "the essence," "I can't do that" or "it's not possible" and "bravo" or "congratulations." Lastly, rather than using "blacklist," choose "allow list" and "block/deny list."

Exclusive LGBTQ+ language includes words and phrases such as "Ms.," "Mr.," "Mrs.," "maternity and paternity leave," "husband," "wife," "boyfriend," "girlfriend," "what are your preferred pronouns?," "transgendered" and "a gay/transgender." To be more inclusive consider using words and phrases such as "parental leave," "parental time off," "partner," "spouse" and "what pronouns do you use?" You can use first names instead of titles or opt for non-gender specific titles like "Mx" and "M." Also, use "a gay/transgender person" and "trans," "transgender" or "transgender people."

These are just a few examples of common workplace language that can inadvertently exclude individuals. There are other areas, such as age, where exclusion can happen.

Here are some general guidelines to follow. Strive to avoid words or phrases that carry biases, use slang or expressions that discriminate against specific groups of people. Avoid generalizations about individuals, cultures, countries or regions. Avoid idioms, metaphors, jargon, acronyms or cultural phrases with negative historical connotations. For example, phrases like "hit it out of the park" and "throw a spanner in the works" can hinder effective communication and make people feel confused, excluded or uncomfortable. If you have questions for your colleagues, consider the impact these might have before you ask them. Reflect on how your questions might affect the person you are addressing. Ask yourself, "would I appreciate it if someone asked me that question?" Would you ask your colleagues the same question? As a general rule, if you would not ask your Grandma, it's best not to ask your colleague!

Let us now consider the **clarity of a message** and how it is delivered. Imagine this scenario. In response to evolving work dynamics, the HR department decided to amend the company's remote working policy to provide employees with more flexibility. They chose to communicate these changes through a memo.

The memo was filled with complex legal jargon and vague terminology. For example, it stated, "Pursuant to a reassessment of our work modalities, the telecommuting policy shall be subject to a phased transitional approach, encompassing eligibility criteria . . ."

What do you think the issues are with this memo? Firstly, the memo used complex and unclear language. It failed to explain the meaning of the "phased transitional approach" or specify the eligibility criteria for remote working. Imagine that it continued without giving clear examples or guidelines for employees to follow. So, what happened as a result of receiving this memo? Employees were left confused and uncertain about how the changes could affect their ability to work remotely and what steps they needed to take to qualify. The choice of a memo may not have been the most effective way to get that message across.

Vague or unclear language can be not only frustrating but also detrimental to effective communication. Think about when you were in a meeting and a message lacked clarity. It can create distance, confusion and tension between the people who are trying to communicate. Specificity is the key to overcoming these challenges. When you communicate with clarity and precision, you remove ambiguity. Being specific means using clear and straightforward language when you are communicating.

So how can you ensure your message is delivered clearly? Firstly, use simple language to ensure your communication is received and understood as intended. Avoid complex language, including idioms and metaphors. Don't use big, complicated words if you can say it simply. Secondly, consider the appropriate form of language for the specific setting and audience, often referred to as "register." Imagine you are talking with an older member of your family. You are likely to use a formal register, addressing them politely, whereas when you talk with your friends, you are likely to use an informal register, with relaxed, casual language. Thirdly, avoid using jargon or acronyms. Some people may not know what they mean and feel uncomfortable asking for clarification. Fourthly, minimize the use of verbs such as "could" or "might" as non-native speakers may misinterpret or become confused by their meanings, leading to further confusion. Also, take into account the other person's fluency in the language you are using for communication. If they are not fluent, be patient and make your requests using direct language. Lastly, if you are uncertain whether your message has been understood, consider asking the person to reflect back what they heard. This ensures that your message has been interpreted as intended.

Was the choice of a memo to convey this policy change to the entire workforce the most appropriate method? Could there have been a more effective way to communicate this message? What approach would you have taken in this instance?

Keep in mind that there are many **methods** to transmit a message to someone, including through telephone calls, video calls, emails, reports or instant messages.

Before you communicate a message, take a moment to assess your options and determine the best way to convey it effectively. Take yourself through this checklist and ask yourself these questions. How urgent is my message? Do I need immediate feedback from the people involved? Do I need a documented record of the communication? If I send an email, is it important that I follow that up with verbal communication? Does any part of the message contain complicated, controversial or private information? Is the message intended for internal or external recipients to the organization?

Now, consider the people you are communicating with. What are their levels of oral and written communication skills? What is their first language? In which language are they most comfortable communicating? What are their personal communication preferences when interacting with you?

Take these factors into account before communicating with someone. This will help you to select the most appropriate channel to effectively convey your message.

Now let's focus on a crucial aspect that often poses challenges for many people. Did the other person **receive your message** as intended? Successful communication hinges on the receiver accurately interpreting your message. The extent to which they understand your message is influenced by various factors, including their comfort level, knowledge about the subject, receptivity to the message, the nature of their relationship and the level of psychological safety they feel with you.

Frequently, in conversations, we are in a hurry and tend to assume that our message has landed as we intended, quickly moving on to the next topic. When we communicate in this way, we are less likely to notice that someone has been triggered or if there has been any misinterpretation. It's important not to make assumptions. How the person responds will give you valuable insights into how they interpreted and received your message. Pay attention to verbal and non-verbal communication cues. Without this feedback, you will not know if your message landed in the way you intended it to.

If your message hasn't been received as you intended, you have the opportunity to take corrective action by clarifying any misunderstandings. This can be initiated by asking the other person to reflect back what they understood. Listen attentively to their response and then clarify any points that have been missed or misunderstood.

If you don't receive any feedback or their feedback appears to conflict with their body language, consider asking them to clarify what they heard. This opens up the space for you to address any potential miscommunication and ensure your message was received in the way you intended.

Receive

Similar to Communicate, there are a number of factors that influence how you receive and interpret a message. In this section, we will delve into key aspects to consider to ensure you receive a message as it was intended before exploring strategies you can employ to enhance your ability to interpret messages accurately.

Let's begin with a scenario. A manager is having a one-on-one conversation with their team member, PJ. The purpose of this meeting is to discuss the progress of a project and address some concerns. However, PJ had a challenging morning. An unresolved argument with their partner at home has left them feeling emotional and confused. There is ongoing construction work outside the office building, causing loud noise, and the busy traffic outside is adding to the distraction.

As the conversation progresses, the manager shares some feedback on PJ's recent work but PJ is finding it hard to focus due to their emotional state and the external distractions. At one point the manager mentions the need for PJ to take on additional responsibilities for the project, which triggers PJ's stress further, as they were already feeling overwhelmed. Struggling to concentrate and feeling triggered by the discussion about extra workload, they nod and give vague responses, unable to fully engage in the conversation.

Do you think PJ received the messages the manager was attempting to get across? In this scenario, several factors influence PJ's interpretation of the manager's messages, making it challenging for them to receive the intended messages.

Your interpretation of messages is influenced by many factors, including your past experiences, state of mind, attitude, knowledge, skills, perceptions, culture, social conditioning, thoughts, triggers, personal agenda, physical environment, the presence of others and noise. Many of these factors were explored in Pillar 1. In this section, we will delve into your state of mind, noise and your listening filters before discussing strategies to help you interpret messages as intended.

State of mind is a crucial factor. PJ's state of mind in the scenario wasn't optimal due to an unresolved argument at home. When you are not in the right headspace, feeling anxious, agitated, frustrated, sad, angry or depressed, or if you feel tired, stressed or overwhelmed, you are less likely to receive messages in the way they were intended.

When you are receiving a message, ask yourself "Am I in the most appropriate frame of mind to receive this message?" Consider not only your physical environment but also your mental state at that moment. Be aware of your emotions and take appropriate actions. This may involve self-care before, during or after a meeting or asking the person to reschedule the meeting or reconvene after you have had time to reflect on the conversation.

Noise can significantly interfere with how you interpret the messages you hear. Noise manifests in various forms, both external and internal. External noises are those present in your physical environment, while internal noises originate from within.

External noises can be categorized into three main types: background sounds, external environmental sounds and immediate vicinity sounds. Background sounds include distractions like the TV, radio, conversations of others, ringing phones and moving chairs. External environmental sounds include traffic, weather conditions, construction work and machinery. Immediate vicinity sounds involve disturbances like pets making noise or moving around, someone attempting to join your conversation and notifications from mobile devices.

Internal noises incorporate factors such as your thoughts and emotional triggers that can disrupt your listening or lead you to interpret messages through personal filters. Your personal agenda may also affect how you perceive the message as you may attempt to steer the conversation toward a specific outcome. Your relationship with the individuals present during the delivery of the message plays a role, especially if you do not feel comfortable or safe while listening to the message. Lastly, your mental state of mind contributes to internal noise, especially if it is not conducive to active listening.

Listening filters play a crucial role in influencing what you hear, often causing you to misinterpret and internalize messages differently from their original intent. To identify your specific listening filters, try this:

1. Describe your job or something that you have enjoyed doing. This will help you to identify your *size filter* – whether you tend to focus on details (a detail person) or see the big picture (a big picture person).
2. Reflect on a time when you have achieved success. What did it feel like? Pay attention to the words you use to describe that feeling. This will help you to identify your *movement filter*. Are you motivated by moving toward goals or away from certain situations?
3. Consider what led you to choose your current career or work style. This will help you to identify your *involvement filter* – whether you prefer association or disassociation with particular aspects of your work.
4. What aspects of your work are the most important to you? This will give you an indication of your *timing filter* and will offer insights into whether you prioritize past, present or future.
5. Lastly, reflect on whether you prefer to follow steps and procedures when solving problems or making decisions, or if you are more inclined to explore options and possibilities before reaching a conclusion. This will help you to identify your *procedures and options filter*.

Now, we are going to explore strategies to enhance your ability to interpret messages as they were intended. We will explore presence, clarifying and listening.

Presence is a key aspect that we identified in Pillar 1, signifying a strong connection to your Authentic Self. Let's explore three real-life examples of presence in action.

Example 1. You are attending the annual conference when you see a colleague you know from another team across the room. Keen to catch up, you approach them and start talking, but you notice that they seem distracted. They are not fully present in the conversation. They keep glancing over your shoulder, more interested in the new people entering the room than in your conversation. Their responses are short and disconnected as though they are only half-listening to what you're saying. You have something really important you want to get an update on from them but realize that your colleague's focus isn't on the conversation, so you hold off on asking for the update.

Example 2. Picture yourself in a team meeting where a guest from another team unexpectedly joins. Your manager requests everyone to introduce themselves and provide a brief project update from their perspective. Caught off guard, you begin mentally crafting your own contribution. As a result, you unintentionally tune out during your colleagues' introductions and progress updates. When it's your turn to speak, you realize you've missed vital information that directly impacts an aspect of your current work.

Example 3. Next, imagine you are in a debate about the best solution to an issue your team is facing. During the discussion, one of your team members presents an idea with which you disagree. Instead of actively listening to their idea and its details, you find yourself mentally crafting a counterargument while they are still explaining their proposal. You are "Gap Listening," where you are listening for the gap when the person finishes speaking so you can jump in and tell them why their idea won't work. However, in doing so, you may miss the crucial point where they address your concerns while explaining their proposal.

Here are a few ideas on how to stay present in a conversation. When someone talks to you, completely stop what you are doing and give them your full attention. Turn down all distractions, including background noise. Focus your eyes, ears, energy and intention on the person you are with. Listen attentively, tuning into their energy, emotions and unspoken words. Get fully absorbed in your interaction with that person. Be curious and ask questions. Reframe what you heard to make sure you understand correctly and be in the conversation to serve them, to help them. Pay attention to your emotions. If you are triggered, respond appropriately right there by asking for clarification. This helps resolve conflicts and ensures you have not misunderstood the message. You could also create an anchor. When you notice your mind has drifted off, use a physical gesture like touching your watch, bracelet, your nose or something in your pocket to bring your attention back to the present moment. When you give your full attention to people in conversations, you emotionally connect with them and create an environment where you can both thrive.

I have mentioned a few times that tension often arises from mishearing, misinterpreting or unclear expectations. To ensure you grasp a message as intended, it is important to **clarify** you have heard what the speaker intended.

Asking questions is a valuable approach, but the type of question you ask depends on your goal. Here are different question types tailored to specific outcomes.

Clarification, if you need to better understand the message, you might ask "what makes you say that?," "what do you mean by . . .?," "could you give me an example?" and "can you explain this further?"

If you want to challenge assumptions, you might ask "what are you assuming?," "how can you verify or disprove these assumptions?" and "are there alternative assumptions to consider?"

If you are unsure about the question that was asked, you can seek clarification with "could you explain the purpose of this question?" and "do we all agree this is the question we need to answer?"

If you want to probe reasons and evidence, you might ask "what do you think causes . . . to happen? Why?," "what leads you to believe this?," "what other information do we need to gather?," "how does this evidence apply to this case?" and "is there a reason to doubt the evidence?"

To question viewpoints and perspectives, you might ask "what alternative viewpoints exist?," "what are the strengths and limitations of each perspective?" and "if we adopt this perspective, what else could arise?"

To probe implications and consequences, you might ask "what are the potential consequences of this assumption?," "how does this impact other aspects?" and "is this the most important question, or is there an underlying issue we should address?"

Don't be afraid to ask questions. Strategically using these question types can cultivate clear and meaningful communication, reducing misunderstandings and tensions in the workplace.

Complementing the act of clarifying what you hear through questions is the art of **listening**. You may be familiar with the wisdom on the Greek philosopher, Epictetus, who said "We have two ears and one mouth so that we can listen twice as much as we speak."

Listening is undeniably a critical skill in the workplace, yet it is not commonly taught within our educational system. Let's delve into some key principles of effective listening.

Non-judgmental listening involves listening without passing judgment and having the ability to separate your personal feelings on a subject when listening. By practicing non-judgmental listening, you can fully grasp someone and their experiences, free from the distractions or biases of your own experiences, thoughts and personal agenda. This form of listening creates a safe space where the speaker feels comfortable to bring their Authentic Self to the conversation and can openly share their experiences.

Active listening is just that – active. When actively listening, you make a conscious effort to hear not just the words that are spoken, but the complete message that is being communicated. Often in conversation what people say does not capture the full picture. Active listening requires attentive listening, understanding both the explicit and implicit aspects of what the other person is communicating and responding thoughtfully to what you've picked up from the conversation.

To practice non-judgmental active listening, begin by reflecting on your current state of mind. Are you in a good head space to listen? Is something bothering you or have you had a recent negative experience that could affect your ability to listen effectively?

Use verbal cues to show you are listening, including acknowledging you have heard the speaker, summarizing their points and repeating back what you understood. This shows you are attentive and engaged in the conversation.

Use non-verbal cues, such as maintaining positive body language, making eye contact, respecting personal space, and using facial expressions and appropriate gestures.

Empathize with the speaker without the need to agree or share your own experiences. Avoid interrupting and allow them to express themselves. Actively listen and let them know you are there to offer help and support.

Be mindful of cultural differences when engaging in conversations with individuals whose ethnicity or cultural experience may differ from your own. Remember certain verbal and non-verbal cues, such as eye contact, gestures and personal space, can communicate different things. If you are unsure, ask the person you are speaking with about their preferred communication norms and comfort levels.

Incorporate techniques like paraphrasing to validate and clarify the information you've received. This involves restating what you've heard in your own words. You can use phrases like "so, am I right in thinking . . .?" or "from what you've shared, it seems . . ." or "what I am hearing is . . ."

To gain further clarity and understanding, you can use phrases like "tell me more about . . .", "how did you feel when . . .?" and "what do you mean when you say . . .?"

If you sense that the individual is not sharing something with you, either consciously or subconsciously, and you are noticing something coming to the surface, you can gently express your observation by saying "I don't know where this is coming from and it may not be relevant but I sense that . . ."

When you notice that the individual might be feeling lost or overwhelmed, offering reassuring questions or comments in a calm and supportive manner can be beneficial, such as "take your time," "tell me your thoughts," "would you like me to repeat the question?" or "would it help if I reworded the question?"

It's also helpful to have a phrase ready that redirects your focus back to the individual when you find your attention drifting away, such as "stop, this isn't my issue" or "concentrate on the person." This will refocus your attention on the individual when you feel your mind wandering.

Maintain an open-minded approach, aiming to uncover the core of their message while being attuned to both verbal and non-verbal cues, in addition to their actual words.

Exchange

In our global study, when participants were asked, "Which one of these do you struggle with the most?," 45 percent indicated they had the most difficulty with the exchange of communication, followed by 30 percent facing challenges when communicating a message and 25 percent struggling with receiving a message.

It is not surprising that Exchange is the aspect people struggle with the most; a conversation involves a number of dynamic and interconnected factors. In this section, we will delve into two key areas. First, we will explore the essential aspects to consider in a conversation. Then, we will discuss strategies to enhance your conversations and improve the effectiveness of the exchange.

Let's begin by exploring three basic constructs of a conversation: opening a conversation, turn-taking and closing a conversation.

Opening a conversation often involves the use of small talk. Imagine meeting someone for the first time at a conference while waiting in the lunch queue. In these first few minutes of conversation, diving into the complexities of your work, family life or hobbies is highly unlikely. Instead, you're likely to engage in small talk, which is a social skill used as an opener or icebreaker. Small talk isn't about sharing ideas or information; it's about finding common ground and building rapport with others.

Imagine you have met someone for the first time at a conference. What topics come up in those first few minutes of conversation? Typically, you might discuss how your day is going, the weather, current events, something in your shared environment or even a recent TV show. If you see someone you know at the conference, your small talk might delve a bit deeper into topics such as food, hobbies, family, work projects or updates about your work role.

It's important to recognize that we all have different personalities, preferences and work styles. Some people enjoy small talk, while others may find it less appealing. Some individuals are comfortable discussing their personal lives, while others prefer keeping conversations strictly professional. Some colleagues are introverted, while others are extroverted, and this influences their willingness to engage in small talk.

During meetings, you may notice varying approaches among your colleagues. Some may arrive early and actively participate in small talk before the meeting starts. Others might arrive early but refrain from engaging in small talk, or they may arrive on time or slightly late to avoid having to engage in extensive small talk. Keep in mind that not everyone will feel at ease with lengthy small talk, with some individuals preferring to keep this to a minimum, beginning meetings promptly.

Next, let's discuss **turn-taking.** In simple terms, turn-taking involves one person listening while the other person speaks, and as the conversation progresses, these roles are flipped back and forth. It's a basic rhythm of communication. Inclusive turn-taking is when different team members speak one after the other, cultivating a collaborative dialogue. Exclusive turn-taking happens when individual members monopolize the conversation, potentially hindering effective communication.

Turn-taking involves several communication and social skills that some individuals may find challenging. These skills include recognizing when it's appropriate to begin speaking, signaling your intention to speak or that you are listening, holding the floor when you're talking, acknowledging when others want to contribute, bringing your contribution to a concise conclusion to create space for others, avoiding dominating the conversation, inviting others to contribute their thoughts and waiting for an appropriate moment to interject without interrupting the speaker. You may have encountered situations in meetings where some of these elements were poorly executed or completely disregarded.

Lastly, effectively **closing a conversation** can be crucial for maintaining rapport with your colleagues. It's essential to respect the time you've allocated for the conversation and bring it to a close within the time frame discussed at the start of the conversation.

When concluding a conversation, whether in a group setting or one-on-one, summarize the key points discussed, outline any actions that were agreed and assign responsibilities for those actions. Determine how you will follow up, whether it's through scheduling another meeting or sending an email when the tasks are completed. If individuals have additional thoughts or information to share after the conversation, establish the best platform for everyone to communicate further. Don't forget to express gratitude for everyone's time, contributions and expertise.

If you find that you haven't addressed everything within the allocated time, acknowledge this and suggest scheduling another conversation to ensure all agenda items are covered, for all parties involved. Sometimes, it's necessary to conclude a conversation before everyone is ready, perhaps due to upcoming meetings or other commitments. It's important to respect these constraints and bring the conversation to a close.

What else should you be aware of in a conversation? We've already delved into triggers in detail in Pillar 1, where we explored common triggers, what happens when you are triggered and their close connection to stories. You've also taken steps to identify your own triggers and have started the process of releasing some of the stories associated with them.

I want to add one more crucial point about triggers here. Many miscommunications follow a familiar pattern. You are engaged in a conversation, actively listening to what is being said. At some point, you get triggered, leading you to form a judgment about the situation and what you think is going on. This judgment you just made causes you to have an emotional reaction to what was said.

Here's the key insight: the emotion you experience in that moment is not a direct response to what was said. Instead, it's a reaction (either positive or negative) to the judgment you just made about the content of the conversation.

Be mindful of your triggers during conversations. Afterward, take time to reflect on the judgments you made and how you interpreted the information you heard. Also notice whether you tend to **respond or react** during communication exchanges with your colleagues. How can you tell the difference? While your colleague is speaking, are you already formulating your response in your mind (reacting) or are you actively listening to what they're saying, waiting and responding appropriately?

When you respond, both your conscious and unconscious mind engage, resulting in a more thoughtful exchange. You actively listen to the person and provide a response based on their actual words. When you react only your conscious mind is involved, leading to a less considered exchange.

Consider this scenario. You are in a meeting and you've been triggered. In a reactive state, you start constructing a reply in your mind to defend your actions. However, as conversations naturally progress, the topic shifts and by the time you've crafted your response and speak up, it may no longer be relevant or appropriate, given the additional information they provided whilst you were planning your response.

Now, consider the same meeting, but a different response. You've been triggered, but this time, you choose to respond consciously. In that moment, you recognize your trigger and address it immediately by saying "Can we pause for a moment? I want to ensure I've understood your point correctly. Here's what I heard . . . Is that correct?" This approach gives the other person an opportunity to clarify their message and it opens the space to discuss any new insights that may have arisen as a result of that clarification.

Another important aspect to consider is **code-switching.** Code-switching occurs when an individual adapts their appearance, communication style, mannerisms or behavior based on their surroundings or the people they are interacting with. It's a survival technique that allows someone to seamlessly navigate different situations, whether personal or social, and it's quite common in the workplace. However, it's essential to recognize that code-switching comes with a significant psychological toll so being aware of it is crucial.

Now, you might wonder why people engage in code-switching. There are several reasons to consider. Code-switching can be a way to avoid potential violence, confrontation or harm. Some individuals code-switch to fit in with the dominant workplace culture and achieve a sense of belonging. It can also be a strategy to attain specific goals such as a promotion, respect, advantages or power. People may code-switch to suppress aspects of their Authentic Self or to make others feel more comfortable.

Examples of code-switching behaviors include changing your name to avoid standing out, shortening your name for ease of pronunciation, altering your natural hairstyle or clothing to conform to workplace norms, adjusting your accent, modifying behaviors and mannerisms or adopting traditional gender characteristics.

Lastly, I'd like to address a common question I often receive; the matter of **off-limits conversations** and whether there should be rules about them in the workplace. There are certain topics that are typically avoided in work conversations, such as politics, religion, controversial subjects or any topic where you're aware that your personal values don't align with the company's values. Right? Every individual has unique values and perspectives on these topics and many people choose not to discuss them in the workplace. This is a personal choice and one that is to be respected.

When it comes to discussing these sensitive topics, it's essential to remember that you're operating within a professional setting. There's an expectation that you adhere to professional boundaries and align with the company's values. However, this doesn't mean that these topics should be completely off-limits, especially if they are relevant to your work. Instead, the focus should be on creating a safe and respectful space for such discussions.

Healthy debate should be encouraged and differences of opinion should be respected. In these conversations seek to understand, ask questions and engage in meaningful discussions rather than arguments, loaded conversations or contentious debates. If you observe inappropriate comments, behaviors or microaggressions, don't hesitate to speak up and, if necessary, activate your conflict resolution strategy. To make the most of these discussions, actively apply the communication techniques outlined in this Pillar and be mindful of triggers, whether they affect you or your colleagues.

Let's now look at strategies to enhance your conversations and improve the effectiveness of the exchange. You will learn more about asserting your idea, interrupting, disagreeing, managing conflict and microaggressions and challenging someone.

Assertiveness

Assertiveness is the skill of respectfully and confidently expressing your thoughts, feelings, needs and boundaries while respecting others' perspectives and rights. What is the difference between being passive, assertive and aggressive? Passiveness involves not taking action and letting things happen to you. It includes avoiding stating your preferences, fear of speaking up, weak communication and prioritizing other people's needs over your own.

Aggression lies at the other end of the spectrum. Aggression is hostile and includes arguing, making decisions for others without listening, confrontation, insults, shouting, intimidation, verbal abuse and bullying. Overly assertive individuals may exhibit aggressive characteristics.

In the middle of that spectrum lies assertive communication, a valuable skill that involves expressing yourself confidently and respectfully. To be more assertive, start by clearly and positively conveying your thoughts and feelings while making direct requests. Use "I-Statements" (see Chapter 7, "Pillar 4") to effectively communicate your emotions and practice saying "no" calmly and directly when necessary. Consider the needs of both yourself and others, remain open to constructive feedback and respond respectfully. Avoid overgeneralizing and use clear verbs in your messages. Don't hesitate to speak up when needed, maintain eye contact and employ welcoming body language. Keep your emotions in check and be mindful of your triggers. Remember you can't control others.

Examples of assertive language are "Thanks for thinking of me, but I'm going to say no this time." "Unfortunately, I can't take on any more tasks/projects at the moment." "I don't agree with that. I believe it will/I see it this way . . ." "I respect your perspective, but let's agree to disagree."

Interrupting

Interrupting can be uncomfortable, but it's sometimes necessary to bring a meeting back on track, to clarify your understanding or to encourage more diverse voices to be heard.

Here are a few guidelines on how to interrupt. Use their first name to get their attention. Acknowledge the person or idea you are interrupting. Summarize or build on their idea. Involve another person. Bring them back to the topic originally presented if the conversation has gone off track.

Here are some positively framed phrases you can use. "Sorry to interrupt but I'd like to make sure I understood correctly." "Can I add something here?" "I'd be interested to hear what X thinks." "I think this is a great topic we need to discuss. But for today, do you mind if we jump into the other points to make sure we address those?" "I'm sorry to interrupt but I just noticed the time."

Disagreeing

It's perfectly normal to have differing perspectives, opinions and ideas when working with colleagues, and you should feel comfortable expressing your disagreements. These differences should be seen as opportunities for learning rather than as threats or conflicts. Disagreement is a natural part of the creative process so if you have a different opinion or perspective, speak up.

When engaging in respectful disagreement, start by communicating calmly and respectfully, showing appreciation for your colleagues' effort in presenting their ideas. It may have taken them a lot of effort to speak up in front of you. Before expressing your disagreement, it's essential to check for understanding. Make sure you've heard the person correctly and fully understand their perspective. Rephrase their idea if needed for clarification. Next, consider your intentions and agenda. Be clear about why you're disagreeing and what outcomes you are aiming for. Are you raising a question, expressing a concern or proposing an alternative idea? Knowing your intention helps keep the conversation positive and productive. Identify your specific concerns and the elements you agree with and disagree with. Determine what would make you comfortable with supporting a proposed solution.

When engaging in a disagreement within a conversation, approach it as a constructive dialogue, not a challenge or argument. Ensure you fully understand the other person's viewpoint before expressing your disagreement. Focus your disagreement on the topic, not on personalities and people. Focus on solutions, not problems. Focus on facts, avoid assumptions. Use "I-Statements" to express your perspective clearly. Be specific about what you agree with and what you don't, presenting your reasons succinctly, followed by your ideas or perspective.

Compromise when necessary. Remember, aim for a win-win outcome rather than a win-lose scenario. What has to occur for all parties to be happy with the suggestions? Use positive language when discussing differences and seek mutual understanding by saying things like "This is what I understand from your proposal . . . This is where I agree with you, because we do agree on several points . . . and this is where I disagree . . . These are the bits I still don't quite understand. Could you explain your thinking to me?" It's essential not to take sides but to think independently and draw your own conclusions.

Incorporating disagreement into the creative process can be valuable. For every idea, challenge it with at least three counter-reasons why it might not work. When you build this into the creative process it sets the precedent for finding new perspectives and exploring them in a safe space.

Managing Conflict

In the workplace, conflicts often arise from three primary sources: miscommunications, misunderstandings and differences in values and perspectives. When faced with miscommunication or misunderstanding, it's essential to address the issue promptly. Conflict happens when you have unclarified expectations or you have been triggered. Recognize and manage your triggers and learn to handle your emotions effectively when triggered. Pay attention to non-verbal cues, such as defensiveness, which may indicate someone has been triggered.

Stay present in the moment and assess whether you're responding thoughtfully or reacting impulsively. Clarify what you believe you've heard and ensure your message was received as intended. Express your expectations clearly to minimize future misunderstandings.

Develop a conflict resolution strategy with your team, outlining steps to resolve conflicts when they arise. This strategy will be a helpful reference and starting point in conflict resolution situations.

To create an effective conflict resolution plan, ensure everyone in the team is included and engage in a discussion. Begin by exploring how each team member individually responds and reacts during conflict situations, identifying which values might trigger negative reactions. Explore how you can work with this information, identifying the approaches that will ensure everyone can hear different perspectives from the team, to minimize tension and conflict on a daily basis.

When conflicts inevitably arise, the first step is to refer to the conflict resolution plan. This document outlines the steps you have agreed to take to resolve conflicts, including a "first intervention," "second intervention" and next steps if the second intervention does not resolve the conflict.

Ensure every team member has access to the conflict resolution plan. In the event of conflict, remind team members of the agreement you made and follow the outlined steps to resolve the issue. Remember, make sure that expectations are clearly expressed and clarify what you hear to make sure you have interpreted the message accurately.

Microaggressions

Microaggressions are subtle actions or comments that target marginalized individuals or groups and are a form of discrimination. They can occur intentionally or accidentally and manifest as everyday put-downs directed at those outside mainstream society. Marginalized groups encompass individuals, groups or populations that endure discrimination and exclusion because of uneven power relationships. This may be due to factors such as race, gender identity, sexual orientation, heritage, age, health status, physical ability, language or religion. Microaggressions can take various forms, including verbal, behavioral or environmental.

Verbal microaggressions occur when individuals make offensive or disrespectful comments directed at marginalized groups. Examples include mispronouncing someone's name and requesting a shorter, easier version for convenience, or assuming non-White colleagues are not from English-speaking countries and complimenting their English proficiency. Other examples involve asking questions like "Where are you really from?" or saying things like "I don't see color when I look at you," which can be hurtful. Praising someone for "overcoming" their disability or using statements like "I'm not (racist/sexist/homophobic); I have (Black/female/gay) friends" can also be considered microaggressions. Inquiring about the dynamics of a lesbian relationship with questions like "Who is the man?" is another example.

Behavioral microaggressions involve actions that discriminate against or harm marginalized individuals or groups. Examples include avoiding eye contact when someone is speaking, ignoring individuals during meetings and in the workplace, disregarding their instructions and seeking clarification from others, interrupting someone while they're speaking, physically distancing from or holding your breath when around certain individuals, excluding people from senior meetings due to perceived neurodiversity, refusing to use gender-neutral pronouns under the pretext of it being "too difficult" and failing to use an individual's known pronouns. Another example is assuming that an older colleague cannot use or learn to use technology.

Environmental microaggressions involve subtle discrimination within society due to inadequate representation, inclusion and diversity. This often manifests through failing to provide accessible facilities or buildings; naming buildings or rooms exclusively after White, heterosexual, cisgender men; and excluding People of Color from executive positions.

If you experience a microaggression, you have the choice of how to respond. It's essential to consider your emotional well-being, as responding to microaggressions can be emotionally draining, especially if they occur frequently. It's perfectly acceptable not to respond if you choose not to.

If you do decide to address the microaggression, take a moment to determine whether you'd like to respond immediately or at a later time, privately or publicly. One effective approach is to briefly discuss the incident with the person involved and arrange a follow-up conversation. This allows both parties to reflect and consider their responses. During the discussion, express how the microaggression made you feel and why it is significant. Focus on addressing the behavior itself, not targeting the individual, and use "I-Statements" rather than "You-Statements." Seeking social support and practicing self-care techniques can be beneficial during these situations. Here are some examples of language you can use when addressing a microaggression: "I know you didn't realize this, but when you said . . . or behaved in this way . . . it was hurtful/ offensive because of . . ." or "I noticed that you made this comment or exhibited this behavior. I used to do or say similar things, but then I learned that . . ."

If you find that you have committed a microaggression, it's essential to avoid reacting defensively. Instead, take the time to actively listen to the person who has brought it to your attention. Make an effort to empathize and understand their perspective. Avoid trivializing the situation with phrases like "I didn't mean it" or "It was just a joke" as this can discredit and invalidate the other person's experience. Verbally acknowledge the impact of your actions. Let the person know that you've heard what they've said, recognize the pain or impact you've caused and express your commitment to being more thoughtful and intentional in the future. A sincere apology is crucial but remember that making amends involves more than just words. It requires self-education and behavioral change. Don't expect immediate forgiveness;

it may take time. If the individual is open to further discussion, consider asking questions to gain insight into their experiences with microaggressions and how you can provide support. Take the initiative to educate yourself; avoid relying on the individual to educate you. Share your knowledge and resources about microaggressions with your colleagues and friends.

Challenging Someone

At times, you may find it necessary to constructively challenge someone at work, whether it's to motivate team members to achieve their full potential or to address behavior or language that is unacceptable.

I am often asked about how to effectively challenge inappropriate behavior in the moment, so here are some guidelines. Firstly, consider your safety and comfort. If you feel safe doing so, calmly and directly speak up when you hear or see inappropriate language or behavior directed at a colleague. For example, you could say "Your language/behavior is inappropriate."

If you do not feel safe speaking up directly, explore other options. Can you intervene or interrupt the behavior discreetly? Is it possible to discreetly remove the colleague who is experiencing inappropriate behavior from the situation, for example by saying, "X, I urgently need to speak with you"? In some cases, it may be necessary to report the incident to someone in authority, such as your line manager, their line manager, the line manager of the individual affected by the inappropriate behavior or the HR department.

After an incident, there are two crucial perspectives to consider. First, if you witness someone using inappropriate language or engaging in improper behavior toward a colleague, it can be constructive to have a one-on-one conversation with them.

Taking this approach gently and with an educational slant can potentially influence their future behavior. Begin by explaining why you'd like to speak with them. Then, clearly identify the specific inappropriate behavior or language you observed. Be specific. Ask them if they are ok. They may be experiencing something that is affecting their behavior in the workplace. Listen to understand their current situation, which could involve stress from personal or work-related factors. Offer support or guidance if they are going through a challenging time. Explain why the behavior you witnessed is unacceptable in the workplace and discuss how it might affect the targeted individual. Encourage them to consider whether an apology or further discussion with the affected individual is necessary. Focus on the future and integrating positive behaviors.

Second, reach out to the individual who was the target of the inappropriate behavior. Let them know that you witnessed the incident and that you are happy to discuss it with them if they wish. Ask if there is any way you can offer support or assistance. If they would like some additional support, guide them to available resources. Ask if they would like to discuss the incident with their line manager, HR or other well-being support channels. Let them know if you have reported the incident to someone else and offer to help them with any further discussions they may want to have.

Pillar Highlight Summary

Drawing upon the foundation of heightened emotional intelligence and the insights gained into the factors that influence your performance and behavior at work, cultivated through Pillar 1, the Pillar 2 Highlights set in motion a profound and lasting transformation, one that deeply influences both your professional and personal interactions and relationships. Through your exploration of the three Dimensions and Pillar Highlights within Pillar 2, you gain a comprehensive understanding of the fundamental elements driving successful communication in the workplace, setting you on a path toward mastering the art of effective workplace communication.

These newly acquired skills empower you to not only effectively express your personal feelings, needs and concerns but also to develop a heightened sense of empathy, allowing you to connect more deeply with your colleagues. You become proficient in the art of communicating messages accurately as intended and adept at accurately interpreting messages received from others. As a result, you engage in more productive, positive and nurturing conversations with your colleagues.

By embracing and implementing the three indispensable elements of the Communication Cycle, you unlock a wealth of benefits, strengthening your ability to navigate complex workplace interactions with confidence. This transformative process encourages non-judgmental, active listening; enhances your capacity to recognize and interpret both verbal and non-verbal cues; and equips you with the skills to communicate with clarity and intention, thereby facilitating open and honest dialogues. Additionally, this process increases your awareness of the emotions, reactions and motivations of others, empowering you to respond thoughtfully and appropriately to their needs and concerns.

Next, you will find the Pillar 2 Pledges and a series of self-reflective questions, providing you with valuable opportunities to assess your communication skills and workplace interactions.

Pillar 2 Pledges and Self-Reflection Questions

Here are the Pillar 2 Pledges and questions for self-reflection. We ask you to commit to these pledges and discuss them regularly in team meetings.

Pillar 2 Pledges

1. I express my feelings, needs and concerns with my line manager and team.
2. I strive to deliver clear messages when I communicate.
3. I practice active, non-judgmental listening.
4. I recognize and interpret non-verbal cues in conversations.
5. I ask questions to clarify.
6. I deal with miscommunications and misunderstandings promptly.
7. I strive to stay present when I am communicating with others.

Pillar 2 Self-Reflection

To what extent do you agree with the following statements? Score yourself for each of the statements.

If you strongly disagree, score yourself 1 point. If you somewhat disagree, score yourself 2 points. If you neither agree nor disagree, score yourself 3 points. If you somewhat agree, score yourself 4 points. If you strongly agree, score yourself 5 points.

1. I have the ability to express my feelings, needs and concerns with my line manager and team.
2. I effectively convey my message to others, ensuring it is understood as intended.
3. I excel at active, non-judgmental listening, focusing on truly hearing rather than formulating responses.
4. I can identify and interpret non-verbal cues from others.
5. I am skilled at asking questions to clarify people's statements, ensuring accurate understanding.
6. I promptly address miscommunications and misunderstandings with colleagues.
7. During conversations, my mind remains focused and does not wander or begin to construct responses before others finish speaking.

Each of the statements refers to a Pillar 2 Pledge. If you score less than a 4 for any of these statements, revisit the relevant section(s) of Pillar 2. Anything under 5 means you have room for improvement. If you score less than a 3, make improvement a priority.

Summary

The heart of Pillar 2 lies in effective communication, serving as the crucial foundation for successful workplace interactions. Unfortunately, our education system doesn't teach these vital skills, highlighting the urgency and need to equip individuals with the necessary tools to navigate and excel in diverse workplace communications. When people lack these necessary communication skills, it can make them feel unsafe, impacting on their ability to express their Authentic Self at work and engage in productive collaborations with colleagues. Effective communication is a vital factor that contributes to creating an environment where everyone can thrive. With the Communication Cycle as your guide, you possess the means to excel in any workplace interaction.

Next on our journey is Pillar 3, where we will immerse ourselves in the realm of team collaboration.

Note

1. For more information about the Psychological Safety Institute and our services, training programs and resources: www.thepsi.global.

6

Pillar 3: Collaboration

Pillar 3 is Collaboration and is dedicated to the art of cultivating a work environment where teams can truly thrive. Building upon the foundation laid by Pillar 2, it places a strong emphasis on empowering teams to intentionally design their work environment to facilitate collaboration. As you navigate the intricacies of workplace collaboration through Pillar 3, you will not only create stronger bonds between team members but also establish the ideal conditions for teams to thrive and consistently achieve outstanding results together.

In our global study, 49 percent of organizations stated that their top priority is to create an environment where teams can thrive, and they reported facing challenges in areas such as creating safe spaces and managing team dynamics.

In this chapter, we will delve deeper into strategies and techniques to address these challenges head-on, to build a culture of collaboration within your teams. We will explore the importance of safe spaces and cultivating positive team dynamics, among other key areas. With Pillar 3 as your guide, you have the opportunity to transform your workplace into a hub of innovation, creativity and unparalleled productivity. So, let's begin with the framework and methodology we use in Pillar 3.

Pillar 3 Framework

First Principle: This is how we work together as a team. This is the fundamental concept on which Pillar 3 is based.

Dimensions. Pillar 3 has five Dimensions, each offering a unique perspective to explore and measure the First Principle. In Pillar 3, teams ask five key questions, providing a practical framework for teams to understand and apply the First Principle. Question 1 is "What are our goals?" Question 2 is "How can we create a safe space for everyone?" Question 3 is "What is the work we need to do?" Question 4 is "How can we get the most out of ourselves and the team?" Question 5 is "How do we keep moving things forward?"

Pillar Highlights. Within Pillar 3, you will find several Pillar Highlights, which represent key areas of emphasis within the CollabZen Methodology (explained below). These Pillar Highlights offer detailed insights, facilitating a deeper understanding and practical application of the First Principle. We will delve into these Pillar Highlights in detail in the Pillar Highlights section later.

As you engage with Pillar 3, leveraging the CollabZen Methodology you will acquire the knowledge and skills necessary to create a highly conducive environment for effective teamwork and collaboration. You will explore and implement proven strategies to drive your team toward success.

With the CollabZen Methodology, you will have the tools you need to establish a culture of trust and collaboration among your team members. You will unlock the full potential of each individual and cultivate high-performing teams that consistently deliver outstanding results. This powerful approach empowers you to maximize productivity and drive innovation within your workplace, paving the way for unprecedented levels of success and growth, for individuals, teams and the organization.

Pillar 3 is the one where you create an environment where teams can thrive. It addresses the critical need for cultivating collaboration and empowers teams to achieve their full potential. While Pillar 2 hones your individual interpersonal skills, Pillar 3 is dedicated to the art of harnessing collective strengths. By mastering the principles within this pillar, you'll not only nurture an environment of trust and collaboration but also empower your teams to reach unparalleled heights of success. Just as the Communication Cycle transforms relationships on a personal level, the CollabZen Methodology is your guide to transforming teams into powerful units that consistently deliver exceptional results.

Pillar 3 Methodology: The CollabZen Methodology

The CollabZen Methodology underpins Pillar 3, providing teams with a comprehensive framework to cultivate effective teamwork and collaboration within the workplace. Comprised of five key elements, as shown in Figure 6.1, it empowers teams to thrive and achieve their goals in a calm and focused environment.

By adopting the CollabZen Methodology, teams intentionally design their work environment to facilitate exceptional collaboration and teamwork. This approach cultivates a sense of belonging among team members, creating a safe and supportive space where everyone can thrive.

The methodology revolves around five essential elements that are vital for establishing an environment conducive to team success. These elements include clearly defined goals to provide clear direction for the team, establishing a safe space that encourages open communication, identifying and assigning appropriate roles to ensure efficient workflow, cultivating and nurturing positive team dynamics to enhance collaboration and communication and implementing a structured approach for making decisions.

Ultimately, the CollabZen Methodology equips teams with a powerful toolkit to collaborate effectively in a calm and focused workplace setting. By utilizing this methodology teams can streamline their efforts, working harmoniously toward their objectives with ease and efficiency, resulting in a high-performing team that consistently achieves its goals.

The first element of the CollabZen Methodology is known as "Goals" and aligns with the Dimension "What are our goals?" In Goals, teams focus on a comprehensive exploration of the collective vision, goals and objectives and their alignment with individual and team tasks and responsibilities.

The second element of the CollabZen Methodology is known as "Safe Space" and aligns with the Dimension "How can we create a safe space for everyone?" In Safe Space, teams focus on cultivating an environment where every team member feels safe and valued.

The third element of the CollabZen Methodology is known as "Roles" and aligns with the Dimension "What is the work we need to do?" In Roles, teams focus on defining and allocating roles and responsibilities, ensuring that each team member contributes effectively to the team's collective objectives and tasks.

The fourth element of the CollabZen Methodology is known as "Dynamics" and aligns with the Dimension "How can we get the most out of ourselves and the team?" Within Dynamics, teams concentrate on fine-tuning their interpersonal interactions, aligning communication and work preferences, understanding personality styles and establishing clear work boundaries. All these efforts combine to unlock

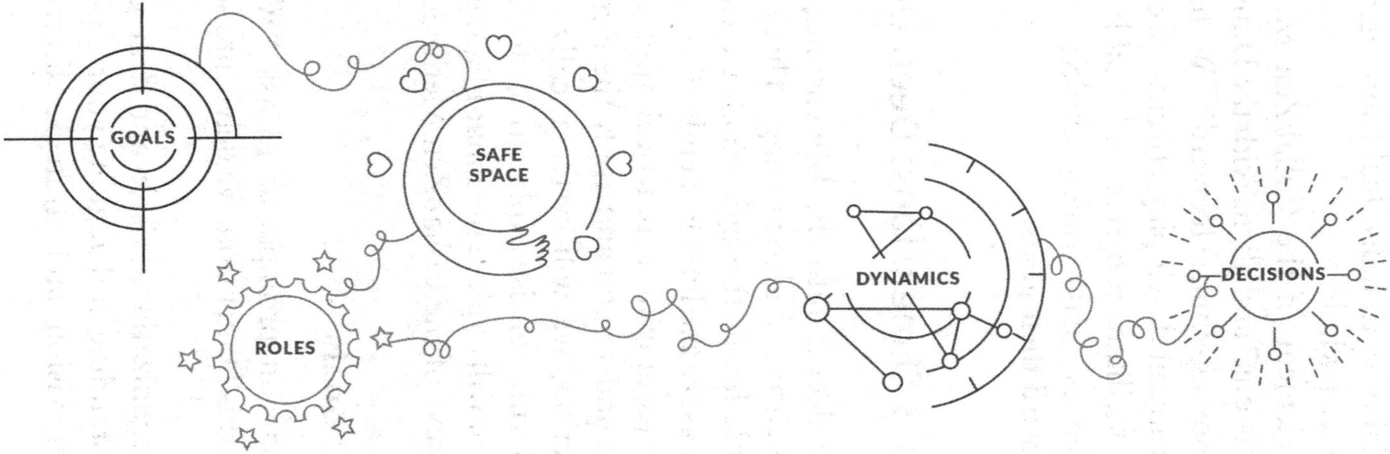

Figure 6.1 The CollabZen Methodology

the full potential of both individual team members and the collective team as a whole.

The fifth element of the CollabZen Methodology is known as "Decisions" and aligns with the Dimension "How do we keep moving things forward?" Within Decisions, teams concentrate on developing effective decision-making processes that facilitate progress and enable the team to navigate challenges, make timely choices and maintain momentum toward their goals.

Pillar 3 Dimensions: Deep Dive

Now let's dive deeper into the Dimensions, providing a more comprehensive understanding. These Dimensions serve as valuable lenses through which we can effectively explore and measure the First Principle. They are presented as questions, encouraging a practical approach for individuals to both understand and apply the First Principle.

In this section, we will systematically explore each Dimension, offering concise explanations for clarity. In the next section, you will explore the Pillar Highlights in detail, within the context of the CollabZen Methodology.

Dimension 1: Goals

The first Dimension prompts us to ask "What are our goals?" Within this Dimension, we delve into several essential elements.

First, the organizational vision and strategic plan. This involves understanding and aligning your aspirations with the overarching vision and strategic direction of your organization.

Second, the team vision, goals and objectives. You consider how these connect to the organization's vision and strategic plan, forming the foundation for your team's purpose and direction.

Third, individual objectives. You examine how individual team members' objectives intersect with the team's collective goals, including your own. To ensure clarity and alignment, it's essential that each team member understands how their individual objectives contribute to the team's shared goals and vision.

Fourth, alignment and interdependencies. Understanding how your personal goals align with those of your teammates and the broader team is crucial. You explore potential interdependencies and synergies.

It's vital to emphasize that when goals and objectives remain unclear or unaddressed within a team, it can lead to confusion, misalignment and missed opportunities for collaboration and innovation. This lack of clarity can hinder progress and limit the team's ability to achieve its collective vision. Therefore, seeking clarification and guidance when needed is essential to keep everyone on the same page and ensure a cohesive and effective team dynamic. Remember, this conversation is not a one-time event; it should be revisited regularly to keep everyone aligned and informed.

Dimension 2: Safe Space

The second Dimension prompts us to ask "How can we create a safe space for everyone?"

In our global study, when we asked "Do you feel safe in your team meetings?" a significant 67 percent responded positively. However, this leaves a concerning 33 percent who do not feel safe during these meetings. This lack of safety can have profound consequences. When team members don't feel safe, they are less likely to bring their Authentic Self to the meeting, their communication skills may not operate at their optimal level, and this can lead to disengagement among team members, fostering an environment where miscommunications are more likely to occur.

Consider what happens when you don't feel safe within your team meetings. Open dialogue becomes a challenge, conflicts may remain unresolved and misinterpretations can arise. To address this challenge, I developed a checklist summarizing the key elements for creating safe spaces. This checklist includes the importance of establishing ground rules, implementing effective conflict resolution strategies, utilizing your Approaching Issues Framework, setting clear expectations, addressing inappropriate behavior and nurturing positive team dynamics.

In Pillar Highlights we will delve deeper into these elements, providing you with practical insights and strategies to ensure your team meetings are both safe and productive environments.

Dimension 3: Roles

The third Dimension prompts us to ask "What is the work we need to do?"

Clarity around roles and responsibilities within your team is really important. Ensure that everyone, including yourself, is clear about the following: What your role involves and the specific responsibilities it encompasses. The roles and responsibilities of each team member. The collective responsibilities that the team shares and how each team member will contribute to these shared tasks.

Lastly, the expectations that team members have of each other.

Not having clarity on these elements can have significant consequences. When roles and responsibilities are vague or misunderstood, teams may experience confusion, duplicate efforts or leave tasks unaddressed. This can hinder progress and collaboration and lead to inefficiencies.

If at any point you find yourself uncertain about these crucial aspects, ask for clarification and guidance. In doing so, you help create a team environment where everyone understands their roles, responsibilities and how they contribute to the collective work, cultivating a more productive and harmonious team dynamic.

Dimension 4: Dynamics

The fourth Dimension prompts us to ask "How can we get the most out of ourselves and the team?"

To illustrate the significance of team dynamics, let's look at a scenario. Picture a bustling marketing agency, where two employees, S and J, are working closely together on a high-profile client project. They have been assigned as co-leads for the project, responsible for overseeing its entire journey from conception to completion. Both are talented and experienced in their roles, but they possess vastly different personality traits and work styles.

S is an extrovert who thrives in social settings and is known for their assertive and proactive approach. They are results-oriented and look for ways to drive the project forward swiftly. They value efficiency and believe in making quick decisions to meet deadlines.

J is an introvert and a meticulous planner who prefers a more thoughtful and methodical approach to projects.

They value thorough research, detailed analysis and careful consideration of options before making decisions. They believe in minimizing risks and ensuring that every aspect of the project is well structured.

As the project progresses, the fundamental differences in S and J's personalities and work styles become increasingly evident.

S tends to make rapid decisions without extensive discussion, believing it keeps the project on track. J seeks more data and analysis before committing to a course of action. They often clash over the pace and depth of decision-making.

S prefers quick face-to-face meetings and concise updates, while J prefers written reports and in-depth discussions. Their differing communication styles lead to misunderstandings and frustration.

S's assertiveness sometimes causes them to override J's input, leading to tension. J feels that their opinions and expertise are undervalued, leading to resentment when their contributions are discarded in discussions about the project's direction.

The personality clash between S and J has significant consequences. Their constant disagreements and delays in decision-making slow down the project's progress, resulting in missed deadlines and a compromise in the team's overall efficiency. The ongoing conflicts create a tense atmosphere within the wider team, affecting morale and job satisfaction. Other team members are also affected by the tension and stress. The project's outcomes are compromised. The clash between S's quick decision-making and J's meticulous planning often leads to suboptimal choices that negatively impact the project's overall success.

Both S and J become increasingly disengaged from the project, as they find it challenging to work with each other. This disengagement affects their overall job satisfaction and motivation.

With this scenario in mind, let's explore measures that can be taken to resolve issues with team dynamics and enhance collaboration.

To navigate the intricacies of team dynamics effectively, I developed a checklist summarizing the key elements for consideration. This checklist includes the following:

- Clearly defining what team members expect from one another.
- Understanding and respecting each other's personal and work boundaries.
- Recognizing individual work preferences and styles.
- Acknowledging varying communication preferences within the team.
- Identifying how team members prefer to celebrate achievements.
- Gaining insight into the diverse personality types within your team and identifying strategies to improve communication, collaboration and productivity.
- Establishing an Approaching Issues Framework (discussed later in this chapter) for addressing challenges and issues that arise.
- Addressing specific dynamics that arise within remote, virtual or hybrid teams.

This checklist serves as a practical guide to optimize team dynamics, ensuring that both individual team members and the team as a whole achieve their full potential. Further exploration of these elements will be covered in-depth within the Pillar Highlights section, offering practical insights and strategies to enhance team dynamics and collaboration.

Dimension 5: Decisions

The fifth Dimension prompts us to ask "How do we keep moving things forward?"

As a team, it is crucial to consider the following aspects. How will you make decisions to help you achieve your team goals? How will you ensure an inclusive decision-making process? How will you prioritize tasks and projects to align with the team's objectives? How will you distribute ownership of tasks and resources?

Consider this real-life scenario a client shared with me. At a leading technology corporation, a cross-functional team was tasked with launching a groundbreaking product to secure a competitive edge in the market. The team consisted of engineers, marketers and designers, each bringing valuable expertise to the table. However, they lacked a clear decision-making strategy.

What impact did this have? They told me that when it came to crucial decisions such as product design, pricing and marketing strategy, the team frequently found themselves in long debates without a clear process to guide them. Hours turned into days, and days into weeks, as team members struggled to reach a consensus. The product launch date had to be rescheduled multiple times, causing frustration among team members and raising doubts about the company's commitment to innovation.

Individual agendas and inter-departmental rivalries took precedence over the collective team goals. Engineers pushed for features that they considered were technically superior, whereas marketers insisted on strategies they believed would maximize sales, resulting in conflicts and delays. With unresolved disagreements, progress ground to a halt. Valuable resources were drained on debates and revisions, leaving the team demotivated and demoralized.

The prolonged decision-making process destroyed their competitive advantage, providing rivals in the industry with the opening to launch similar products and capture the market share that could have been theirs.

The team's inability to make key decisions efficiently had a significant impact on project timelines, competitiveness and the overall dynamics within the team. This highlights how neglecting to establish a clear decision-making strategy can lead to confusion, project delays and potential conflicts within the team, ultimately delaying the achievement of your goals.

Establishing a clear decision-making process within teams is crucial for achieving your goals effectively and maintaining a competitive edge.

Pillar 3 Highlights

Pillar 3 covers a wide range of strategies to create an environment where teams can thrive. For the Pillar Highlights, we will focus on two key aspects that most organizations prioritize: team dynamics and safe spaces.

In this overview, we will cover the basics. However, it's important to emphasize that our specialized resources, including our live training sessions, the Psychological Safety Toolkit and Authentic Self Journal, e-learning programs and retreats, offer a comprehensive suite of guidance and activities that will support you to create an environment where teams can thrive. The reason for not delving into these resources here is because every individual and team has unique needs. To effectively navigate the complex challenges that may arise, they require the guidance and support of experts who can tailor solutions to their specific requirements. More information about our resources can be found on our website, details of which can be found in the endnotes.[1]

Let's delve into these highlights and explore the key elements that play a significant role in enhancing workplace collaboration, using the CollabZen Methodology as our framework.

Team Dynamics

To enhance team dynamics, several crucial conversations should take place, focusing on the following areas: personal and work boundaries, work, communication and celebration preferences, the Approaching Issues Framework and personality types. Let's briefly look at each of these aspects.

Personal Boundaries

Personal boundaries are the limits and guidelines that individuals establish to protect their physical, emotional and mental well-being. These boundaries define the line between what is acceptable and unacceptable behavior toward you and others. Personal boundaries can be physical, emotional, mental and spiritual. Here are some examples of the different types that emerged during a meeting within a team I worked with, where the topic of personal boundaries was discussed.

One team member started the conversation by sharing their personal boundaries related to **physical space**. They emphasized the importance of having their personal space respected, both in the office and during virtual meetings. They prefer a quiet workspace with minimal interruptions and value their privacy. They also communicated their preference for limited physical touch and interactions, which they believe helps them maintain focus and comfort during work.

This encouraged another team member to open up about their **emotional** boundaries. They discussed their willingness to share personal information and express feelings in a professional context. They value open and honest communication but mentioned that they are selective about accepting feedback. They prefer constructive criticism delivered with empathy, as it allows them to process feedback more effectively and maintain their emotional well-being.

Another individual discussed their **mental** boundaries and personal beliefs. They emphasized the importance of respecting their personal beliefs, values and opinions, both in work-related discussions and general interactions. They value diverse perspectives but underlined the need for respectful conversation when differing opinions arise.

Lastly, a team member shared their **spiritual** boundaries. They expressed their strong observance to specific religious beliefs and practices. They value understanding and respect for their spiritual beliefs and requested that discussions around religious topics be handled with sensitivity and respect.

Setting and maintaining personal boundaries are crucial for your physical, emotional and mental well-being, both in and outside of the workplace. Clearly defining these boundaries and effectively communicating them to your colleagues are essential.

To initiate a conversation about personal boundaries, consider scheduling a team meeting where everyone can openly share their boundaries. Encourage an atmosphere of respect and understanding, emphasizing that these boundaries exist to promote well-being and productivity. Discuss how these boundaries can be respectfully asserted if they are crossed, ensuring that all team members feel safe and heard. By understanding and supporting each other's boundaries, you can build a stronger and more productive team. This conversation will help you to create a workplace where everyone can thrive while respecting each other's individual boundaries and well-being.

Work Boundaries

Work boundaries play a crucial role in maintaining a healthy work-life balance. They help individuals separate their professional lives from their personal lives, ensuring well-being and productivity. Work boundaries can be related to time, communication, tasks, personal (as above) and space. Here are some examples of the different types in action.

You initiate a discussion with your team around work boundaries where one of them reveals their **time** boundaries. They set specific work hours from 10 a.m. to 6 p.m., dedicating those hours to work tasks and client interactions. Outside of these hours, they prefer not to engage in work-related tasks or discussions.

Another colleague has strong **communication** boundaries. They have established clear guidelines for how and when they will communicate with colleagues. They prefer emails for non-urgent matters, as this allows time to process information at their own pace. For critical or time-sensitive issues, they prefer phone calls or instant messaging.

Another member of the team shares their **task** boundaries. They prioritize tasks and delegate responsibilities to prevent overworking and burnout. They are clear about their capacity and communicate effectively with team members. When tasks start to pile up, they proactively redistribute responsibilities to ensure everyone's workload remains manageable, contributing to a more balanced workload within the team.

Another colleague reveals their **personal** boundaries. They distinguish between work-related information they share with colleagues and what they keep private. They believe in transparency but are mindful of their personal space. They set boundaries to protect their private life, maintaining positive working relationships with colleagues while protecting their privacy.

Lastly, another team member discusses their **space** boundaries. They have meticulously created a separate and organized workspace at home. This virtual workspace is distinct from their personal living space, allowing them to switch between work and relaxation modes effectively.

Initiating a conversation about work boundaries is a proactive step toward a healthier work environment and enhanced communication between team members. Discuss these boundaries openly, addressing how they can be respectfully asserted if crossed. Emphasize that respecting these boundaries not only benefits individuals but also enhances overall team dynamics and well-being.

Work Preferences

A work preference refers to an individual's preferred way of working or performing tasks and can include a variety of factors such as the work environment, work schedule, work style, communication preferences and job responsibilities.

Work preferences can vary widely from person to person and may be influenced by personal values, skills, interests and experiences. Here are some examples of work preferences in action.

During a team meeting, you initiate a discussion about work preferences. One of the team members expresses their **work environment** preference. They thrive in a quiet workspace, where they can focus deeply on their tasks. They value minimal distractions and find that a serene environment enhances their productivity. In contrast, another team member prefers a more dynamic and collaborative space, where spontaneous interactions and ideation sessions fuel their creativity. Embracing these differences, you can create a workspace that caters to both preferences, designating quiet zones and collaborative areas.

You begin to explore **working schedule** preferences with the team. One individual reveals their preference for a flexible schedule that allows them to balance work and personal life effectively. They value the freedom to adjust their work hours to accommodate personal commitments and find this flexibility enhances their overall well-being. On the other hand, another team member prefers a structured schedule with set hours, as it helps them maintain a routine and structure their day effectively. Recognizing these distinct preferences, you implement a flexible work schedule policy that accommodates both approaches.

You then delve into **work style** preferences with your team. One individual expresses their inclination toward independent work. They value autonomy and enjoy tackling tasks on their own, finding that it allows them to concentrate and deliver quality results. Another team member prefers a collaborative approach, relishing the opportunity to work closely with team members to generate ideas and solve problems collectively. Recognizing the value of both styles, you encourage team members to choose the approach that suits their tasks and projects, promoting a balanced work dynamic.

Next, you discuss **communication** preferences. One team member shares their preference for written communication, favoring email and instant messaging for their clarity and record-keeping. This method allows them to process information thoughtfully. In contrast, another team member values face-to-face communication or phone conversations for important discussions, as they provide a deeper connection and immediate feedback. Acknowledging these distinct preferences, your team implements a communication protocol that combines both methods to enhance efficiency and clarity.

Lastly, you explore **job responsibility** preferences. One individual expresses their preference for a role that allows them to focus on a specific set of tasks or responsibilities. They find deep satisfaction in becoming an expert in their field. On the other hand, another team member thrives in a more varied role with a range of tasks and projects. They enjoy the diversity of challenges it brings and believe it fuels their personal and professional growth. Recognizing these preferences, you adjust roles and responsibilities within the team to maximize individual strengths and create a well-rounded team.

Initiate a conversation about the work preferences of everyone in the team. Discuss individual preferences and preferred working styles and explore how everyone can express their full potential. Embrace these differences as strengths and explore ways to leverage them for the collective success of your team.

Communication Preferences

Communication preferences at work refer to the ways in which people prefer to communicate and receive information in a professional setting. Common communication preferences at work include the following.

During a team discussion focused on communication preferences, a team member expresses their preference for **verbal** communication. They value face-to-face conversations or phone calls when discussing complex topics or making important decisions. They believe that verbal communication allows for immediate clarification and a deeper understanding of nuances in discussions.

Another team member shares their communication preference for **written** communication. They emphasize their comfort with email and instant messaging, as it allows them to carefully process their thoughts and have a written record of conversations. They appreciate written communication for its clarity and reference.

This encourages another team member to discuss their preference for **visual aids** in communication. They find that graphs, charts and presentations help them better grasp complex information and data. They suggest incorporating visual aids when discussing project updates to enhance understanding among team members.

The same team members highlight their preference for face-to-face communication. They value in-person interactions as they allow them to interpret **body language** and non-verbal cues effectively.

Timing was then discussed where one individual shared their preference for morning communication, as they feel most alert and focused during that time. The team agrees to schedule important discussions and meetings in the morning to accommodate this preference.

These scenarios demonstrate various communication preferences within a team. By initiating a conversation about these preferences and aligning on preferred communication methods and timing, the team can enhance the clarity and effectiveness of their communication and collaborative efforts, ultimately leading to improved productivity and teamwork.

Celebration Preferences

Like your working style and work preferences, you also have specific preferences when it comes to receiving recognition and rewards. There are five main ways people like to be rewarded. Feedback, gifts and perks, quality time, acts of service and physical touch. Let's look at each of these briefly.

During a team discussion focused on celebration preferences, a team member expresses their preference for **feedback** as a form of recognition. They value verbal praise for their efforts, finding it motivating and encouraging. They appreciate it when team members provide words of encouragement or positive feedback or acknowledge their achievements during meetings. They believe that sharing success stories with other teams also boosts morale.

Another member of the team reveals their preference for **gifts and perks** as a way of feeling rewarded. They appreciate thoughtful gifts, cards and tokens of gratitude to acknowledge their contributions. They value tangible items as symbols of recognition and they enjoy receiving event tickets or gift certificates as rewards. They also believe in the value of mentorship as a rewarding experience.

Excited by the conversation, an individual highlights their preference for **quality time** as a form of celebration. They value acknowledging workplace anniversaries with small celebrations, team lunches or social events and trips. They believe that spending time together strengthens team bonds and encourages a sense of camaraderie, making celebrations more meaningful.

Another member of the team discusses their preference for **acts of service** to feel appreciated. They value help from team members to finish or participate in projects or tasks. They believe that offering to help a colleague who may be overwhelmed with their workload or taking on simple, low-level tasks to support high-level projects demonstrates a strong team spirit and collaboration.

One individual mentions their preference for **physical touch** to feel appreciated. They enjoy high-fives, handshakes, fist bumps and sensory-friendly gifts, such as a spa day, as gestures of recognition. The team agrees to be mindful of physical boundaries and cultural differences while celebrating achievements.

These scenarios illustrate various celebration preferences within a team. By initiating a conversation about these preferences and acknowledging and celebrating achievements in alignment with individual preferences, the team can create a more inclusive and meaningful celebration culture that respects personal boundaries and cultural considerations. Don't forget to discuss how you want to celebrate as a team too, when you achieve your goals. Make sure this celebration fulfills everyone's preferences in some way.

Approaching Issues Framework

Establishing a framework to address challenges encountered while working toward team goals is crucial. By agreeing on a proactive course of action before issues arise, you'll save time and effort, while also ensuring clarity on everyone's role.

As a team, discuss the following questions to create the foundations for your framework. How will you identify the issue? Are there specific meetings or methods for identifying them? Take all issues to a Curiosity Session (see Chapter 7, "Pillar 4") to be discussed. What is the best way for you to generate solutions? Take the issues that you have identified and explored in Curiosity Sessions to Creativity Workshops (see Chapter 8, "Pillar 5"), where you will begin to generate solutions and creatively problem-solve as a team. What approach will you use to develop an action plan and what needs to be considered in this? How will you implement the action plan? How will you monitor progress and how often will you check in? How do you want to celebrate the success of this team goal?

Remember to activate the Approaching Issues Framework whenever an issue arises. This framework will guide your team toward effective issue resolution and goal achievement.

Personality Types

We have already explored a scenario where a clash in personalities was evident. Understanding different personality types in your team can make or break effective collaboration.

Let me introduce you to a few individuals from a real-life team that I have worked closely with. To respect their privacy (and others throughout the book), I have omitted their names and specific identifiers. Let's call them B, S and C.

B is a self-professed highly extroverted individual. They are outgoing and social and thrive in group settings. In team meetings, B is the one initiating discussions, sharing ideas and making connections with colleagues. They feel energized by social interactions and are always ready to lead group projects or collaborate with others.

S is an introvert who thrives in a calm and focused work environment. They excel in tasks that require deep concentration and analytical thinking, making them a valuable asset for research-oriented work. S prefers to work independently and approaches meetings with attentive listening and thoughtful contributions. Unlike B, S tends to reflect before offering their input.

C is emotionally unstable and often experiences stress and anxiety in high-pressure situations. This emotional instability becomes evident when they face tight project deadlines or demanding clients, sometimes leading to visible signs of distress. They tend to need extra reassurance and support during challenging times to maintain their emotional equilibrium. They also exhibit traits associated with psychoticism. They are known for their unconventional thinking and behavior, frequently taking risks and exploring innovative, out-of-the-box solutions to problems. However, their approach is perceived as unconventional and even controversial by more traditional colleagues.

In contrast to C, S is emotionally stable. They are calm and composed, even in highly stressful situations. S's ability to manage their emotions adds to their reputation as a reliable and steady team member. Their colleagues turn to them for guidance during times of crisis. S adheres to established norms and values in the workplace. They follow structured processes and guidelines, believing in the importance of established procedures for maintaining order and efficiency within the team.

In this workplace scenario, I have introduced you to Eysenck's Personality Theory, which offers insights into how individuals with different personality dimensions can coexist and contribute uniquely to the team.[2]

Think back to the iceberg presented to you in Pillar 1. Personality is one component of your identity. Personality consists of a set of psychological traits that influence how you interact and adapt to intrapersonal (within the mind: memories, dreams, your thoughts, emotions, desires, fantasies or motivations), physical and social environments.

These traits manifest as predictable patterns of behavior. You can't change or transform your personality. It is hard-wired in the brain. Personality traits are a habitual pattern of behavior, thought and emotion. They are consistent and long-lasting and influence your emotions, thoughts and actions.

On the other hand, personality states are temporary and situation specific, like feeling angry or upset on one day but not necessarily the next.

Let's take a quick look at Eysenck's Personality Theory which places significant emphasis on three primary dimensions of personality. The first is Extroversion versus Introversion. The second is Neuroticism versus Emotional Stability. The third is Psychoticism. Re-read the scenario above. Can you identify which team members exhibited which personality trait?

Extraversion versus introversion indicates an individual's level of social engagement, neuroticism versus emotional stability reflects an individual's emotional reactivity to stress and psychoticism reflects an individual's level of impulse control and risk-taking behavior.

While learning about Eysenck's theory, it's important to note that not all individuals will exhibit the same behaviors or preferences in a work setting. Other factors such as personal values, individual experiences and the specific demands of a job can also influence work behavior. It's also essential to recognize that these traits are just one aspect of an individual's personality and should not be used to make assumptions or judgments about their capabilities or potential in a work environment.

Extroversion versus Introversion According to Eysenck's theory, extraverts have a lower baseline level of cortical arousal than introverts. This means they require more external stimulation to reach the same level of arousal as introverts. They seek out external stimulation to increase their arousal levels and satisfy their need for excitement and social interaction, which provides them with the energy and engagement they thrive on.

For example, in a fast-paced environment, an extroverted sales manager constantly seeks external stimulation to boost their arousal levels. They thrive on team meetings, networking events and client interactions, finding excitement in each interaction. Their willingness to embrace new challenges and their enthusiasm for socializing not only energizes them but also motivates their team, driving productivity and creating a vibrant, collaborative atmosphere that benefits the entire department.

Introverts have a higher baseline level of cortical arousal than extroverts, which means they are overstimulated by external stimuli. Introverts may find external stimulation overwhelming or exhausting and may prefer quieter or more solitary activities that allow them to reduce the amount of external stimulation they experience.

For example, in a bustling open-plan office, an introverted software developer often finds the constant chatter and activity overwhelming. Unlike extroverted colleagues who thrive on interaction, they prefer quieter, focused work in a secluded corner. To reduce external stimulation, they use noise-canceling headphones to create a cocoon of concentration, immersing themselves in coding tasks or intricate problem-solving. This preference for a calmer work environment allows them to maintain optimal productivity and mental clarity, highlighting the introverted need for a less stimulating workspace.

Neuroticism versus Emotional Stability High levels of neuroticism arise from excessive activity of the autonomic nervous system, which is linked to the body's Fight or Flight Response.

Let's revisit the real-life example you were introduced to earlier to observe the differences between the two. C, with high neuroticism (emotionally unstable), reacts strongly to stressful situations. When faced with tight project deadlines or unexpected changes, they become visibly anxious, leading to emotional instability and difficulty concentrating. This anxiety sometimes escalates to the point of causing physical symptoms like headaches. In contrast, S, who is generally emotionally stable, maintains a calm demeanor even in challenging circumstances. They approach setbacks as opportunities for growth and adapt well to change. This difference in emotional response influences their performance; C's high neuroticism occasionally leads to missed deadlines and strained relationships with colleagues, while S's emotional stability creates a more positive and productive work environment, allowing them to handle stress and uncertainty effectively.

Three key points to note here. First, it is important to note that individuals high in emotional stability are not immune to experiencing stress or negative emotions. Second, people with high neuroticism scores may not necessarily be considered neurotic but are more likely to be susceptible to experiencing neurotic problems, such as emotional instability, anxiety, distress, obsessive-compulsive disorder, PTSD and social anxiety disorder. Third, it is important to note that high levels of neuroticism do not prevent an individual from being successful in their job. With proper support, self-awareness and coping strategies, individuals with high neuroticism can learn to manage their emotions and thrive in their role.

Psychoticism Individuals who are high in psychoticism tend to exhibit traits such as aggressiveness and impulsivity and may lack empathy and concern for others, which can have negative implications for their behavior in a work setting.

In the scenario above, C displays traits associated with high psychoticism, which can manifest as disruptive behavior in a workplace. C's impulsiveness often leads to actions without considering the consequences, resulting in uncooperative behavior and conflicts with colleagues. They lack empathy and concern for the feelings and needs of their team members, making it challenging to collaborate effectively. Their aggressive tendencies can escalate workplace disputes and hinder open communication, ultimately creating a tense and unproductive atmosphere.

It is important to recognize that individuals with high levels of psychoticism may have other positive qualities that could benefit their work performance, such as creativity or assertiveness. Nonetheless, individuals high in psychoticism should be aware of their tendencies and work to manage them effectively in a work setting.

What happens when traits are combined? This is the bit when it becomes even more fascinating.

When extroverted behaviors are combined with emotional stability, individuals tend to be sociable, outgoing and often take on leadership roles with ease. However, when extroverted behaviors combine with emotional instability, it can result in restlessness, unpredictability and impulsiveness, potentially leading to erratic interactions in the workplace. On the other hand, emotionally stable introverted behaviors manifest as passivity, thoughtfulness and reliability, creating a calm and controlled work demeanor. In contrast, emotionally unstable introverted traits may lead to moodiness, anxiety and reserved tendencies, which can impact communication and social engagement within a team. This interplay of personality traits adds depth to our understanding of how individuals navigate the intricacies of the workplace.

In Chapter 3 we presented you with the results about personality from our global study. We asked "Which of these personality traits best describes you, in the workplace the majority of the time." Respondents identified themselves as follows: 39 percent stated they are introvert and emotionally stable; 34 percent stated they are extrovert and emotionally stable; 14 percent stated they are introvert and emotionally unstable; and 13 percent stated they are extrovert and emotionally unstable. Consider the impact that has on team dynamics and collaboration.

Is it possible to change your personality? While personality is generally considered to be hard-wired in the brain and not easily transformed, some level of change is possible. Although it may be challenging to transition from one end of the personality spectrum to the other, various factors such as life experiences, self-reflection, intentional effort and psychotherapy can contribute to gradual personality changes over time.

Now imagine, you have a team of eight people. With such a diverse mix of personality variations in the workplace, it's no surprise that communication and collaboration can sometimes be challenging. Each team member has unique traits and preferences that should be acknowledged and respected. By investing time in getting to know your colleagues' boundaries, preferences and their personalities, you increase the likelihood of effectively navigating communication and creating an environment where everyone can thrive.

You might be wondering how all this relates to psychological safety. Applying Eysenck's Personality Theory, team members who score high in extroversion and low in neuroticism (emotionally stable) are more likely to feel psychologically safe in the workplace. Team members who score low in extroversion (introverts) and high in neuroticism (emotionally unstable) are less likely to feel psychologically safe in the workplace.

Psychometric tests have gained popularity in the workplace as valuable tools for identifying individual team members' strengths and limitations. The ultimate goal is to enhance team effectiveness and productivity by helping organizations understand how team members can collaborate more efficiently based on their individual characteristics and skills.

To facilitate team discussions about different personality types, a variety of personality assessment tools are available, including the Myers Briggs Type Indicator, DISC Assessment, 16 Personality Factors, Emotional Quotient Inventory (EQ-i) and the Big Five Personality Traits.

In summary, I encourage you to organize a series of team discussions where you initiate conversations about the following topics: personal and work boundaries; work, communication and celebration preferences; the Approaching Issues Framework; and personality types. The goal is to deepen your understanding of each team member and explore how this knowledge can be leveraged to create an environment where everyone can thrive and collaborate more effectively.

Creating a Safe Space

To create a safe space, there are several considerations that organizations often overlook. We will explore these in this section. First, it is essential to understand that creating a safe environment is the responsibility of everyone, not just one individual. It is crucial for effective communication and collaboration, employee well-being, productivity, curiosity, creativity and innovation. By investing time and effort now, you can save a significant amount of both in the future.

The second thing to consider is that the sense of safety is an individualized experience. While you may perceive your team meetings as a safe space where everyone can bring their Authentic Self to work, discuss their tasks and openly reflect on their progress, this might not be true for everyone in the team.

Creating a safe space for your team requires careful consideration and clear guidelines. It doesn't just happen. The following sections discuss some steps to follow.

Setting the Scene

Begin by asking your team members what they need and want to feel safe within the team. Use their responses to guide your next steps.

Next, devise and regularly update your team's ground rules. Ground rules establish expectations and provide a framework for holding team members accountable for their behavior. They work best when devised and agreed upon by the whole team. Focus on the following areas: behavior, contribution, communication, presence and participation.

Here are a few examples of ground rules: "Meetings will start and end on time." "Meetings will follow an agenda prepared by the team, which is circulated before the meeting." "Video meetings require everyone to have their cameras turned on." "Disagreement is considered a natural part of meetings. Disagreements focus on issues, not people." "If we have a problem or misunderstanding, we discuss it."

Ground rules help establish expectations for workplace behavior and create a sense of accountability. Ensure that your ground rules are disseminated to everyone in the team, are introduced at the beginning of working together (every session) and reviewed regularly. As a team, decide how you will enforce these rules, when necessary, and remember that anyone can initiate this protocol.

Create a well-defined conflict resolution strategy that outlines how to initiate conversations and the steps to take when resolving conflicts. This strategy should emphasize open and constructive communication as the first step toward addressing issues. See Chapter 5, "Pillar 2," for more information on what to include in this.

Establish an "Approaching Issues Framework" within your team as discussed earlier in this chapter. This framework should provide a structured approach to addressing concerns, as well as setting expectations for transparency and collaboration in problem-solving.

Clearly communicate expectations for workplace behavior. Create and share guidelines for appropriate conduct and outline the consequences for violations. Make it explicit that discrimination, harassment and bullying will not be tolerated. This clarity helps set boundaries and standards for respectful interactions.

Ensure that every team member knows how to recognize and address inappropriate behavior. Offer training and resources to educate the team on identifying and dealing with such behavior. Encourage a culture where individuals feel empowered to speak up if they witness or experience inappropriate behavior.

Invest time in getting to know your team members on a personal level. Understand their boundaries, preferences and personality types. Building these connections promotes empathy and helps you tailor your interactions to create a more supportive and respectful environment.

By implementing these foundational practices, you will establish a solid base upon which to build a safe and inclusive space for collaboration. With these foundational elements in place, you can then shift your focus to other critical aspects, such as communication, collaboration, meetings and your team's well-being. Let's look at each of these in detail.

Communication

Communication is a fundamental element when it comes to creating a safe and productive space for both individuals and teams. Building on the skills and knowledge acquired from Pillar 2 and the Communication Cycle, here are essential communication practices that will help you when creating a safe and inclusive space.

Create clear channels for team members to provide honest and constructive feedback. Develop a protocol for addressing concerns within the team. Define how team members can raise issues, who they should reach out to and the steps involved in resolving these concerns. Transparency in this process is crucial.

In addition to the basic ground rules, define any specific expectations you have for communication within the team. These expectations can relate to the tone of discussions, response times or any other factors that contribute to a respectful and productive environment.

Encourage team members to ask questions and ask for clarification if they don't fully understand something. This helps prevent misunderstandings and promotes clear communication.

Discuss and implement strategies to ensure that every team member's voice is heard. This may involve techniques such as round-robin discussions or rotating meeting facilitation responsibilities to prevent one person from dominating conversations.

Schedule regular team check-ins to provide a platform for team members to share updates, discuss progress and address any emerging issues in a collaborative manner.

Misunderstandings, miscommunications and conflicts are inevitable in any team. The key is to address them promptly and constructively. Develop a conflict resolution plan that addresses issues based on facts and focuses on solutions, not blame.

Collaboration

To promote effective collaboration within your team and create a safe space for all team members, consider these important practices.

Regularly engage in discussions about the Pillar 3 dimensions of Goals, Roles and Decisions. This collaborative approach helps align everyone's efforts.

Recognize and appreciate the diversity of knowledge, experience, skills and perspectives within your team. Diversity enhances problem-solving and innovation. Encourage and celebrate contributions from everyone, irrespective of their background.

Establish a clear plan to distribute workloads fairly and equitably among team members. Avoid overburdening certain individuals while others are underutilized. Regularly review and adjust projects to ensure a balanced workload.

Show respect and kindness in all your interactions. Avoid making offensive comments or jokes that may offend or marginalize others. Be mindful of how your actions and words can impact the well-being and comfort of your team members.

Trust is the foundation of effective collaboration. Maintain trust that has been built within the team by respecting confidentiality. Safeguard sensitive information and respect your team members' privacy. When handling personal information, maintain discretion and be sure to adhere to data protection regulations.

These practices not only enhance collaboration but also promote creativity, productivity and a sense of belonging among all team members.

Inclusive Meetings

Meetings serve as critical forums for collaboration and decision-making within a team, when done right. To ensure these are effective and inclusive and to encourage participation and contributions in meetings, consider the following best practices.

Firstly, eliminate any unnecessary hierarchies and power dynamics and respect each other's time by starting and ending meetings punctually.

Before the meeting, communicate clear expectations to team members. Let them know if they will be expected to contribute and tell them upfront the topics for discussion. Share relevant information in advance to provide team members with different personalities and working styles the time for reflection and preparation.

For virtual or hybrid meetings, clearly communicate whether cameras and microphones are necessary, allowing team members to prepare. Be flexible and prepared to respond in the moment if someone is unable or uncomfortable with using their camera or microphone during the meeting.

Establish clear channels and methods for contributing ideas before, during and after the meeting. Consider using online collaboration tools, such as shared documents or project management software, to enable asynchronous contributions. This will accommodate different schedules and work styles.

During meetings, ensure that everyone has an opportunity to contribute and actively participate. Create a supportive atmosphere where team members feel comfortable sharing their thoughts and ideas. Maintain the principles of the Creativity Manifesto (see Chapter 8, "Pillar 5"), where all ideas hold equal value and everyone is encouraged to contribute. Create an environment where every idea is heard and no idea is rejected. Encourage equal participation and seek input from everyone.

Recognize that individuals have different communication preferences and personality types, impacting how they contribute to meetings. Be mindful of these differences and create an environment that accommodates various communication styles.

Encourage open and respectful communication during meetings. Your aim is to create an environment where team members feel safe sharing diverse perspectives and ideas, as well as their fears and concerns. Maintain a culture of mutual respect, where everyone's voice is heard and valued.

After meetings, implement a structured process for following up on ideas and action items. Create a channel for team members to continue to contribute ideas and feedback post-meeting, ensuring that discussions and initiatives move forward effectively.

These practices will help you to create an inclusive and productive meeting where team members are able to collaborate effectively, contribute their unique insights and work together toward shared goals.

Well-Being

A focus on well-being is essential for maintaining a healthy and resilient team. To promote well-being and create a supportive environment, consider the following key practices.

Encourage work-life balance as the foundation of your team's culture. Encourage team members to establish clear boundaries between work and personal life.

Regularly discuss self-care and resilience. Create a space where team members feel comfortable sharing their self-care strategies and resilience-building techniques. This can help reduce stress and promote mental and emotional well-being.

Emphasize the importance of physical and mental health. Encourage team members to prioritize their health by taking breaks when needed, engaging in physical activity and practicing mindfulness or relaxation techniques. Make self-care a regular practice for all team members.

Ensure that everyone on the team is aware of available resources for well-being support. Communicate information about counseling services, employee assistance programs and other resources that can help manage stress, anxiety or other mental health concerns. Promote a stigma-free environment where seeking support is encouraged and normalized.

Implement regular check-ins or wellness sessions to gauge the well-being of team members. These sessions can provide an opportunity for individuals to share their concerns, discuss stressors and receive support from their colleagues.

Establish policies that support well-being, such as flexible work arrangements, time-off policies and stress management programs. Ensure that these policies are communicated and easily accessible to all team members.

Lead by example in prioritizing your well-being. Demonstrate a commitment to self-care and resilience and encourage your team members to do the same. Your actions can inspire others and reinforce the importance of well-being practices.

Prioritizing well-being within your team will create an environment that fosters not only individual health and happiness but also collective strength and resilience. This contributes to higher morale, productivity and a positive team dynamic. Don't neglect your team's well-being.

Next, we will address three common topics in the context of creating safe spaces: addressing unsafe environments, cultivating participation and decision-making within the safe space.

Unsafe Environments

I am often asked "How do you address an unsafe environment in the workplace?" Begin by following the "Setting the Scene Guidelines." Make sure everything is in place from these guidelines. Once you have these, depending on the nature of the issue, you can initiate a conversation using the agreements related to ground rules, conflict resolution, Approaching Issues, expectations, personal and work boundaries or inappropriate behavior. If you don't have these elements in place, the resulting conversation will be much harder to initiate. By following the "Setting the Scene Guidelines," you establish agreements and strategies that empower you to address inappropriate behavior and cultivate safer working environments, as well as reducing the stress around how to address the issue.

Participation

A note on participation. In collaborative spaces, participation can be categorized into five distinct levels, as illustrated in Figure 6.2. Imagine yourself in a team meeting. You will observe individuals at various points along the Participation Spectrum.

Level 1: Observing. Passive. At this level, individuals predominantly listen and observe during discussions. They don't actively contribute or engage in the discussion.

Level 2: Responding. Reactive. This level involves responding to questions and participating when directly asked but mainly in a reactive manner. They don't actively initiate discussions and do not contribute spontaneously.

Level 3: Contributing. Proactive. Participants actively listen and spontaneously contribute thoughts and ideas without waiting for prompts. They take the initiative to share their perspectives, relevant information, insights and ideas to add value to the conversation. They actively engage in discussions, making the conversation more dynamic.

Level 4: Engaging. Interactive. Here, individuals not only listen and contribute ideas but also actively engage in problem-solving and solution-oriented discussions. They go beyond offering thoughts and insights; they actively participate in discussing and implementing existing ideas and solutions, sharing personal ideas and solutions and taking actions to move the discussion forward.

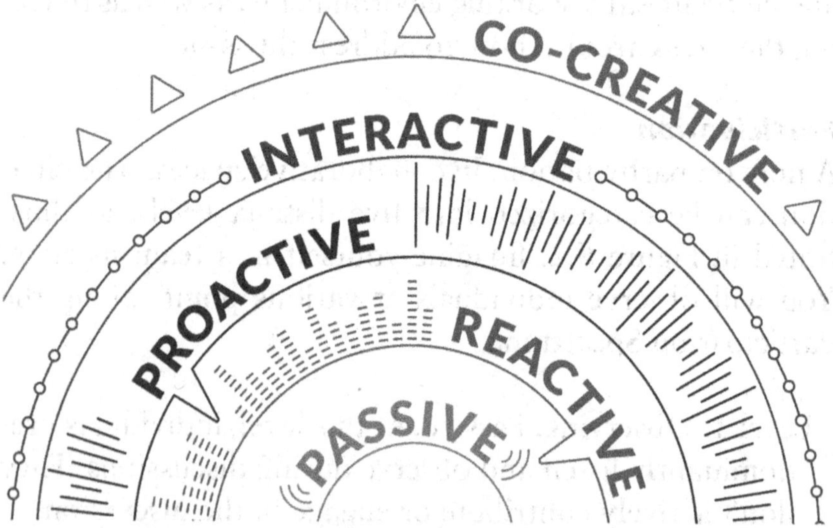

Figure 6.2 The Participation Spectrum

Level 5: Collaborating. Co-Creative. At the highest level, participants actively listen, respond, offer thoughts and ideas and collaborate closely with the team. They co-create solutions in a highly interactive manner. Collaboration goes beyond discussing existing solutions; they actively work to co-create innovative solutions that wouldn't be possible individually. They work in a highly interactive manner, building upon each other's ideas and the collective intelligence in the room and collectively shape the direction of the conversation to create something new and impactful.

In summary, individuals at Level 1 are passive. They observe and listen without active participation. At Level 2, individuals are reactive. They respond to questions and prompts. Engagement is primarily reactive, waiting for cues to participate. At Level 3 individuals are proactive. They contribute insights and ideas to enrich the conversation. At Level 4 individuals are interactive. They actively contribute and take on the role of active problem-solvers or solution providers. At Level 5 individuals are co-creative. They are focused on creating something new together, co-creating innovative solutions through a tightly integrated, interactive and synergistic approach.

Chances are, you've experienced these various levels during your own meetings. When you attend meetings, take a moment to reflect on your own level of participation and consider why you're at that level. Also, observe your colleagues' levels of engagement, with no judgment.

The goal is to create a safe space where everyone feels comfortable operating at Levels 4 and 5. By increasing your awareness of your participation level, you become better equipped to create a more inclusive, collaborative and secure environment for all.

Decision-Making

Here are steps to guide your team toward effective decision-making, whilst maintaining the safe space.

Establish a process for making decisions as a team. Start by discussing and agreeing on a decision-making process that the team can use. This process could involve identifying the decision, gathering relevant information, discussing options, evaluating pros and cons and selecting the next steps.

Determine the criteria that will be used to evaluate possible solutions. Consider factors such as feasibility, cost, time, impact on stakeholders and alignment with team goals and values.

Encourage active participation. Actively involve all team members in the decision-making process. Emphasize that every team member's input is valuable, as diverse perspectives can uncover blind spots and hidden opportunities.

Encourage open and respectful discussion among team members. Allow team members to express their opinions, ask questions and ensure everyone has an opportunity to contribute to the conversation. Recognize that communication preferences and personality types vary among individuals, which will impact on how they contribute to the discussion.

Strive to reach consensus among team members on the best course of action. Consensus doesn't require unanimous agreement, but it means that everyone can support the decision and commit to its successful implementation.

After making a decision, define clear next steps and follow through to ensure effective implementation.

Be sure to distribute ownership of tasks and allocate resources fairly among team members to ensure everyone has a stake in the decision's success.

By following this guidance, you will set your team up to make well-informed decisions and to be able to work together effectively to achieve common objectives.

Pillar Highlight Summary

By embracing the five indispensable elements of the CollabZen Methodology, you embark on a journey that yields profound and lasting transformation. This transformation centers on team collaboration and cultivating an environment where teams can truly thrive. Through your exploration of the five Dimensions and Pillar Highlights within Pillar 3, you gain a comprehensive understanding of the fundamental elements to enhance workplace collaboration, setting you on a path toward cultivating high-performing teams.

Teams that embrace the CollabZen Methodology can expect a wide range of valuable benefits. They will experience a surge in innovation, faster decision-making and a clearer alignment of roles. This newfound clarity will raise communication standards and cultivate greater inclusivity within the team, resulting in team members who are not only more engaged and happier but also thriving in the workplace. This, in turn, will contribute to a stronger sense of belonging within the team and create a culture of ownership and accountability. All of these are underpinned by a solid foundation of trust, respect and effective communication.

The organization will witness a transformation that leads to remarkable benefits. Project success rates will soar, setting a new standard for excellence and bringing about a surge in productivity, heightened customer satisfaction and substantial revenue growth. There will be a noticeable elevation in employee satisfaction, marked by higher retention rates and a significant reduction in employee turnover. This collaborative work environment, characterized by thriving teams, will not only enhance the organization's productivity but also contribute to its overall success and sustained growth.

Next, you will find the Pillar 3 Pledges and a series of self-reflective questions, providing you with valuable opportunities to assess your collaboration skills, as well as evaluating your approach to creating an environment where your team can thrive.

Pillar 3 Pledges and Self-Reflection Questions

Here are the Pillar 3 Pledges and questions for self-reflection. We ask you to commit to these pledges and discuss them regularly in team meetings.

Pillar 3 Pledges

1. I regularly clarify my objectives and how they fit into my team's goals and vision.
2. I know my team's ground rules and assert these rules when necessary.
3. I apply the agreed conflict resolution strategy, when needed.
4. I communicate the expectations I have of my team members.

5. In meetings and project work, I contribute fully – answering questions, offering my thoughts and contributing ideas/solutions with my team.
6. I communicate with my team at agreed times, to update on projects and progress against team goals.

Pillar 3 Self-Reflection

To what extent do you agree with the following statements? Score yourself for each of the statements.

If you strongly disagree, score yourself 1 point. If you somewhat disagree, score yourself 2 points. If you neither agree nor disagree, score yourself 3 points. If you somewhat agree, score yourself 4 points. If you strongly agree, score yourself 5 points.

1. I consistently clarify how my objectives align with my team's goals and vision.
2. I actively participate in creating and updating our team's ground rules and confidently assert them when necessary.
3. My team has a clear conflict resolution strategy and I am comfortable applying it when necessary.
4. I effectively communicate my expectations to my team members to enhance our collaboration.
5. I actively participate in meetings and project work by answering questions, offering my thoughts and contributing ideas/solutions.
6. I consistently communicate with my team at agreed times to provide updates on projects and progress against team goals.

Each of the statements refers to a Pillar 3 Pledge. If you score less than a 4 for any of these statements, revisit the relevant section(s) of Pillar 3. Anything under 5 means you have room for improvement. If you score less than a 3, make improvement a priority.

Summary

At the core of Pillar 3 lies the essence of collaboration and the art of cultivating an environment where teams can truly thrive. By embracing the CollabZen Methodology, you intentionally design your work environment, one that is conducive to exceptional collaboration and teamwork. Creating an environment where teams thrive is a goal that many organizations focus on, recognizing its vital role in achieving success. However, the journey toward a thriving team environment goes far beyond simply arriving at the destination; it demands attention to every step along the way.

Organizations often prioritize Pillar 3, dedicating substantial efforts to cultivate collaboration and teamwork. However, what they may not fully grasp is the importance of building a solid foundation, a foundation that is established through the principles presented to you within Pillars 1 and 2. Overlooking the critical work needed to lay this foundation can leave organizations wondering why they haven't achieved the thriving team environment they aspire to. When Pillar 1, Pillar 2 and Pillar 3 are implemented successfully, you create an inclusive and thriving workplace, empowering both individuals and teams to realize their full potential.

Next on our journey is Pillar 4, where we will shift gears and look at curiosity and its role in enhancing your collaborative efforts.

Notes

1. For more information about the Psychological Safety Institute and our services, training programs and resources: www.thepsi.global.
2. For more information about Eysenck's Personality Theory: https://hanseysenck.com

7

Pillar 4: Curiosity

Pillars 4 and 5 are different from the earlier Pillars. These Pillars take the building blocks we have laid and elevate them to new heights by providing structured opportunities for continuous learning, innovation and creativity.

Pillar 4 is Curiosity and is dedicated to igniting a culture of innovation and curiosity within your organization. It places significant emphasis on the power of reflective practice, feedback and the pursuit of learning and development.

In our global study, a surprising 51 percent of respondents revealed that the organizations they work for do not actively encourage them to reflect on and learn from their work, both as individuals and within teams. The question arises: are these organizations missing out on valuable opportunities for personal and professional growth and innovation?

In this chapter, you will journey into the heart of Curiosity. We will delve into the transformative world of Curiosity Sessions, providing guidance on how to run these effectively and outlining the crucial ground rules needed to ensure their success.

Let's begin our exploration of Curiosity and its role in igniting a culture of innovation and continuous learning within your organization.

Pillar 4 Framework

First Principle: This is how we improve what we do. This is the fundamental concept on which Pillar 4 is based.

Dimensions. Pillar 4 is built upon a single Dimension, providing a lens through which we explore and measure the First Principle. Within Pillar 4, teams are guided by one key question: "How can we improve what we do and how we work together?"

Pillar Highlights. Within Pillar 4, you will find several Pillar Highlights that offer in-depth insights into this Dimension. Here, you will gain a comprehensive understanding of the methodology behind Curiosity Sessions.

As you actively integrate Curiosity Sessions into your team's routine, you will develop the essential skills of reflection and inquiry. These sessions serve as a catalyst, igniting innovative thinking, fueling curiosity and embracing continuous learning.

Pillar 4 is the one that questions to ignite a culture of innovation and curiosity. It encourages individuals and teams to question their approaches, enhance team collaboration and challenge the status quo.

Pillar 4 Methodology: Curiosity Sessions

Curiosity Sessions form the foundation of Pillar 4, providing structured opportunities for reflective practice and refining approaches, thereby enhancing collaboration and effectiveness. By immersing yourself in these transformative sessions, you will ignite a culture of innovation and curiosity, propelling your team toward new levels of growth and success.

These scheduled sessions offer a dedicated and structured time for reflection, exploration and experimentation – inviting individuals to step out of their daily routines, challenge themselves and embrace the possibilities of what could be.

As you dive deeper into Pillar 4, you will discover the power of questioning to ignite a culture of innovation, transforming your approach to learning and development. Regularly engaging in Curiosity Sessions will empower you to extract valuable insights from the past to tackle current challenges.

With an unwavering commitment to self-reflection, fueled by an insatiable curiosity and a growth mindset, you will transform every experience into an opportunity for learning and evolution.

Creating a culture characterized by continuous learning and experimentation, driven by an unquenchable thirst for growth and development, will propel your team toward new heights of innovation, performance and productivity, positioning both you and your team for sustained success in an ever-changing world.

Pillar 4 Dimensions: Deep Dive

Pillar 4 is centered on a singular Dimension, with a primary focus on enhancing team collaboration and refining work processes.

Curiosity Sessions are designated times in your diary to reflect as a team.

Why is this important? In the daily hustle and bustle of work, you are likely to charge forward with your projects and tasks. Which is great. But what happens when you take a moment to stop and reflect on what you are doing? It's during these pauses that new ideas emerge and you find alternative approaches to the challenges you face. Sometimes, a simple conversation with a colleague can spark an idea that helps you to move forward from a roadblock. It may seem counterintuitive, but stepping back and pausing can lead to real progress.

Imagine, you have a project-focused meeting with your team. You are stuck on something, they are stuck on something and maybe the team dynamics are not working so well at the moment. In this meeting, you all voice what is going on for you and the challenges you are facing. What happens? Your team members start to think of possible solutions for you, and you for them. A colleague might ask you to elaborate on something or ask a question that sparks something within you, and in that moment you feel an internal shift that helps you to move past the issue that is blocking your thinking. When you openly discuss any frustrations you are feeling, not directed at a person but because of a situation, you mentally release something and allow the space to discuss how you can strengthen how you all work together. These moments of reflection and discussion can significantly improve team dynamics and problem-solving. Ideas flow, solutions emerge and magic happens. Truly.

Giving your team a regular opportunity to pause and reflect will transform the way you work together. However, it is crucial to use this time constructively. It is not an opportunity for negativity, gossiping or projecting onto your team members. It is a dedicated time for reflective practice and feedback, aimed at enhancing collaboration, refining skills and facilitating personal growth.

What benefits might you experience from reflective practice? There are many benefits such as managing yourself more effectively (time, processes), developing insights into your skills, competencies and behaviors, heightened self-awareness, increased mental resilience, enhanced emotional intelligence and better decision-making.

There are various different models for reflection, such as Gibbs' Reflective Cycle (1988), Rolfe et al.'s "What, So

What, Now What" model (2001) and Kolb's Experiential Learning Model (1984).[1]

Additionally, in Curiosity Sessions, you also need to consider learning styles of individuals and using different feedback models, which are detailed in the resources within our Psychological Safety Toolkit and Authentic Self Journal. More information about our resources can be found on our website, details of which can be found in the endnotes.[2]

Pillar 4 Highlights

Pillar 4 highlights focus on two key aspects, the principles behind the Curiosity Sessions and the Curiosity Manifesto.

Curiosity Sessions

To run successful Curiosity Sessions, follow these essential guidelines.

Before Curiosity Sessions

Regular scheduling. It is crucial to hold Curiosity Sessions regularly, ideally every 4 weeks. These sessions should not exceed 90 minutes, with a scheduled break after 45 minutes.

Setting ground rules. Before diving into Curiosity, establish ground rules for how the session will be conducted and how the team will collaborate during the session. At the beginning of every Curiosity Session, remind everyone of the ground rules that were agreed.

Role rotation. Facilitate Curiosity collectively as a team. There is no hierarchy in these sessions. Rotate roles among team members, including facilitator, timekeeper and note/action-taker. Create a schedule to ensure everyone has an opportunity to take on each role.

The Structure of Curiosity Sessions

Curiosity is split into three parts. Part 1 is updates, Part 2 is reflections and Part 3 is the round-up.

Part 1: Updates. During this section, each team member has a maximum of three minutes to provide an update on their progress toward individual and team objectives. Share achievements since the last Curiosity Session, current projects and any obstacles hindering progress. After each update, invite concise team contributions, focusing on adding value to the individual. If you don't have anything to add that is valuable, move on to the next person to offer their contribution.

Part 2: Reflections. This section involves group reflection, where questions are posed and everyone has the opportunity to respond. Key questions include: What has worked over the last four weeks? What has not worked? What mistakes or errors can we learn from? How can we improve the work we have produced – individually and as a team? How have we worked together as a team? What improvements can we make to improve our future teamwork? What are the blockers to achieving our team objectives? What can we do to unblock these?

Part 3: Round-Up. This is the time to set and record action items resulting from the discussions.

Curiosity Manifesto

Next is the Curiosity Manifesto. It outlines the key principles for cultivating a culture of curiosity and effective communication within the team. It sets expectations for how team members should engage during Curiosity Sessions.

The Curiosity Manifesto

1. **Commitment.** Every team member commits to attending Curiosity Sessions consistently.
2. **Preparation.** Prior to each session, individuals prepare their updates for thoughtful engagement.
3. **Open-Mind.** We approach Curiosity Sessions with an open mind, promoting inclusivity to encourage diverse perspectives and innovative ideas.
4. **Respectful Listening.** During contributions, we give full attention to the speaker, showing respect by not interrupting.
5. **Thoughtful Engagement.** Active participation is encouraged and any questions or insights that arise during the speaker's presentation are noted for later discussion.
6. **Feedback.** The speaker collects feedback and contributions from the team, which are followed up with individuals after the session.
7. **Collaboration.** We embrace a culture of collaboration, actively contributing our expertise to the team while learning from one another.
8. **Solution Focused.** Discussions are solution focused, aimed at overcoming challenges and enhancing our work together.
9. **Actionable Insights.** We promptly implement agreed-upon changes and improvements, holding ourselves accountable to ensure they enhance our work and processes.

As you embrace the Curiosity Manifesto, you chart a path toward cultivating a culture of inquiry and open dialogue. These principles will guide your interactions during Curiosity Sessions, elevating the environment to one where you can authentically express yourself while strengthening team communication and collaboration.

Feedback

As part of the Curiosity Sessions, you may be invited to give and receive feedback. For some, giving and receiving feedback can be uncomfortable, so let's briefly explore how to make the most of these feedback interactions.

When you think about receiving feedback from others, what comes to mind? Do you envision criticism or someone suggesting that your work isn't good enough? Perhaps you associate feedback with negative emotions like anxiety, a knot in your stomach, defensiveness or the need to justify your actions.

Feedback is someone's perspective or opinion, offering a valuable learning opportunity. It is not a personal judgment on you or your abilities.

Listening to other people's perspectives and feedback is essential for personal and professional growth while strengthening your relationships. Feedback is a catalyst for skill development and improvement. Gathering feedback from a variety of sources provides a more rounded view.

Here are guidelines to help you and your team to receive feedback effectively.

Ensure you are in the right headspace and feeling positive before receiving feedback. Fatigue, stress or overwhelm can lead to fixating on areas for improvement.

Have a team discussion about individual preferences for receiving feedback, specifying areas of interest and how much feedback you would like. Setting clear parameters in advance will ensure you get the most out of the experience.

Ask clarifying questions to understand how to improve. What did I do well? What could be improved and how? How can I approach things differently next time? What opportunities exist for me?

Phrase your questions positively. For example, ask "What can I do better?" instead of "What am I doing wrong?"

Be open to sharing incomplete work with your colleagues, be curious and invite their perspectives, ideas and potential solutions to any challenges you may face. Create a space for them to contribute their thoughts and ideas and if you find their ideas valuable, build upon them. Collective intelligence is a powerful thing!

Now, a few guidelines on how to give feedback. When giving feedback, it's valuable to have structured models to guide your approach. I will briefly outline a few for your consideration.

The Situation-Behavior-Impact (SBI) Model involves three key components. First, describe the specific situation or context in which the event that you are referring to happened. Then, explain the behavior itself, providing specific details. Finally, articulate how this behavior impacted you, the team, clients or stakeholders. The SBI model helps you offer clear and constructive feedback.

Another effective feedback model is the STAR Method, which stands for Situation, Task, Action and Result. Begin by setting the scene with the situation or context in which the event unfolded. Then, narrow down to the specific task or action you want to address. Next, describe the actions taken by the person in that situation. Finally, consider the outcome of these actions and how they influenced others. The STAR method provides a structured framework for discussing performance and outcomes.

The Example-Effect-Change/Continue (EEC) Model is a versatile feedback approach. Start by providing an example of the behavior or action under consideration. Then, explain the effect this action had, whether positive or negative. What sets the EEC model apart is its forward-looking nature. Depending on the feedback's nature, you can suggest changes for future improvement or encourage the person to continue their effective practices. It's a well-rounded model that not only addresses the past but also focuses on shaping future behavior and outcomes. What should the person change to improve their behavior, output or work methods? Or perhaps they did a great job and you want to let them know to keep working this way.

The IDEA feedback model simplifies the process of providing effective feedback into four key steps. First, you identify the specific aspect or behavior that requires feedback. Then, you describe the situation or behavior in detail, offering context and reasons for addressing it. The third step, encourage, underscores your intention to support and assist the person, making it clear that the feedback aims at growth, not criticism. Finally, you conclude with action, providing clear, actionable steps for the person to implement and improve based on the feedback received. This structured approach ensures clarity, understanding and a forward-looking focus on continuous improvement.

The I-Statement method is a straightforward approach to providing feedback that aims to minimize defensive responses in the person. I-Statements are a simple way that helps describe a problem tactfully.

A You-Statement tends to be accusatory, such as "You don't care about my workload." In contrast, an I-Statement takes responsibility for feelings, like "I feel overwhelmed when you increase my workload because I'm already at capacity. I would appreciate it if you could delegate tasks or reevaluate priorities with me." The method follows a four-step process, involving "I feel . . ." where you take responsibility for your feelings, "when you . . ." stating the behavior that is a problem, "because . . ." stating what it is about the behavior or its consequences that you don't like and "I would like it if . . ." where you offer a preferred alternative or compromise. This approach helps you to address problems and promote open dialogue.

These models offer structured and effective ways to provide feedback, ensuring that your feedback is specific, constructive and goal oriented.

Next, you will find the Pillar 4 Pledges and a series of self-reflective questions, offering you a structured framework to evaluate and strengthen your commitment to reflective practice, nurturing curiosity and cultivating continuous learning within your team.

Pillar 4 Pledges and Self-Reflection Questions

Here are the Pillar 4 Pledges and questions for self-reflection. We ask you to commit to these pledges and discuss them regularly in team meetings.

Pillar 4 Pledges

1. I prioritize attendance at Curiosity Sessions.
2. I ask for and give constructive feedback to my team.
3. I proactively share my knowledge, expertise and experience with the team.
4. I discuss the things that haven't worked, errors and mistakes with my team.
5. I actively engage in personal and professional development.

Pillar 4 Self-Reflection

To what extent do you agree with the following statements? Score yourself for each of the statements.

If you strongly disagree, score yourself 1 point. If you somewhat disagree, score yourself 2 points. If you neither agree nor disagree, score yourself 3 points. If you somewhat agree, score yourself 4 points. If you strongly agree, score yourself 5 points.

1. My team regularly dedicates time to reflect on our work and collaborative processes, and I make attending Curiosity Sessions a priority.
2. I actively engage in the exchange of constructive feedback with my team.
3. I take the initiative to share my expertise, knowledge and experiences with my team.
4. I openly discuss issues, errors and mistakes, encouraging a culture of learning and improvement within my team.
5. I proactively invest in my personal and professional development, consistently seeking opportunities for growth.

Each of the statements refers to a Pillar 4 Pledge. If you score less than a 4 for any of these statements, revisit the relevant section(s) of Pillar 4. Anything under 5 means you have room for improvement. If you score less than a 3, make improvement a priority.

Summary

As we conclude our exploration of Pillar 4, centered on igniting innovation through the transformative power of Curiosity Sessions, we recognize their profound impact on individuals and teams. These sessions empower individuals to authentically engage in collaborative spaces, communicate with effectiveness, nurture the environment where they can thrive and drive innovation, all while experiencing significant personal and professional growth.

Organizations that wholeheartedly commit to the practice of regular Curiosity Sessions reap a multitude of benefits. These include heightened self-awareness among team members, leading to more informed and strategic decision-making processes. Both individual and collective performance levels soar, creating a collaborative environment that transcends organizational silos, thereby promoting cross-organizational learning and cohesion. The free exchange of experience, knowledge and skills becomes the norm, contributing to elevated confidence and self-esteem among team members, while also increasing their visibility within the organization. This culture of curiosity not only fuels innovation but propels the entire organization toward unprecedented levels of success and growth.

Next on our journey is Pillar 5, where we will delve into creativity and its role in increasing engagement and productivity.

Notes

1. G. Gibbs (1988). *Learning by doing: A guide to teaching and learning methods*. Further Education Unit. G. Rolfe, D. Freshwater and M. Jasper (2001). *Critical reflection in nursing and the helping professions: A user's guide*. Basingstoke: Palgrave Macmillan. D. A. Kolb (1984). Experiential learning: Experience as the source of learning and development (Vol. 1). Englewood Cliffs, NJ: Prentice-Hall.
2. For more information about the Psychological Safety Institute and our services, training programs and resources: www.thepsi.global.

8

Pillar 5: Creativity

Like Pillar 4, Pillar 5 is different from the earlier Pillars.

Pillar 5 is Creativity. It offers a unique perspective on generating solutions to drive growth and success within your organization. This Pillar places significant emphasis on problem-solving and creative thinking, key drivers of innovation, engagement and profitability.

In Pillar 3, you were introduced to the Participation Spectrum, where you explored the five distinct levels of participation in collaborative settings, a framework highly relevant in the context of creative idea contribution. As you consider your role in the creative process ask yourself, which of the following resonates with you?

- I am passive (Level 1). I keep my ideas to myself and don't share them.
- I am reactive (Level 2). I share my ideas only when prompted.
- I am proactive (Level 3). I openly share my ideas to add value to the conversation.
- I am interactive (Level 4). I actively contribute my ideas and implement existing ideas.
- I am co-creative (Level 5). I am dedicated to creating something new, building upon the collective intelligence and ideas in the room.

So, where do you sit on this spectrum?

Our global study sheds light on the prevailing approaches to creativity within organizations. When collaborating with others, respondents were asked to describe their participation in the creative process: 40 percent of respondents revealed that they are operating at Level 3, proactive, whilst

60 percent stated they are operating at Level 4, interactive. This was really encouraging, but it prompts the question: are you potentially missing out on the transformative power of Level 5, where individuals actively build upon collective intelligence to create innovative solutions? And are you missing out on increased employee engagement and valuable opportunities for growth?

In this chapter, you will dive into Creativity, exploring the dynamic realm of Creativity Workshops and their transformative power. You will be provided with guidance on effective workshop facilitation and the crucial ground rules to ensure their success.

Let's begin our journey to unlock the power of Creativity, generating innovative solutions that not only boost employee engagement but also drive revenue growth and success for your organization.

Pillar 5 Framework

First Principle: This is how we solve problems. This is the fundamental concept on which Pillar 5 is based.

Dimensions. Pillar 5 is built upon a single Dimension, providing a lens through which we explore and measure the First Principle. Within Pillar 5, teams are guided by one key question: "How do we problem-solve?"

Pillar Highlights. Within Pillar 5, you will find several Pillar Highlights that offer in-depth insights into this Dimension. Here, you will gain a comprehensive understanding of the methodology behind Creativity Workshops.

As you actively integrate Creativity Workshops into your team's regular routine, you will nurture and enhance your problem-solving and creative thinking abilities. These workshops ignite an innovative, growth mindset, enabling individuals to tap into their untapped creative potential.

Pillar 5 is the one that generates solutions to drive growth, transcending boundaries. It is the rocket fuel behind the success and growth of individuals, teams and your organization.

Pillar 5 Methodology: Creativity Workshops

Creativity Workshops form the foundation of Pillar 5, providing structured opportunities to hone your problem-solving skills and develop creative thinking. These workshops are designed to empower both individuals and teams to navigate challenges effectively.

Within these scheduled workshops, you'll find dedicated time to address individual and team-specific issues systematically, encouraging participants to break away from routine and embrace the potential for innovative solutions.

Creativity Workshops provide teams with a platform to explore original concepts and gain fresh perspectives, nurturing a culture of experimentation and creativity. This, in turn, enhances problem-solving capabilities, resulting in more innovative solutions that drive growth and success for your organization.

As you delve deeper into Pillar 5, you'll experience a transformative shift in your problem-solving and creative thinking abilities. You'll learn to thrive in ambiguous and uncertain situations, unlocking fresh perspectives and unconventional approaches to overcome challenges. Armed with a versatile toolkit of strategies and techniques, you'll be equipped to break down complex problems and unleash your full creative potential.

Mastering these skills will position you as an inspirational and empowering leader within your team. Your ability to generate solutions that transcend conventional thinking will facilitate a culture of innovation and growth. As a valuable asset to your team, you'll unearth new possibilities, boost engagement and, ultimately, drive revenue growth for your organization.

Pillar 5 Dimensions: Deep Dive

Pillar 5 is centered on a singular Dimension, with a primary focus on problem-solving.

Creativity Workshops are designated times in your diary to generate ideas and experiment as a team.

You are unique, with a very different background, skills and knowledge from everyone else. You were hired for this very reason.

When someone in your team faces a challenge with a project, do you openly share your ideas – no matter how abstract or unconventional they may seem, drawing from your unique life experiences? Or do you hold back because you want to fit in and be accepted by your colleagues? Now imagine a scenario where a friend seeks your input on a challenge they are facing. In this context, you are more likely to share your ideas freely because you feel safe, knowing you won't be judged.

In your day-to-day work, creative thinking opportunities are often limited, with a strong focus on meeting targets and achieving specific outcomes. However, by dedicating time each month for your team to come together and discuss the challenges you are facing while actively considering different perspectives, you can transform your thinking and cultivate the emergence of new ideas. It is like when you ask a question, you actively seek an answer. When a team member presents a challenge, you collectively work to find a solution.

During Creativity Workshops, you will develop and hone your problem-solving and creative thinking abilities. These workshops provide a safe space for you to generate fresh ideas and explore alternative approaches to achieving both your personal objectives and the team's goals. These workshops give you the time to carve out your own creativity, knowing you will not be judged or criticized and your ideas will be heard and valued.

Dedicating time to problem-solving and creative thinking offers numerous advantages to individuals within an organization. First and foremost, it enhances your problem-solving skills, providing you with a structured framework to tackle challenges effectively. These workshops nurture the development of creative thinking, encouraging individuals to explore innovative and unconventional solutions. Also, such opportunities boost confidence by creating a safe space for sharing ideas without fear of judgment. This growth in problem-solving and creative thinking skills contributes to personal development and overall skill enhancement. Ultimately, it increases engagement, job satisfaction and motivation among employees, enriching their professional journey.

Within a team context, the benefits of dedicated problem-solving and creative thinking time become even more pronounced. Regular workshops of this nature foster improved team collaboration, as members learn to share ideas, communicate openly and draw from each other's diverse perspectives. This open dialogue enhances team dynamics and relationships. Furthermore, it nurtures a culture of innovation where new ideas are valued and explored collectively, leading to more comprehensive and effective solutions. As teams become better at identifying and addressing issues proactively, overall efficiency in problem-solving increases, contributing to a more cohesive and productive working environment.

At the organizational level, dedicating time to problem-solving and creative thinking yields significant advantages. It promotes a culture of innovation within the company, facilitating the development of cutting-edge products, services or processes. This innovative edge provides a competitive advantage in a constantly evolving market landscape. Additionally, higher employee retention rates are observed, as engaged individuals are more likely to stay within the organization, reducing turnover. Enhanced productivity and efficiency, stemming from effective problem-solving, result in cost savings and contribute to revenue growth. Overall, a reputation for cultivating a creative problem-solving culture helps the organization attract top talent and establishes it as a forward-thinking industry leader.

Pillar 5 Highlights

Pillar 5 highlights revolve around two key elements – the principles underpinning Creativity Workshops and the Creativity Manifesto.

Creativity Workshops

To ensure the success of your Creativity Workshops, it is vital to follow these essential guidelines.

Before Creativity Workshops

Regular scheduling. Hold Creativity Workshops regularly, ideally every two weeks. These workshops should not exceed 90 minutes, with a scheduled break after 45 minutes.

Setting ground rules. Before delving into the creative process, establish ground rules for how the workshop will be conducted and how the team will collaborate during your time together. At the beginning of every Creativity Workshop, remind everyone of the ground rules that were agreed.

Role rotation. Facilitate Creativity collectively as a team. These workshops operate without a hierarchy. Rotate roles among team members, including facilitator, timekeeper and note/action-taker. Create a schedule to ensure that each team member has an opportunity to take on each role.

Topics for Creativity Workshops. Workshops are dedicated to addressing various aspects, including identifying blockers that are stopping you from achieving your personal and team objectives. Use the time to explore opportunities for improvement and streamlining, to tackle work-related issues that require creative solutions and to generate fresh ideas to overcome challenges, both as a team and individually.

Agenda setting. Before each Creativity Workshop, an "agenda" is defined, and any team member can propose topics to include in this agenda. This agenda is circulated to everyone before the workshop starts, ensuring transparency and active participation in the creative process.

The Structure of Creativity Workshops

Each agenda item is allocated a maximum of 20 minutes. The person proposing the agenda item has a maximum of 4 minutes to provide the team with the necessary context. A dedicated 10-minute slot is designated for individual idea generation by the team. Following idea generation, 6 minutes are allocated for presenting the ideas. All ideas are recorded so the person can take these away from the workshop.

For every idea generated, you must attempt to identify at least three counter-reasons why it might not work. This exercise fuels the development of robust ideas and solutions.

The person that initiated the agenda item retains all the generated ideas for personal reflection. If further deliberation is required to reach a consensus on the solution, it is put on the next Creativity Workshop agenda.

After Creativity Workshops

When you have decided on the idea to address the problem that has been identified, discuss it with your team, then put the chosen idea into action to resolve the issue. Maintain an open line of communication with your team to ensure they are informed of the progress and the ultimate outcome.

Remember, you have permission to question existing practices and question whether they need to be re-evaluated and improved.

Creativity Manifesto

Next is the Creativity Manifesto. It outlines the key principles for cultivating a culture of innovative thinking and effective problem-solving within the team. It sets clear expectations for how team members should engage during Creativity Workshops.

The Creativity Manifesto

1. **Playfulness.** We approach Creativity Workshops with a relaxed and playful mindset, creating an atmosphere conducive to creative thinking.
2. **Inclusive Participation.** Every team member actively shares ideas and potential solutions.
3. **Active Listening.** We commit to actively listening to every idea presented.
4. **Equal Value.** Within Creativity Workshops every idea holds equal value.
5. **Embrace Every Idea.** No idea is dismissed outright.
6. **Collective Building.** We actively build upon ideas, creating a collective and collaborative approach to innovation.
7. **Embrace Silence.** In creative thinking, silence and reflection are valuable; we don't need to fill every moment with noise.
8. **Diverse Perspectives.** We embrace the diversity of perspectives, experiences, skill sets and expertise that each team member brings to the table.
9. **Unrestricted Creativity.** Every team member is empowered to express their creativity without the confines of predefined limits.

As you embrace the Creativity Manifesto, you embark on a journey to nurture a culture of innovative thinking and effective problem-solving. These principles will be your guiding light during creative endeavors, creating an environment where your creativity can flourish, challenges can be tackled and team collaboration can thrive.

Overcoming Creative Blocks

Creative blocks, which everyone encounters from time to time, can be overcome effectively. If you ever find yourself facing such a block, consider these approaches.

Engage in Creativity Workshops with your team, to give you structured time to collaborate and generate ideas with other people. Discussing your challenges with others can lead to fresh insights, a different perspective or trigger new ideas. Group collaboration can be particularly effective during dedicated Creativity Workshops. Our Psychological Safety Toolkit and Authentic Self Journal offer a comprehensive set of strategies and tools to help you unlock your creativity, generate ideas and overcome creative blocks during these workshops. It serves as a valuable resource to support your journey toward becoming a more innovative and effective problem-solver. More information about our resources can be found on our website, details of which can be found in the endnotes.[1]

Embrace a growth mindset. Instead of viewing creative blocks as obstacles, see them as opportunities for growth and learning. Understand that creative blocks are a natural part of the creative process and they can lead to breakthroughs if approached with patience and perseverance.

Stepping away from a problem for a while can help you return to it with a clearer mind. Short breaks or longer vacations can recharge your creative energy and provide a fresh outlook.

Sometimes, a change in scenery can do wonders for creativity. Step away from your usual workspace and find a new location, whether it's a park, coffee shop or a different room in your office. The novelty of a change in environment can help stimulate fresh ideas.

Practicing mindfulness or meditation techniques can help clear your mind and reduce stress, both of which can contribute to creative blocks. Taking a few minutes to focus on your breath or engage in mindful activities can free up mental space for creative thinking.

Maintain a journal where you jot down ideas, thoughts and observations regularly. Reviewing your past ideas can inspire new ones and serve as a creative resource during blocks.

Explore sources of inspiration outside your usual field or domain. Read books, watch documentaries, attend art exhibitions or listen to music that is unrelated to your current project. Sometimes, cross-pollination of ideas from diverse sources can break creative barriers.

Engage in creative exercises or games that challenge your thinking. Activities like lateral thinking puzzles, word association games or visual ideation can stimulate creativity and help you overcome blocks.

Don't be afraid to embrace failure or setbacks. Often, creative blocks arise from the fear of making mistakes or producing subpar work. Accept that not every idea will be a masterpiece and failure is part of the creative journey.

Remember that creative blocks are temporary and common for everyone. By experimenting with different strategies and maintaining a mindset of curiosity and exploration, you can effectively overcome these obstacles and continue to nurture your creative thinking abilities.

Next, you will find the Pillar 5 Pledges and a series of self-reflective questions, offering valuable insights into your approach to cultivating team creativity and promoting effective problem-solving.

Pillar 5 Pledges and Self-Reflection Questions

Here are the Pillar 5 Pledges and questions for self-reflection. We ask you to commit to these pledges and discuss them regularly in team meetings.

Pillar 5 Pledges

1. I prioritize attendance at Creativity Workshops.
2. I actively contribute to Creativity Workshops, bringing unique ideas from my personal experience, skill set and expertise.
3. I actively look for solutions to problems experienced within the team.
4. I am proactive in implementing a solution.

Pillar 5 Self-Reflection

To what extent do you agree with the following statements? Score yourself for each of the statements.

If you strongly disagree, score yourself 1 point. If you somewhat disagree, score yourself 2 points. If you neither agree nor disagree, score yourself 3 points. If you somewhat agree, score yourself 4 points. If you strongly agree, score yourself 5 points.

1. My team regularly dedicates time to collaborative problem-solving, and I make attending Creativity Workshops a priority.
2. I proactively contribute during Creativity Workshops by sharing my ideas, skills, knowledge and experience with my team to enhance our collective problem-solving capabilities.
3. I consistently and proactively seek solutions to address challenges and issues encountered within the team, actively contributing to problem-solving efforts.
4. When I identify an idea that can address a team problem, I proactively put it into action to resolve the issue.

Each of the statements refers to a Pillar 5 Pledge. If you score less than a 4 for any of these statements, revisit the relevant section(s) of Pillar 5. Anything under 5 means you have room for improvement. If you score less than a 3, make improvement a priority.

Summary

As we conclude our exploration of Pillar 5, which revolves around the transformative potential of Creativity Workshops, we recognize their profound influence on individuals, teams and the organization's overall growth and success.

These workshops empower individuals to unleash their creativity, collaborate effectively and maintain a consistent culture of innovation and experimentation.

Organizations that fully embrace regular Creativity Workshops stand to experience a wide range of benefits. These workshops create a broader and deeper pool of perspectives and ideas, accelerating the creative process and enhancing problem-solving and creative thinking. Individuals develop valuable strategic thinking skills while experiencing increased staff morale, fun and happiness, and the strengthening of relationships and trust within teams. There is also a notable boost in workplace engagement and interaction. Creativity Workshops act as a catalyst for identifying new products, methods and processes, ultimately driving innovation, engagement and profitability. With increased productivity and revenue generation, these workshops contribute significantly to the organization's success by generating solutions that drive growth.

Note

1. For more information about the Psychological Safety Institute and our services, training programs and resources: www.thepsi.global.

9

Summary

In this book we have delved into the 5 Pillars of Psychological Safety in depth. As we near the conclusion, I'd like to address two common questions that often arise.

Firstly, many of our clients inquire about how these principles apply to remote teams. Creating psychological safety for remote teams hinges on the same core principles as those for teams in physical workplaces, with a few additional considerations.

Effective communication takes center stage when working with remote teams. In a remote setting, the informal interactions that typically occur before and after meetings or during a casual walk to a meeting room are often missed. To bridge this gap, it's essential to place more emphasis on social elements for remote teams. This includes creating opportunities for team building and socialization, such as virtual "water-cooler" moments, team lunches, coffee chats and dedicated spaces for pre- and post-meeting catchups.

Additionally, scheduling weekly social points for non-work-related discussions, alongside the usual channels for feedback, collaboration, Curiosity Sessions and Creativity Workshops, can foster a sense of connection and camaraderie. Leveraging video conferencing whenever possible can also help remote team members feel more connected and establish a stronger sense of presence.

To further support remote teams, establish clear expectations regarding communication protocols, work hours, team goals and available resources.

Here are specific areas of focus within the 5 Pillars that are particularly relevant for remote teams:

- Pillar 1: Emotions, triggers, expectations and personal boundaries.
- Pillar 2: The Communication Cycle.

- Pillar 3: Safe space (including ground rules and conflict resolution), team dynamics and scheduling regular check-ins.

Related to this first question about applying these principles to remote teams, we are often asked: "How do you know if you have issues in a remote team?" Signs of potential problems manifest in similar ways to hybrid and onsite teams, and may include team members who remain silent during meetings or discussions, lack active participation in team goals or projects and don't actively contribute their ideas, opinions, concerns, knowledge, experience or expertise unless prompted directly. Reluctance to collaborate, awkward silences in response to questions, tensions among team members, frequent misunderstandings and a lack of feedback-seeking can also signal issues. Additionally, if team members appear dissatisfied with their work or team environment, withhold personal information, resist turning on their camera and microphone or if there's a high turnover of staff, it's essential to address these indicators promptly to ensure the team's well-being and productivity.

The second question we often encounter is how to engage the whole organization in adopting the 5 Pillars of Psychological Safety. Achieving this requires a collective effort and a commitment to long-term cultural change. Here are some thoughts on how to accomplish this.

Begin by emphasizing the vital role of leadership. Leaders at all levels should not only endorse but actively champion the implementation of the 5 Pillars. Their visible commitment sets the tone for the entire organization.

Encourage leaders and managers to lead by example. When employees see their leaders actively practicing and embedding the Pillars, it reinforces their importance and encourages adoption.

Conduct regular assessments, including the use of the psychological safety diagnostic tool, Lux (discussed in Chapter 3), to gauge the organization's progress in implementing the Pillars and to identify areas for improvement. Lux provides valuable insights into the current state of psychological safety within the organization, enabling targeted interventions and tracking progress over time. Use the feedback and recommendations from Lux to refine your approach continuously.

Establish a transparent communication plan to keep employees informed about the progress of this cultural transformation. Use various channels such as newsletters, meetings and internal social platforms to keep everyone updated.

Provide comprehensive training programs that educate employees at every level about the importance of psychological safety and the practical application of the 5 Pillars. Consider rolling out our comprehensive resources, including the Psychological Safety Toolkit designed for leaders and managers, the Authentic Self Journal for all employees, our e-learning modules and bespoke live training sessions tailored specifically for leaders and managers. These resources provide practical guidance and tools to support the implementation of the Pillars and ensure that everyone has access to the knowledge and skills needed to contribute to a psychologically safe workplace. More information about our resources can be found on our website, details of which can be found in the endnotes.[1]

Encourage cross-functional teams or working groups to collaboratively explore how the 5 Pillars can be integrated into their specific areas of work. This fosters a sense of ownership and involvement.

Implement recognition programs that acknowledge individuals and teams for their contributions to creating psychologically safe workplaces. Highlight success stories and share them as examples throughout the organization.

Create feedback loops where employees can provide insights and suggestions regarding the implementation of the 5 Pillars. Make sure that feedback is actively considered and acted upon.

Pair experienced employees with newcomers or those who may need extra support in understanding and applying the 5 Pillars. Mentorship and coaching can reinforce the importance of psychological safety.

Link the implementation of the 5 Pillars to performance evaluations and career development discussions. This underscores their significance and encourages alignment with organizational goals.

Celebrate milestones and achievements along the way. Whether it's the completion of a successful training program or the positive impact of the 5 Pillars on workplace culture, these celebrations help maintain momentum.

Recognize that creating psychologically safe workplaces is an ongoing journey. Encourage a culture of continuous learning and improvement, adapting the implementation of the 5 Pillars as needed.

By following the guidance laid out in this book, organizations can cultivate a workplace where every employee feels valued, supported and psychologically safe.

Throughout the pages of this book, you have been introduced to the 5 Pillars of Psychological Safety and the methodologies behind each of them. Armed with the tools and insights provided in this book, you are now equipped to take an active role in creating a psychologically safe environment for yourself and your team.

Starting with Pillar 1, you explored the concept of the Authentic Self and learned strategies to empower you to bring your Authentic Self to work, enabling you to thrive in any workplace scenario.

Pillar 2, you delved into the Communication Cycle and gained a comprehensive understanding of the fundamental elements that drive successful communication in the workplace, setting you on a path to mastering the art of effective workplace communication.

In Pillar 3, you explored the CollabZen Methodology, where you discovered how to intentionally design your workplace environment so teams can thrive, facilitating exceptional collaboration and teamwork by harnessing collective strengths.

When Pillar 1, Pillar 2 and Pillar 3 are implemented successfully, you create an inclusive and thriving workplace, empowering both individuals and teams to realize their full potential.

In Pillar 4, you ventured into Curiosity Sessions, focusing on reflective practice to ignite a culture of innovation and curiosity, propelling your team toward new levels of growth and success.

Finally, in Pillar 5, you embarked on a journey through Creativity Workshops, concentrating on generating solutions to drive growth within your organization.

Together, these 5 Pillars form a comprehensive framework that cultivates psychologically safe, inclusive and forward-thinking workplaces. Serving as a powerful catalyst, these Pillars drive a transformative shift in workplace culture. With a strong emphasis on authenticity, effective communication and collaboration, as well as personal and professional mastery, innovation and creativity, the 5 Pillars stand as cornerstones for cultivating a dynamic and thriving work environment. The 5 Pillars of Psychological Safety empower individuals and teams to create work environments where people thrive.

Now, it is over to you.

Note

1. For more information about the Psychological Safety Institute and our services, training programs and resources: www.thepsi.global.

Acknowledgments

My heartfelt gratitude goes to the following individuals. Firstly, to those at Wiley: Annie, for choosing me and having faith in what I might produce. I am so grateful for you putting your trust in me. Tom, your insightful editing and constructive challenges have been invaluable in shaping something I am incredibly proud of. Thanks to the designers, marketing, publicity and all the team behind the scenes whose collective efforts brought this book to fruition.

To Theresa for your amazing graphics and dealing with the back and forth so expertly. You are a joy to work with and I love what you have created, both here and in our other collaborations.

To my friends whose active encouragement, thoughtful insights, helping with choosing one or the other and unwavering support have always had my back. Thank you for putting up with me disappearing for months on end and replying to your messages in my head, instead of for real. You are all amazing humans. Special and biggest thanks to Helen, Rachel, Ruth, Catherine, Cátia and Amy.

There are very few people in this world with whom I feel incredibly safe. Mum, thank you for being one of those people, loving me for who I am and being there to listen at the end of the day, through the good and bad. Auntie Net, thank you for being the constant in my life where I have always felt valued and loved. You are a treasure. Liz and

Cliff, for adopting me, making me part of your family and welcoming me into your lives.

And lastly, Paula. My everything. Thank you for putting your trust and love in me. For creating a home and space that I can retreat to and experience comfort and true safety. For believing in me, encouraging me, challenging me and for making me think and be a better human. It is true, relationships are your biggest teacher. I am who I am because of you.

Oh, nearly forgot. Lumi and Shadow. Lumi, thank you for helping me write this book by creating absolute chaos during the writing process. Sitting on my head, jumping all over my keyboard and screaming your appreciation for the words I write was really helpful in honing creativity and patience! Shadow, thank you for being the complete opposite and providing moments of respite and peace in my days. You are a dream. After the chaos, I am grateful for animal therapy at the end of each day.

About the Author

Gina Battye is the founder and CEO of the Psychological Safety Institute. Her mission is to create work environments where people thrive.

Gina's expertise has been sought after by the world's largest multinational corporations, spanning countries and cultures.

As the visionary behind the 5 Pillars of Psychological Safety, the Hierarchy of Psychological Safety and Lux, the psychological safety diagnostic tool, Gina's groundbreaking contributions have earned widespread recognition. Her work has been featured extensively in global press outlets, and she serves as an advisor for TV and film.

Gina lives in Yorkshire, UK with her partner and two fluffs. Her passions include travel, turtles and rocks and in her spare time she loves to walk, learn Portuguese and make journals.

www.thepsi.global

Index